KTO STUDIES
IN
AMERICAN HISTORY

Consulting Editor: Harold M. Hyman
William P. Hobby Professor of History
Rice University

JAMES WILSON

From McMaster, John and Frederick B. Stone,
Pennsylvania and the Federal Constitution 1787–1788
(New York: Da Capo Press, Inc., 1970), frontispiece

By permission of the Historical Society of Pennsylvania

JAMES WILSON

Geoffrey Seed

kto press

A U.S. Division of Kraus-Thomson Organization Limited

Millwood, New York

First printing 1978

Printed in the United States of America

Library of Congress Cataloging in Publication Data

Seed, Geoffrey
  James Wilson.

  (KTO studies in American history)
  Bibliography: p. 217
  Includes index.
  1. Wilson, James, 1742–1798.   2. Statesmen—
United States—Biography.   3. United States—
Politics and government—Revolution, 1775–1783.
4. United States—Politics and government—1783–
1809.   5. Pennsylvania—Politics and government—
1775–1865.   I. Title.   II. Series.
E302.6.W64S44   973.3'092'4 [B]   78-2034
ISBN 0-527-81050-9

CONTENTS

PREFACE

I am indebted, as are all who are interested in James Wilson, to C. Page Smith whose biography *James Wilson: Founding Father, 1742–1798* presents with discernment the scanty evidence concerning Wilson's life, and to R. G. McCloskey whose introduction to his edition of *The Works of James Wilson* contains a brilliant analysis of his political and legal ideas. Both of these scholars have helped to raise Wilson from the obscurity in which he has so undeservedly languished for so long. It is hoped that this study of his contribution to the ideas on which the United States of America was founded, and which were reflected in its subsequent growth, will take the process a stage further and will encourage others, undeterred by the paucity of the material for such studies, to undertake additional research into the life of one of the most important of the Founding Fathers of the American nation. It is hoped also that it will appeal not only to the professional scholar but equally to those whose interest is more general.

I am deeply grateful for the assistance and advice of those who have shared in the preparation of this book. In particular I am indebted to Dr. Patricia Lucie for her perceptive comments and for ideas which have greatly enhanced whatever merit the work might possess; to Professor Harold Hyman for many valuable suggestions all of which are reflected in the following pages; to my wife, for her careful reading of the manuscript and for the removal of many stylistic infelicities and obscurities, ambiguities, and repetitions in the argument; and to Miss Glynis Williams for her admirable and expeditious typing of the manuscript and for bringing to light blemishes which had escaped previous scrutiny.

Geoffrey Seed
University of St. Andrews

Note: Quotations from James Wilson's writings do not necessarily reproduce exactly the form given in the source cited, which in any event often does not itself reproduce exactly the form of Wilson's original draft. Spelling, including in general the elimination of the capitalization of nouns, is modernized, and Wilson's prolific and frequently unnecessary use of underlining, italics, and capitalization of whole words, is ignored except when particular emphasis is clearly appropriate. For the sake of consistency, and in the interests of harmony of style, indirect quotations (e.g., from the Records of the Federal Convention) are similarly treated.

JAMES
WILSON

CHAPTER 1

*Concerning James Wilson's
early life in Scotland, his settlement
in America, and the part he
played in the revolt
against Britain.*

James Wilson was born in Scotland in 1742, and brought up on his father's farm at Carskerdo, near Ceres in the county of Fife. His father, William Wilson, was an elder of the Church of Scotland,[1] and he and his equally devout wife saw to it that their seven children were given a strictly religious upbringing. Robert Annan, James Wilson's cousin who lived in the Wilson home for several years, described the Wilson parents thus: "His father was distinguished for gravity, piety, and good sense; . . . His mother remarkable for a fine person, a superior genius, sound piety and elevation of sentiment." It is evident that they wished James, their eldest son, to enter the ministry of the Church of Scotland, and to that end provided him with a sound classical education at Cupar Grammar School, from which he proceeded to the nearby University of St. Andrews. There he was awarded a bursary which covered most, if not all, of his expenses. In his four years as an Arts student he studied the compulsory subjects of Latin, Greek, philosophy, science, and mathematics, and from the extent of his library borrowings of works on ancient history it seems possible that he attended also the optional classes of the recently appointed professor of civil history. Wilson then proceeded to St. Mary's, the theological college in the university, to study Divinity with a view to ordination in the Church of Scotland, but after only one year there the death of his father forced him to leave St. Andrews and, according to his cousin, he became "a tutor in a gentleman's family."

This is all we know with reasonable certainty of Wilson's early life in Scotland.[2] It has often been asserted that he studied in turn at the universities of Edinburgh and Glasgow, but there is no clear evidence of this, and the records of those universities reveal no trace of him. In any event, it is likely that whatever intellectual stimulus was given him by formal education came mainly from St. Andrews. Rare as it would have been in England or America for the son of a none-too-affluent small farmer to have entered a university, it was not so in Scotland. Wilson was unusual only in the kind of success he achieved; many scores of Scottish boys of similar background went to and from the Scottish universities impelled by the same motives and often achieving success differing only in degree. But few can have been endowed with the ambition so strong and the intellect so powerful which enabled Wilson to achieve a degree of fame and fortune that put him among the outstanding men of his time, or have been so lacking in the virtue—commonly attributed to the Scots—of prudence, want of which, in his lifetime, led to the sacrifice of the reputation he coveted so highly.

Though direct evidence is lacking, there is little doubt that Wilson's life in Scotland profoundly affected his attitudes throughout his life. It is not easy to define in what way this was so. But it is reasonable to assume that the Scottish view of civil and ecclesiastical government, with its powerful democratic overtones, made almost self-evident to Wilson political concepts which in America seemed impractical or even dangerous to others. And in a more narrowly intellectual sphere the influence of the Scottish common-sense[3] philosophy which Wilson absorbed in his youth remained with him throughout his life. The uniqueness of Wilson's approach to American political problems almost certainly derives from his Scottish roots. More than this it would be unwise, and unnecessary, to assert.

In the mid-eighteenth century America attracted many able and ambitious Scots who found their opportunities in Scotland inadequate and who were insufficiently well connected politically to hope for rapid advancement in England. It was natural for Wilson to look across the Atlantic for the means of satisfying his intense craving for power and wealth, the more so as his relative Robert Annan was already in America. He arrived in New York in 1765 and went at once to Philadelphia where, in 1766, he accepted an appointment as instructor in Latin at the College of Philadelphia, which granted him an honorary M.A. "in consideration of his merit and his having had a regular education in the universities of Scotland." It was not, however, as a pedagogue that he expected to gain the distinction he aspired to, even though he quickly achieved a reputation as a man of unusual ability and learning. Assessing the scope for advancement, he quickly realized that the study of the law would open the door to the material and political opportunities he sought, and accordingly, with the financial cooperation of Robert Annan, he began his apprenticeship under John Dickinson.[4] Characteristically, Wilson embarked on his studies with intense energy and meticulous care. His notebooks have survived, and they reveal the painstaking care and the perceptive insight that marked his entire career.

In a sense, Wilson's subsequent reputation as a political thinker and legal scholar was based on his ability to assimilate the philosophical scholarship of St. Andrews with the legal scholarship of Philadelphia—a combination that was unique in the America of his day. And it cannot reasonably be doubted that Wilson's view of the relationship with Britain was colored if not conditioned by his association with the man who became one of the foremost political thinkers of the Revolution. In 1767, after less than a year of intensive study, Wilson was sufficiently equipped to begin his career as a lawyer. He moved to Reading, a rapidly growing frontier community then of about a thousand inhabitants, where he hoped to achieve the position and affluence which were prerequisites to the next stage in his progress. For it was already clear that Wilson had no intention of remaining a small-town lawyer concerned, however successfully, only with local affairs. Success he did achieve, but in the expectation of finding even greater opportunities he moved in the autumn of 1770 to Carlisle.

In the meantime Wilson had advanced his interests by his marriage to Rachel Bird,[5] whose brother, Mark, became his partner in business enterprises which gave a new dimension to his efforts to attain prosperity. Wilson was undoubtedly deeply enamored of Rachel, and it was fortunate for him that the match gave him extensive opportunities for material advancement as well as personal happiness.

In Carlisle Wilson quickly established himself among the leading citizens, several of whom were also emigrants from Scotland. His practice grew rapidly, most of it arising from the frontier situation in which occasions abounded for litigation over land. His activities and his reputation spread far beyond the limits of Cumberland County, reaching even Philadelphia, where Robert Morris and his partner, Thomas Willing, appointed him to represent them in a land case, marking the beginning of an important relationship in his life and leading to an ever deeper involvement in land speculation. It was already clear that land was becoming an obsession with him. Ever alert to opportunities for the increase of his wealth and influence, the situation in Pennsylvania, especially on the frontier, seemed to point to transactions in land (it may not be fair to call it speculation) as the best means of achieving his aims. Already in his early days in Carlisle it seems that his rapidly growing wealth was largely on paper: much of what he earned, or could borrow, he invested, and then as throughout his life his commitments left him deficient in liquid assets.

It was at this early stage of his career in America that Wilson began to involve himself in political activity on behalf of the Whig cause. Whatever may have been the extent to which his ideas were influenced by his Scottish democratic background, or his association with John Dickinson and other Whig activists, it is probable that much of his incentive came from his deep interest in the economic growth of America, especially in expansion and development in the West. It was evident to those involved that the main obstacle to rapid expansion and the full satisfaction of personal ambition was the policy of the British government which in general aimed at achieving what was probably an unattainable balance between colonial, Indian, and Canadian interests, as well as the interest of Britain in maintaining the imperial economic structure. Successive British governments sought, at times clumsily, to keep four balls in the air at once, and to solve the problem of reconciling the white settler interests of the seaboard with the interests both of the indigenous population of the interior and those of the conquered French, while at the same time ensuring that British interests were safeguarded. The immensely complicated nature of this task need not concern us; it is sufficient to point out that the almost limitless expansionist aspirations of the colonists were bound to conflict with the Indian need for a guarantee of their territorial and cultural integrity, and that British policy seemed to many in America to be weighted in favor of the Indians.

The reluctance of Britain to authorize the Vandalia scheme[6] aroused serious misgivings which were eventually confirmed by the territorial clauses of the Quebec Act.[7] It seemed to Americans that the conflict could most easily be resolved by a new political arrangement which would restore unequivocally to the colonial assemblies the control of land policy which had been unquestionably theirs before 1763. Not independence necessarily, but at least a sufficient measure of legislative and administrative autonomy, would provide a practical solution to a practical problem. It is in this context that Wilson's first major essay in political theory should be regarded.

Wilson apparently wrote his pamphlet *Considerations on the Na-*

ture and Extent of the Legislative Authority of the British Parliament in 1768 or perhaps early in 1769 when he was still at Reading, but withheld publication until August 1774,[8] when controversy over the Coercive Acts and the Quebec Act was at its peak, when the time seemed ripe for men of ambition to advocate openly the cause of the colonies, and when a major blow had been struck at the aspirations of territorial expansionists. The final version of the pamphlet emphasized the adverse effect of the authority claimed by Parliament on the political rights of the colonies and omitted a reference in the original draft to the effect on the prosperity of the colonies. Like all Whig polemicists, Wilson narrowed the issue to that of the inadequacy of the British Parliament and government to the needs of the seaboard colonies. With clear logic he sought to prove that Parliament's claim to authority over the colonies was untenable, and that only a relationship with the Crown had any validity for the colonies. He disputed even the claim that imperial trade regulation required parliamentary authority. The idea that any other set of interests existed within the empire never occurred to him. There could be no claim opposed to those of the colonies for the possession of western lands, and Indians and Canadians were dependents, fit objects for colonial domination. The kith and kin arguments, or assumptions, so familiar to later generations of British imperial statesmen, were as implicit in Wilson's *Considerations* as in most contemporary political writings.

Wilson's political ideas as they had emerged at this time are revealed in a speech he prepared for delivery in a Pennsylvania convention in January 1775 and in an address submitted to the Continental Congress in 1776, as well as in the more widely known *Considerations*. Regarding the relationship with Britain, the views of Wilson were not significantly different from those that prevailed widely among Whigs at that time, though if Wilson's assertion is true, that he in fact wrote his *Considerations* around 1768 and refrained from publishing it until 1774, then perhaps he can justly claim to have helped to pioneer what became a fairly conventional view.

Throughout his life, Wilson persistently laid stress on the democratic basis of government. Government derived its authority from the people, and any proper system must ensure that the rights and interests of the people were adequately safeguarded. In Britain, this was achieved by the system of representation and by the fact that rulers and ruled shared the same set of common interests. The British people possessed a number of safeguards against any abuse of power. They elected the House of Commons, with provision for ensuring that the electorate was truly "free" by excluding from the franchise those who might, through dependence on the Crown or on another person, not be fully capable of exercising an independent judgment. Those they elected would be desirous of retaining the respect and good will of their constituents, with a further safeguard the frequency of elections, enabling the electorate to reelect those they approved of, and to reject those who had acted contrary to their interests. Moreover, the power of the Commons to vote supplies ensured that executive prerogative could never be used to ruin the interests of the people. Altogether, the British political system ensured that, for the British people, "the first maxims of jurisprudence are ever kept in view—that all power is derived from the people—that their happiness is the end of government."

While extoling the virtues of the British system Wilson had no difficulty in showing that its desirable attributes did not extend to the people of America. Starting from the premise that Americans are entitled to the same rights and privileges as the British, he showed that the system contained no safeguards for them, as it did for the British, that their rights and interests would be preserved. The House of Commons was in no way representative of the Americans; members of Parliament could not be influenced, either in what they do or do not do, by the desire for the respect of nonexistent American constituents or the implied restraint of an American electorate. Not only did members of Parliament have no common interests with Americans; they were not even aware of what American interests were. "Can," Wilson asked, "such members be styled, with any propriety, the magistrates of the Americans? Have those, who are bound by the laws of magistrates not their own, any security for the enjoyment of their absolute rights . . . ?"

In common with many contemporaries, and in accordance with what already was becoming a characteristically American mode of thought, Wilson sought ingeniously if somewhat tendentiously to illustrate from legal and historical precedents that because of their exclusion from a share in the British legislature the colonies were not bound by the acts of the British Parliament. This, however, was no more than a conventional legalistic veneer; the substance of Wilson's case, whether explicitly or implicitly asserted, was that Americans could not possess adequate political rights unless they had sufficient control, through financial restraint or otherwise, over the policy of the government in matters that affected their interests, and that no safeguard could be satisfactory unless it reflected the principle that all legitimate power was derived from the people. It might seem that the only matter of real substance concerned control over policy, and that any emphasis put on democratic principles might be seen as primarily a means to this end. Indeed, this is how Wilson's democratic ideas have often been interpreted, especially in the later context of the Federal Convention, where his vigorous advocacy of democratic principles has been portrayed as no more than a device for strengthening the national government.

The precise significance of Wilson's views will be discussed in various contexts, but it will be useful at the outset to emphasize that Wilson did not at any time use concepts of democracy merely to achieve narrow and immediate objectives; they were in fact basic to his view of political society, and if they were a means to an end, that end was the happiness of the people through the efficient working of American society in its broadest sense. There was no trace of hypocrisy in Wilson's view of a democratic political society.

Though in his writings and speeches of the years 1768–74 Wilson repudiated the authority over America of the British Parliament as it was then constituted, he did not thereby seek, in form at least, the complete separation of Britain and America. After an examination of the nature of the dependence of the colonies on Britain in which he rejected all forms of dependence except that which arose from the connection with the Crown, he considered the practical effects of that relationship. The Crown, he acknowledged, could be a unifying force, through which measures of concern to the empire as a whole could be coordinated, matters involving questions of war and peace, the negotiating of alliances, the avoidance of conflict in the laws of the various separate legislatures within the empire, and the regulation of imperial commercial relationships—though on this last issue he tentatively suggested that the adoption of free trade might obviate any need for central coordination. "The connexion and harmony between Great Britain and us," he wrote in the *Considerations,* "which it is her interest and ours mutually to cultivate, and on which her prosperity as well as ours so materially depends, will be better preserved by the operation of the legal prerogatives of the Crown, than by the exertion of an unlimited authority by Parliament."

It has sometimes been suggested that in seeking to base imperial relationships on allegiance to the king rather than to Parliament, Wilson was putting forward, characteristically ahead of his time, a practical solution to existing problems based on the later apparently successful Commonwealth concept. But this not only is anachronistic in terms of practicability in the eighteenth century, when no British government could conceivably have regarded the concept as other than equivalent to outright independence; it also implies unwarranted assumptions about the real nature of the imperial relationship of a later era. Moreover, it appears that Wilson himself was less than sincere in making his proposal—for although in the *Considerations* he appeared willing to accept the king as an effective coordinating force, in his speech to the Pennsylvania convention in 1775 he implied very clearly that he would not even nominally allow him any part in framing policy. So loyalty to the Crown may perhaps have been no more than a disguise for independence and it is certain that the British government would, rightly, regard it in this light. As a practical solution to present difficulties the suggestion was therefore without merit.

These initial forays into political controversy earned Wilson the degree of prominence he sought and the respect of his fellow Whigs. John Adams, though perhaps as much in criticism of Dickinson, whom he disliked, as in praise of Wilson, described him as a young man "whose fortitude, rectitude, and abilities too, greatly outshine his master's."[9] He was by now a sufficient figure in Pennsylvania to obtain appointment as delegate to the Continental Congress,[10] and there to serve on a variety of committees. Though most of Wilson's activities remain obscure, his involvement in matters concerning western lands is of evident importance. He was becoming more and more active in land deals and there is little doubt that he used his official position to further his own interests and those of his associates. As a member of the Indian affairs committee he was sent to Fort Pitt, the center of an area in dispute between Pennsylvania and Virginia, and his chief concern was to achieve a settlement favorable to the Pennsylvania interests with which he was connected. Thomas Jefferson was warned by Edmund Pendleton of his activities in the matter. Referring to Wilson he urged Jefferson to be on his guard against one of his "brethren in Congress who was an Indian commissioner last summer [i.e., 1775] at Fort Pitt, who stands charged by all the gentlemen then present of directing every speech and treaty with the Indians to the particular emolument of Pennsylvania; and many things unworthy his public character."[11]

The details of Wilson's activities are unknown but there is little reason to doubt his tendency in matters involving his economic interests—whether in land or otherwise—to assimilate his private with the public interest. He was, moreover, concerned to prevent the settlement of the Wyoming valley by men from Connecticut[12]—an issue in which he was later to play a major and successful part—and as early as December 1775, he attempted to persuade Congress to forbid further immigration from Connecticut. He was deeply involved also in efforts to persuade Congress, in 1775, to organize an attack on Detroit, a matter closely connected with his western interests, and advocated by his close associate, Arthur St. Clair.[13] While at Fort Pitt, Wilson wrote to Congress urging them to include an attack on Detroit, to be led by St. Clair, in their plans for the invasion of Canada. Congress rejected the proposal, giving as their reasons the lateness of the season, lack of adequate intelligence, and that the success of the main Canadian enterprise would ensure the fall of Detroit.[14] However, this was merely a question of tactics, and Wilson was an ardent supporter of the Canadian expedition, in the belief that its success would secure the Northwest for development and settlement. Through his friends Arthur St. Clair and William Thompson,[15] both commanding Pennsylvanian troops in the campaign, he kept in close touch with events and, after the failure to take Quebec, renewed his efforts, in collusion with his associates, to bring about an attack on Detroit. The failure of the Canadian enterprise, frustrating his hopes in the Northwest, was a major disappointment to him.

His political writings and his activities as a member of the Continental Congress in the prosecution of the conflict with Britain clearly established Wilson as a vigorous opponent of parliamentary authority and British policy in the colonies. He had not yet emerged, however, as an unambiguous advocate of American independence, and though he was one of the signers of the Declaration of Independence, his enthusiasm was suspect, and he was in fact subsequently accused of having dragged his feet in this vital matter and of having sought to avoid the necessity of formal separation from the mother country. His attitude certainly was unclear enough to give rise to doubts concerning the degree of his commitment to independence. In his writings and speeches of the years before 1776 he had tentatively touched on the issue of independence. In the *Considerations* he avoided any explicit assertion that circumstances might arise in which American interests would necessitate independence but, as we have seen, he envisaged what in practice would be tantamount to independence, and the possibility of appropriate circumstances arising was implicit in his argument. In his 1775 speech to the Pennsylvania convention[16] he went a short step further when he urged Americans to do neither too much nor too little to safeguard their rights and interests. Early in 1776, however, he was much more explicit when, on February 13, he presented an address to the Continental Congress.[17] This address was prepared in association with John Dickinson and others,[18] and while much of the drafting may possibly have been the work of Dickinson, contemporaries attributed it to Wilson, and in introducing it he was not in any way presenting views which were not his own. Though the address expressly denied any desire for independence, it suggested that independence might be forced on the colonies. "We are *desirous,*" it declared, "to continue subjects; But we are *determined* to continue freemen. We shall deem ourselves bound to renounce . . . the *former* character whenever it shall become incompatible with the *latter*." Wilson concluded with the resounding peroration: "That the colonies may continue connected, as they have been, with Britain, is our second wish: Our first is that America may be free." At the same time Wilson showed great concern at the possible consequences of separation. "If one part of the Constitution be pulled down," he warned, "it is impossible to foretell whether the other parts of it may not be shaken and, perhaps, overthrown." What Wilson and his associates had here in mind was the possible effect on the volatile Pennsylvania political structure of the sudden removal of the constitutional relationship. It is this which at least partly explains his ambiguous and hesitant attitude as the decision over independence grew closer.

Until this point was reached Wilson had certainly given no reason to doubt his attachment to the Whig cause. He had been prominent in 1774 in the measures taken in Pennsylvania in preparation for a general congress,[19] he had been a member of the committee which in June 1775, recommended the Continental Congress to advise Massachusetts to set up a new government,[20] and had himself put the suggestion to Congress, and in January 1776 he had introduced a motion that everyone who refused to sign the Association should be disarmed.[21] However, in February and March 1776 Wilson was still clearly in favor of retaining the degree of dependence on Britain which he had acknowledged in the *Considerations*.[22] In May, his concern over the political situation in Pennsylvania became more evident when he opposed the adoption by Congress of a preamble to the resolution of May 15 recommending the colonies to assume all the powers of government. This preamble sought to repudiate all oaths of allegiance to any government under the Crown, and urged the total suppression of the authority of such governments and their replacement by governments deriving their authority from the people. Wilson based his opposition to this measure on the grounds that its adoption would bring about the "immediate dissolution of every kind of authority," and urged that new governments be first properly established. "Before we are prepared to build the new house," he argued, "why should we pull down the old one, and expose ourselves to all the inclemencies of the season?"[23]

The outcome of impetuosity, Wilson rightly foresaw, would be the immediate replacement of the government under the Proprietors by one dominated by the extreme radicals. He did not, of course, express his opposition in quite these terms: the reason he put forward for opposing the measure was the fact that he was the delegate of his constituents—the Pennsylvania assembly whose future was in jeopardy—and he could not properly exceed the authority delegated to him.[24] This was not hypocrisy. Wilson genuinely believed that he was the servant of the people—in this case the assembly—and though he was sincerely opposed to the preamble, he did subsequently endeavor, with success, to persuade the assembly to modify its restricting instructions to its delegates on the broader issue of independence.[25]

When, on June 7, a debate on independence was opened, Wilson was still an advocate of caution, and was clearly having difficulty in assessing the political situation in Pennsylvania. A few days after the debate in Congress, he wrote to General Gates: "Our affairs [i.e., of Pennsylvania] have been in such a fluctuating and disordered situation that it has been almost impossible to form any accurate judgment concerning the turn that things would take."[26] In the debate, he adhered to the line of expediency, arguing that the people of the middle colonies "were not yet ripe for bidding adieu to the British connection." He went on to say, however, "that they were fast ripening, and in a short time would join in the general voice of America."

The chief opponents of a declaration of independence at that time, according to Jefferson, were James Wilson, Robert Livingston, Edward Rutledge, and John Dickinson, with on the other side, according to Rutledge, "the power of all New England, Virginia, and Georgia."[27] The danger in Pennsylvania seemed to be that precipitate action by the Congress might lead the assembly to decide to support Britain, with perhaps dire consequences politically and also to the interests of certain Pennsylvania land speculators. With his concern for properly constituted, moderate government, and with his interest in the West, it is not difficult to appreciate Wilson's dilemma. Anyhow, part of the problem was resolved by a subsequent change in the assembly's instructions to its delegates, in withdrawing the prohibition on voting for independence without instructing them to do so. Moreover, the assembly was now rapidly disintegrating, with the defection of sufficient Whig members to render it impossible to obtain a quorum.[28] Power was passing to the radicals, who organized a provincial convention which met on June 18 and took steps to summon a constitutional convention under radical control. The situation in Pennsylvania changed decisively in the short period between early June and early July, and accordingly when the issue of independence next arose at the beginning of July, Wilson voted in favor, even though at first his delegation divided four to three against, and only the absence of two members, John Dickinson and Robert Morris, threw Pennsylvania's support to the Declaration on July 4.

So Wilson, belatedly and perhaps slightly reluctantly, became in the end a supporter of independence and a signer of the Declaration. It is apparent that before his final vote in favor, he had been widely stigmatized as an opponent and had been acutely embarrassed in consequence. After his vote against independence in June, he persuaded twenty-two of his colleagues in the Congress to sign a memorial, drafted by himself, testifying that his apparent opposition to independence was based on the conviction that, although he supported independence, so momentous a decision should be seen clearly to reflect the desire of the representatives of the people in the various colonies, and the issue should therefore be referred back at least to those colonies whose delegates were bound by instructions to oppose independence. Among the signatories to this document were Sam and John Adams, John Hancock, and Thomas Jefferson, as well as a number who still remained opposed to independence.[29]

Wilson's sensitivity about his public image over the issue of independence was revealed also in the matter of his address to the Congress in February 1776, when he had also shown a reluctance to accept independence as necessary. He informed Madison, though not until some years later, that his purpose then had been "to lead the public mind into the idea of independence."[30] It is likely that as July approached, political events in Pennsylvania were forcing Wilson, and others, to take a firm stand, and this could only be in favor of independence. It was about the same time that the total failure of the Canadian enterprise became clear, and that therefore there seemed little prospect of a change in the British government's Western policy within the framework of the empire. The distinguished and astute Pennsylvania conservative, James Allen, noted regretfully in his diary the sudden conversion to independence around that time of many who had formerly opposed it, and attributed the phenomenon to ambition.[31] The wind was set fair for independence, and Wilson was not one to be left on shore when the crew embarked.

Wilson fully accepted the decision, though a short time before he would have been satisfied with internal autonomy under the Crown, provided it included control of land policy. Events, both in Britain and America, had by July made Wilson's hopes wholly unrealistic, and there was in the end no basic shift in attitude in his acceptance of independence. Clearly however, Wilson, unlike some of the New Englanders, was not at that time an emotional nationalist and had as yet no real sense of an American as distinct from a British ethos. He had not yet made any very significant contribution to the development of the United States, and had his career ended at this point he would be remembered only as a very insignificant signer of the Declaration of Independence and the author of a rather interesting political pamphlet which revealed him as a young man of promise. His close associates, however, already knew him to be a man of consuming ambition, tremendous energy, and great intellectual power, and with a range of vision which enabled him to foresee the future needs of the new country, and to identify its welfare with his own political and material aspirations.

CHAPTER 2

*Concerning some of James Wilson's
thoughts on government
and law.*

Before considering Wilson's major achievements in the making of
constitutions, it will be both useful and interesting to take a look at
his philosophical speculations on the nature of government and law.
The abstract speculations of men of affairs do not always parallel their
practical objectives; with Wilson, however, there was a remarkable
degree of compatibility between theory and practice. Consistency is
not always a mark of statesmanship; but in statesmen it is usually a
mark of sincerity.

The broad philosophical background of Wilson's thought was an
amalgam of natural law concepts, of the Scottish common-sense
philosophy, of a religious outlook based on his Presbyterian upbringing and his later close association with William White, who became
Episcopalian bishop of Pennsylvania, with whom, soon after his arrival in America, he established a lifelong friendship. Wilson was not
unusual in basing his view of politics and society on abstract speculation; rare as it would be in the twentieth century, in the eighteenth
century it was by no means uncommon and gave a quality, much of
which has since been lost, to the practical aspects of political arrangements.

Wilson's view of natural law was a broad one. It was ordained by
God and revealed in part in the Bible, and it placed on man moral
obligations perceivable at times through his conscience—"the voice
of God within us"—and at others through reason. Wilson's view of
natural law was that man should pursue his own perfection and happiness. Happiness, in fact, was the natural consequence of a good con-

science, and was not attainable, as many were then maintaining, by calculations of expediency in line with which actions were assessed by their tendency to promote happiness. Happiness, in other words, was highly subjective, and not an object which could be pursued by conscious efforts. In his philosophy, in apparent marked contrast to his behavior, Wilson was notably nonmaterialistic.

Of more direct relevance to Wilson's view of government was that part of his philosophy which derived from the common-sense or intuitive school associated with Thomas Reid of Aberdeen, which was in Wilson's day highly influential especially in Scotland. The essence of the common-sense philosophy was that the basis of knowledge is intuitive, that there are self-evident truths which provide the premises for logical deduction. As Wilson himself expressed it:

> This philosophy will teach us that first principles are in themselves apparent; that to make nothing self-evident is to take away all possibility of knowing anything; that without first principles, there can be neither reason nor reasoning; that discursive knowledge requires intuitive maxims as its basis; that if every truth would admit of proof, proof would extend to infinity; that, consequently, all sound reasoning must rest ultimately on the principles of common sense— principles supported by original and intuitive evidence.[1]

"The science of morals," he wrote elsewhere, ". . . is founded on truths that cannot be discovered or proved by reasoning. Reason is confined to the investigation of unknown truths by the means of such as are known. We cannot, therefore, begin to reason, till we are furnished, otherwise than by reason, with some truths, on which we can found our arguments. . . . Morality . . . has its intuitive truths, without which we cannot make a single step in our reasonings upon the subject."[2] This intuitive insight, a natural or God-given endowment, could not be inculcated in man by any process of education, yet it was possessed by most men, and was a reliable guide to action. It was in fact the only kind of intellectual attribute most men possessed, and yet it was sufficient to render them capable of conducting their own affairs and, indeed, their relationships with others, in a manner which would benefit society. As Wilson assumed also that man was by nature a social, benevolent animal, it followed that the political judgment of the people could be relied on, and that only good could come of the wide diffusion of political influence. A broad franchise, in other words, was a positive instrument of good government, and the influence of the people could usefully extend not merely to the election of the entire legislative branch, but in fact to all branches of government. The influence of the people in the judicial branch was exercised even through the common law which, being founded on "long and general custom," was based by clear implication firmly on the "free and voluntary consent" of the people.[3] Statute law, being the work of a body chosen by and representing the people, was obviously based on consent, and accordingly this principle permeated the whole judicial system. Wilson firmly refuted the orthodox Blackstonian concept of law as the will of a superior and replaced it by the principle of obligation based on "the consent of those whose obedience the law requires."[4]

Wilson very frequently stressed what to him was the vital principle of government: "that the supreme or sovereign power of the society resides in the citizens at large."[5] Popular consent lay behind every branch of government, since in civil society, which preceded the formation of civil government, all men were equal, and therefore equally free, and accordingly when civil government came into being no man could possess any inherent authority over others—no authority was by grace of God; all was by grace of the people. The sovereignty of the state was no more than the aggregate of the powers and rights of its members. Moreover, government at all times was subordinate to society. "By some politicians," he wrote, "society has been considered as only the scaffolding of government. . . . In the just order of things, government is the scaffolding of society; and if society could be built and kept entire without government, the scaffolding might be thrown down without the least inconvenience or cause of regret."[6] Society, for its part, was the instrument not merely of economic advance but, equally important, of the development of the human mind and personality.[7] For this, far more than for material progress, good government was necessary. By good government Wilson meant balanced government which in accordance with prevailing theories would, by mixing in proper proportions the qualities associated with monarchy, aristocracy, and democracy, produce vigor, wisdom, and goodness. Failure to achieve the right balance would create a danger of tyranny, whichever of the three elements might prevail, and under a tyranny no man could achieve his proper fulfillment. At all times Wilson kept clearly in mind the perfection of man as the aim of society.

Whereas most of his contemporaries put their main emphasis on the liberty of the individual and the rights of citizens, Wilson gave equal importance to the duties of the citizen. To him, liberty and responsibility must go together in the free, well-regulated, contented society. It was a fundamental responsibility of men to obey the laws they themselves had helped to make, and to respect the authority of the officials they had helped to elect. He also expected the citizens of a republic in the event of a conflict between the two to subordinate their own interests to those of the state. "Whenever," he wrote, "a competition unavoidably takes place between his interests and that of the public, to the latter the former must be the devoted sacrifice." Without this, civil government could not be supported. If he was somewhat naive in his view of human nature he was equally naive in his view of the normal relationship between the state and the individual. "Fortunate . . . it is," he went on, "that in a government formed wisely and administered impartially, this unavoidable competition can seldom take place, at least in any very great degree."[8] A state in which private interests were apt to conflict with those of the government Wilson described as tyrannical. More positive aspects of the duties of citizenship were the duty to vote (on more than one occasion he deplored the electoral apathy which was characteristic of the time), the duty of the citizen to inform himself of the nature of public issues, and in particular to acquire a general knowledge of the law. "The public duties and the public rights of every citizen of the United States loudly demand from him all the time which he can prudently spare, and all the means which he can prudently employ, in order to learn that part which it is incumbent on him to act."[9] The idea of the participatory democracy was central to much of Wilson's thinking. Moreover, public-spirited service to the society was the way to personal happiness. "He who acts on such principles and is governed by such affections as sever him from the common good and public interest, works, in reality, toward his own misery; while he, on the other hand, who operates for the good of the whole, as is by nature and by nature's God appointed him, pursues, in truth, and at the same time, his own felicity."[10] Wilson's assumptions may seem unrealistically idealistic, but they were compatible with the philosophy that still had influence in the Pennsylvania environment to which he belonged.

In line with his concept of good government being but the projection of the individual, Wilson in his view of natural liberty envisaged for man the widest possible measure of freedom subject only to his responsibilities to others. Even the exercise of these responsibilities was not in reality a restraint on his liberty, as if all the citizens exercised them equally conscientiously the balance of liberty was even more in their favor. He wrote that under good government—always his basic assumption—"every citizen will gain more liberty than he can lose by these prohibitions. He will gain more by the limitation of other men's freedom, than he can lose by the diminution of his own. He will gain more by the enlarged and undisturbed exercise of his natural liberty in innumerable instances, than he can lose by the restriction of it in a few."[11] Wilson thought of natural liberty as complete liberty of action for the individual, subject only to the avoidance of injury to others. With only this qualification man, whose "dignity and perfection" arose from his voluntary acts, had a right to seek his happiness in his own way, the state having no right to attempt in any way to control him, however foolish or harmful to himself his conduct might be, provided only that no injury was caused to any other person, or his efforts were not thereby diverted from carrying out his public responsibilities.[12] Even in his definition of natural liberty Wilson gave precedence to public duties over private interests. He may have taken an idealistic view of human nature, and he may have oversimplified basic problems of government, but nevertheless he did understand what should be the basis of a better society.

Wilson regarded natural rights more as a safeguard of the weak against the strong than of the citizen against the state, as in any event he never regarded the state as an entity quite distinct from the individual, and in a well-conducted state conflict should not arise. The "wisest and most powerful" in a society must not be allowed, through the exploitation of their wisdom or power, to inflict injury on "the meanest and most ignorant." The right of the ignorant and indolent to their small possessions was as sacred as the right of the clever and active to their large ones.[13] Though Wilson was much concerned with the natural right of man to undisturbed possession of his property, he attached equal importance to man's natural right also "to his character, to liberty, and to safety." As a corollary of these rights, he added the right "to receive the fulfillment of the engagements which are made to him." The right to security from injury, and the right to ensure the honoring of obligations, were to him "the pillars of justice" on which rested the criminal and civil law.[14] In stressing possession of property as a natural right he was not thinking in narrowly materialistic terms. Property to him, at least in theory, was never an end in itself, but always the means to some higher good.[15]

The improvement of both man and society was in Wilson a recurring theme. Progress meant not merely material progress—though that was important—but equally the expansion of the human mind with its consequent benefit to human society. "A progressive state," he said, "is necessary to the happiness and perfection of man. Whatever attainments may be already possessed, attainments still higher ought to be pursued. It is our duty, therefore, to press forward, and to make unceasing advance in everything that can support, improve, refine, and embellish society."[16] "It is," he wrote elsewhere, "the glorious destiny of man to be always progressive."[17]

His faith in moral and material progress was an important element in his general philosophical outlook and, as we shall see, was reflected in his actions as much as more prominent features of his thought. A corollary of this was an interest in education. On one occasion he declared that if he were to have any influence on the growth of society he hoped it would be "in raising the care of education to that high degree of respectability, to which, everywhere, but especially in countries that are free, it has the most unimpeachable title."[18] Education, he believed, was of vital importance to the progressive state, and there was no higher calling than to help prepare young minds "for all the great purposes for which they are intended."[19]

The feature of Wilson's thought, which if not the most fundamental was the most pervasive and influential, was his view of the nature of democracy, which in many ways reflected his views on a wide range of subjects. In effect it epitomizes his whole attitude to man, society, and government. Commenting on philosophical discussion of the nature of sovereignty, he asserted:

> The dread and redoubtable sovereign, when traced to his ultimate and genuine source, has been found, as he ought to have been found, in the free and independent man. This truth, so simple and natural, and yet so neglected or despised, may be appreciated as the first and fundamental principle in the science of government.[20]

The implications of this belief led Wilson inexorably to acceptance of a degree of democracy which seems to have gone much further than any other Founding Father believed expedient, and which based the entire political structure on the authority of the people. Wilson was very fond of employing the metaphor of the pyramid, whose base represented the people. "The pyramid of government," he remarked in 1789, "should be raised to a dignified altitude; but its foundation must, of consequence, be broad, and strong and deep. The authority, the interests, and the affections of the people at large are the only basis on which a superstructure, proposed to be at once durable and magnificent, can be rationally erected."[21] As well as the metaphor of the pyramid, Wilson was fond of using the metaphor of the chain. In the Pennsylvania Ratifying Convention in 1788 he used both together:

> A free government has often been compared to a pyramid. This allusion is made with peculiar propriety in the system before you: it is laid on the broad basis of the people; its powers gradually rise, while they are confined, in proportion as they ascend, until they end in that most permanent of all forms. When you examine all its parts, they will invariably be found to preserve that essential mark of free governments, a chain of connection with the people."[22]

We will see later how Wilson used these concepts in the Federal Convention. That of the pyramid to underline the need for strong government and to show that, contrary to the widespread belief at that time, it was not incompatible with a popular basis, and that of the chain, to emphasize the importance of maintaining at all levels of government a clear connection with the people. Many examples can be given of Wilson's philosophical devotion to the principle of democracy. The vital, or life-giving, principle of sound government was that the supreme power of society should reside "in the citizens at large,"[23] an idea he expressed most trenchantly in the Pennsylvania Ratifying Convention, when he said, "That the supreme power . . . should be vested in the people, is in my judgment the great panacea of human politics. It is a power paramount to every constitution, inalienable in its nature, and indefinite in its extent."[24]

The best measure of Wilson's philosophical commitment to democracy is his attitude toward the suffrage. It is possible to be a theoretic democrat and at the same time a practical aristocrat, but this would almost certainly be revealed by a degree of caution in advocating an extension of the suffrage. Wilson displayed no such caution. He was the only Founding Father of any consequence who asserted with conviction his belief in the principle of one man, one vote.[25] His view of the suffrage put it in an almost mystical light. Its exercise gave a new dimension to human relationships within a state, as well as contributing to the moral development of individuals. "The right of suffrage," he declared in 1789, "properly understood, properly valued, properly cultivated, and properly exercised, is a rich mine of intelligence and patriotism . . . it is an abundant source of the most rational, the most improving, and the most endearing connection among the citizens—and it is a most powerful and . . . a most pleasing bond of union between the citizens and those whom they select for the different offices and departments of government."[26] It would produce in citizens that kind of "pure and genuine patriotism . . . which consists in liberal investigation and disinterested conduct" and as a result "warm and generous emotion glows and is reflected from breast to breast." He who had the right of suffrage in fact stood above the proudest princes, whose sovereignty, after all, was merely derivative, whereas that of the voter was original.[27]

On the essential matter of the extent of the franchise, Wilson was not always precise. He maintained that as to vote for members of a legislature was "to perform an act of original sovereignty" then "no person unqualified should . . . be permitted to assume the exercise of such preeminent power." The boundary of the suffrage was, however, extensive. It should "certainly be extended as far as considerations of safety and order will possibly admit." Defining the boundaries more precisely, he went on: "The correct theory and the true principles of liberty require that every citizen, whose circumstances do not render him necessarily dependent on the will of another, should possess a vote in electing those by whose conduct his property, his reputation, his liberty, and his life, may be all most materially affected."[28] We will see later what this meant in practice; there is certainly nothing whatever in Wilson's statements to suggest that he was not wholeheartedly committed to the democratic principle of direct election, on the basis of manhood suffrage. Nor did Wilson ever even imply the expediency of distortion of the system to restrain the free exercise of democratic rights. He was, for instance, an ardent advocate of equal electoral districts, in order that the assembly elected would reflect fairly the whole society.[29] Wilson was convinced that the mass of the people would exercise the franchise responsibly and that there was nothing to fear from democracy even when carried to its logical limit. He believed that the power, for example, to amend the Constitution would always be used with the greatest care. The people, he was sure, would elect men of wisdom and goodness—few at that time, however democratic, envisaged the election of men of the people—who would preserve the kind of society he wanted, based on respect for property and the rule of law. He was fully aware that the people must exercise their sovereign power sensibly and honestly; otherwise the kind of government he desired could not long exist. "For a people wanting to themselves," he warned on more than one occasion, "there is indeed no remedy in the political dispensary."[30] All power, in other words, resided ultimately in the people, and its proper exercise equally depended ultimately on them.

Direct democracy was Wilson's ideal, though he knew it was impracticable in all but very small political units. "Power," he wrote, "ought to be exercised personally by the people, when this can be done without inconvenience and without disadvantage."[31] Representation, however, was essential to a democratic system in America, and in Wilson's view it should operate strictly on the principle of a simple majority, which "must be deemed the will of the whole"[32] and "should have the same weight and influence, as the sentiments of the constituents would have if expressed personally."[33] At only one point did Wilson depart from the view that a representative body should mirror precisely the opinion of the electors. He asserted that the representative should express·the same sentiments which the people he represented "if possessed of equal information," would have expressed.[34] Apart from the assumption that the people would always elect men of wisdom, education, and position this is the only trace of elitism to be found in Wilson's theory of democracy.

There is a remarkable degree of consistency in Wilson's thought. Throughout his life he adhered to the same principles and displayed the same attitudes, something perhaps impossible to achieve except on the basis of complete sincerity.

al Convention of
are most notable.
ished long before
tal Congress and
utions later. The
ng to Wilson. In
been implicit in
l accustomed to
uthority between
eed, largely over
t the Revolution
ssential issue was
on of governmen-
stronger central
learly displayed,
is attitudes and

—from 1775 to
5 to 1787—but
ade his position
should aspire to.
t with adequate
ress discussed a
h concerned the
d the state gov-
rpose of remov-
Articles that all
hat only certain
onjunction with
orously by Wil-
attempt at that
government was
later of pressing
he outset of the
he need to cen-
ing trade,[3] and
d "labored with
s implications,
ime Wilson re-
ion had already
ndment in the

son's
rs from
relating
s

he cause of an indepen-
roceeded to try to estab-
of the new nation. With
to make a conspicuous
tical organization of the
al system, the economic
nmerce, and her territo-
as Wilson's personal in-
al interest. At the same
olitical affairs of his own
gest that already he saw
on the future of his coun-

ime for the cultivation of
uential friends whose re-
to achieve the warmth of
n in good stead in public
to establish the historical
achieve. Wilson's surviv-
with which his associates
o him several times he has
nat he has been, and is, too
torical reputations tend to
inous correspondence and

It is in the period during and after the Fede
1787 that Wilson's achievements in politics and law
The pattern of his thought, however, was well estab
then, and in many ways his work in the Contine:
outside it foreshadowed his more important contri
emergence of the federal idea in itself owed nothi
practice, if not always recognizably in theory, it ha
the old imperial system, and Americans were w
operating a form of government which divided a
London and the various colonial capitals. It was, in
the question of where the line was to be drawn.th
occurred. Under the Articles of Confederation[1] the
much the same. Wilson was dedicated to a distributi
tal functions which would ensure the creation of :
government than had before existed, and this was
whether explicitly or by implication, in many of
actions in the years following 1776.

His membership in the Congress was spasmod
1777, from 1782 to 1783, and after the war from 17
right at the outset, and consistently thereafter, he :
clear with regard to the kind of government America
His first attempt to provide the central governme:
powers was a total failure. In February 1777, Con
clause in the proposed Articles of Confederation wh:
relationship between the future central government :
ernments. An amendment was proposed with the p
ing any doubt or ambiguity by stating clearly in the
sovereign power resided in the states separately, and
expressly enumerated powers should be exercised in
Congress. Opposition to the amendment was led vi;
son, but in the end only Virginia supported him.[2] An
time to establish even a moderately strong central
premature, yet Wilson missed no opportunity then o:
his advocacy of effective national authority. Right at
discussion, in July 1776, he had urged, successfully,
tralize in Congress the control of Indian affairs, inclu
according to John Adams, he and Wilson, in 1777, h
great zeal" to establish in the Articles, with obvio
voting by population rather than by states.[4] By the
turned to Congress, in 1782, the Articles of Confeder:
been adopted and were in force. Constitutional am

CHAPTER 3

Concerning James Wilson's
activities during the years from
1775 to 1787, in matters relating
especially to politics
and finance.

Having committed himself irretrievably to the cause of an independent America, Wilson with his usual energy proceeded to try to establish himself as one of the foremost statesmen of the new nation. With complete confidence in his ability, he hoped to make a conspicuous contribution in at least four areas—the political organization of the United States, the creation of an effective legal system, the economic development of America in business and commerce, and her territorial expansion to the west. In all of these areas Wilson's personal interest was closely identified with the national interest. At the same time he remained deeply involved in the political affairs of his own state of Pennsylvania. It is tempting to suggest that already he saw himself as a man of destiny, whose influence on the future of his country would be all-embracing.

It is not surprising that he had little time for the cultivation of personal relationships; although he had influential friends whose respect for him was great, he was never able to achieve the warmth of human contact which might have stood him in good stead in public life and which certainly would have helped to establish the historical reputation he deserves but has so far failed to achieve. Wilson's surviving papers are notable for the frequency with which his associates complain that although they have written to him several times he has not replied and for his occasional response that he has been, and is, too busy to write fully but will do so later. Historical reputations tend to depend on conspicuous success or voluminous correspondence and Wilson achieved neither.

It is in the period during and after the Federal Convention of 1787 that Wilson's achievements in politics and law are most notable. The pattern of his thought, however, was well established long before then, and in many ways his work in the Continental Congress and outside it foreshadowed his more important contributions later. The emergence of the federal idea in itself owed nothing to Wilson. In practice, if not always recognizably in theory, it had been implicit in the old imperial system, and Americans were well accustomed to operating a form of government which divided authority between London and the various colonial capitals. It was, indeed, largely over the question of where the line was to be drawn that the Revolution occurred. Under the Articles of Confederation[1] the essential issue was much the same. Wilson was dedicated to a distribution of governmental functions which would ensure the creation of a stronger central government than had before existed, and this was clearly displayed, whether explicitly or by implication, in many of his attitudes and actions in the years following 1776.

His membership in the Congress was spasmodic—from 1775 to 1777, from 1782 to 1783, and after the war from 1785 to 1787—but right at the outset, and consistently thereafter, he made his position clear with regard to the kind of government America should aspire to. His first attempt to provide the central government with adequate powers was a total failure. In February 1777, Congress discussed a clause in the proposed Articles of Confederation which concerned the relationship between the future central government and the state governments. An amendment was proposed with the purpose of removing any doubt or ambiguity by stating clearly in the Articles that all sovereign power resided in the states separately, and that only certain expressly enumerated powers should be exercised in conjunction with Congress. Opposition to the amendment was led vigorously by Wilson, but in the end only Virginia supported him.[2] Any attempt at that time to establish even a moderately strong central government was premature, yet Wilson missed no opportunity then or later of pressing his advocacy of effective national authority. Right at the outset of the discussion, in July 1776, he had urged, successfully, the need to centralize in Congress the control of Indian affairs, including trade,[3] and according to John Adams, he and Wilson, in 1777, had "labored with great zeal" to establish in the Articles, with obvious implications, voting by population rather than by states.[4] By the time Wilson returned to Congress, in 1782, the Articles of Confederation had already been adopted and were in force. Constitutional amendment in the

direction of strengthening the central government was all he could hope to achieve. He was provided with an opportunity of great significance in the furthering of the national cause in the controversy over the issue, made urgent by pressure from a disgruntled army, of the financing of the central government. This was an acutely delicate matter, as the conventional view, arising from the circumstances of the struggle with Britain, was that to endow a central authority with financial independence was to invite tryanny and oppression. Yet without it no effective central government could be created, and Wilson, who consistently denied that efficient centralization and the liberty of the people were in any way incompatible, accordingly became a strong advocate of giving Congress a source of revenue which would enable it to govern effectively.

It is interesting to observe that although little could be achieved, apart from the above-mentioned abortive attempt to base representation in Congress on population, to identify the people with the government, Wilson nevertheless asserted the conviction that remained basic in his thinking, that if the people felt an identification with their government they would support it and, in this instance, willingly contribute taxes which otherwise they would resent and resist. The people should be brought to consider themselves "as the sovereign as well as the subject; and as receiving with one hand what they paid with the other." This was an idealization of political society perhaps, but its logic was impeccable, and it reflected clearly the true democratic convictions of James Wilson.

However, for the moment at least, the ideal was unattainable, and Wilson's immediate concern was much more with the practical problems arising from the withholding from Congress of the power to tax. Already, during Wilson's absence from Congress, an attempt to obtain an independent income—that is, independent of the states—by means of a 5 percent impost, or import duty, had been effectively blocked by Rhode Island. Wilson, therefore, when he took up the issue in 1783 was attempting to find a new practical method of implementing a principle already accepted by the majority in Congress and in the state assemblies. In arguing, as he did, that both justice and practical common sense called for an independent income he was preaching to the already converted. His argument went beyond this, however. His dedication to the cause of a united America under a strong government was again revealed in his observation that "a public debt resting on general funds would operate as a cement to the confederacy, and might contribute to prolong its existence, after

the foreign danger ceased to counteract its tendency to dissolution."

On January 27, 1783, Wilson moved this resolution: "That it is the opinion of Congress that complete justice cannot be done to the creditors of the United States, nor the restoration of public credit be effected, nor the future exigencies of the war provided for, but by the establishment of *general* funds to be collected by Congress."[5] After discussion and amendment it emerged two days later as: "That it is the opinion of Congress that the establishment of permanent and adequate funds or taxes or duties which shall operate generally and on the whole in just proportion throughout the United States, are indispensably necessary toward doing complete justice to the public creditors, for restoring public credit, and for providing for the future exigencies of the war."[6] An examination of the differences between the two versions reveals the strength of the opposition to the kind of government Wilson wanted, and the deep suspicion of the motives behind his proposals. In presenting his resolution, Wilson may well have been seeking more than ostensibly appears, and the final version reflected the most that Congress at that time could be persuaded to accept. The controversy occurred over the phrase "by the establishment of *general* funds to be collected by Congress." It was at once objected that the word "general" could be held to include all possible uses of taxation as well as the collection throughout the states of a particular tax. In other words, it could be interpreted in a way that would give immense power to the Congress of the United States, and evidently there were some who believed this to be Wilson's concealed intention. Moreover, the proposal that these general funds be collected by Congress, and not through the agency of the states, might be held to imply the enactment of a federal law enforced by federal courts. Wilson was in fact expressly accused of having been deliberately vague in his proposals in order that approval of the principle by Congress would be followed by forms of detailed application preconceived by him and his supporters and objectionable to the majority. He was believed, in other words, to be involved in a conspiracy to change the government by stealth, and his denial of the charge, mainly on the grounds that to introduce detail at this stage would be premature,[7] did not carry conviction.

On more than one future occasion Wilson created the suspicion that there was more behind a proposal he was advancing than appeared on the surface. He had a very astute mind, and was aloof and perhaps even secretive by nature; and men such as that tend to be less subtle than they suppose and in consequence arouse suspicion of their mo-

tives and purposes. Throughout his life Wilson was, in his political actions, a frequent victim of mistrust which was usually unwarranted.

In pressing for an independent income Wilson was acting in accord with, and in fact in association with, Robert Morris and his group, whose dedication to the cause of strong government was as great as Wilson's. Yet it would be misleading to suppose that Wilson was merely the spokesman of the Morris group, or that he was in any way a subservient agent. Wilson never at any time expressed a view that was not fully his own; he did in fact differ in one important respect from his associates—in his views regarding the usefulness of democracy in government—and never hesitated to express an independent view when the occasion warranted. He has on occasion been unfairly dismissed as a subordinate and subservient member of an ultraconservative Morris faction, and condemned as an enemy of the people on the basis of guilt by association. It is safe to assume that whatever Wilson said or did accurately reflected his own attitude, whether or not his views were at times colored by self-interest. The views he expressed in the Congress, as elsewhere, though often fundamentally the same as those of Robert Morris, were nevertheless his own, and independently arrived at.

With his original proposal emasculated, Wilson proceeded belatedly to reveal what he considered to be the best methods of raising a central revenue. Accepting the provision of the amended resolution that any taxes should "operate . . . in just proportion throughout the United States," he nevertheless sought to interpret it in a way that would prevent its application to individual taxes, but seek merely to achieve a fair balance of taxes collectively throughout the country. For instance, a land tax that would most affect the South could be balanced by the concurrent imposition of commercial levies which would most affect the East. The nationalizing tendency is clearly evident, though not to a degree that would endanger the states as viable units of government. On the details of taxes which might be imposed, he expressed a preference for a poll tax, again with obvious nationalizing implications, though admitting its impracticability for the reason that as it would be contrary to the constitution of Maryland the necessary unanimous consent to amendment of the Articles could not be obtained. His other suggestions were for a tax on salt, which would press most heavily on the eastern states where it was used extensively in the fisheries; for a land tax of one dollar per hundred acres, which would bear most heavily on the big landowners of the middle and southern states; and, most lucrative of all, for an impost on trade. The details of the proposals are important only in revealing the persistence shown by Wilson in pursuing his aim. They were not peculiar to him, whatever part he may have had in formulating them, being advocated by Robert Morris and others associated with him, nor were they ever implemented, all but the renewed suggestion for an impost being dropped, and the impost again failing of ratification by the states.

As a member of Congress, Wilson did not confine his interest to the major issues of government. He was not, like some distinguished contemporaries, a political prima donna, but a man who eagerly embraced every opportunity of contributing to the affairs of the nation. It might be said, with justice, that he was devoted to the public service, but it must also be said, with equal justice, that he was avid for office, though perhaps as much for the honor as for the power it would bring him. In Congress, Wilson served on a large number of committees, and it is doubtful whether he ever declined a proffered appointment, however minor. Reputation and fame were at all times Wilson's deepest desire.

One of the other issues Wilson involved himself in was the intractable one of whether the financial contribution of the states to the central government should be based on the valuation of property or on population. The point at issue was one of feasibility, since no question arose of the relative power of state and central governments, even though emphasis on people rather than on property might provide a useful analogy to support one of the major proposals later put forward by Wilson with the purpose of creating the most effective possible national government. It may be that Wilson was looking ahead to an opportunity of drastically changing the basis of government, but there is no direct evidence of it and, tempting as it is, it would be unwise to credit him with so great a degree of prescience. It was in accordance with both his practical judgment and his philosophical attitude that in matters of political organization he preferred people to property whenever there was a choice between them.

In Dickinson's original draft of the Articles, provision was made for the allocation of financial contributions on the basis of population. This gave rise to controversy over slavery, as delegates from the southern states wished to exclude slaves from the estimate of population. Wilson was emphatic in his opposition to the proposal, and his hostility was based both on practical and moral grounds. Slaves increased the wealth of a state and therefore should be counted, the more so as they also increased the defense burden, which would fall on all the states; though they produced less than a freeman they consumed less, therefore leaving a comparable surplus for taxation, and moreover Negro women, unlike white women, were part of the labor force. Though he did not make it clear that he opposed slavery for the sake of the Negro, he did reveal an important moral consideration in his contention that slavery was harmful to freemen, and to society in general.[8] However, Dickinson's proposal was rejected, and in the final version of the Articles it was replaced by the value of land and buildings as the basis of the assessment.

When Congress came to consider the method of arriving at the appropriate values difficulties arose, and the Grand Committee to which the matter was referred expressed grave doubts as to the practicability of their task. Wilson, along with Hamilton and Madison, urged the committee to recommend to the states an amendment to the Articles to enable population to be substituted for land values.[9] When this was turned down by the majority, Wilson suggested a formula derived from a combination of the quantity of land and the number of inhabitants, but this was rejected with some indignation by delegates from the South, where the ratio of value to area was less favorable than it was elsewhere for purposes of assessing the state contribution. Further failure to find an acceptable formula led to another revival of the original proposal, with Wilson again strenuously supporting it. On this occasion he asserted that only the impossibility of solving the problem of the slaves had prevented the principle of population from being accepted when the issue first arose. A compromise on the slavery issue was now put forward by Madison, that a three-fifths ratio be established between whites and blacks, and this proposal, which restored the principle of population, Wilson was willing to accept. It was in fact adopted by Congress and sent to the states for their consent—a consent not unanimously granted during the lifetime of the Congress, which therefore had to continue to stumble along on the basis of improvised requisitions often unfulfilled.

Among Wilson's committee appointments was that of chairman of a standing committee of five members set up in January 1777 to "hear and determine" all appeals from the courts of admiralty in the various states. In a sense this was a rudimentary national appeal court, though it would be too fanciful to suggest that Wilson in his youth attained what he most highly coveted at the end of his career, the position of presiding officer over the highest court in the land. Wilson did not himself regard his appointment to this congressional committee as worth very much, especially as he had reason to suppose that his appointment to Congress, shortly to terminate, would not be renewed by the Pennsylvania assembly. But he was already scheming to obtain for himself an executive post which would make him the principal law officer of the United States, and in which he would be safe from displacement through electoral hazards. His opportunity to present his proposals for the creation of this post came with the emergence of the possibility that Congress would set up executive departments headed by nonmembers of Congress and who would be able to devote themselves fully to the duties of their office. Accordingly he wrote to Robert Morris,[10] laying out his proposals and begging for his support in persuading Congress both to adopt the plan and to appoint Wilson to the office thus created. The duties of the officer appointed would be to "manage all admiralty causes, on behalf of the continent," to "conduct all enquiries and prosecutions instituted by Congress," and to "give his opinion upon such questions in the civil and maritime laws, and the laws of nations as shall be stated to him, for that purpose, by Congress" and by various specified boards and committees of Congress. The importance of the first of these duties would be to enable the laws and practices of the various state courts of admiralty[11] to be "brought, as soon and as well as possible, into a system," a matter made more difficult by the introduction of juries into admiralty courts and therefore rendering all the greater the value of an officer who would help to establish uniform practices. The scope of the second function of the office—to conduct enquiries and prosecutions— would embrace investigations of the management of public affairs and the prosecution of public officers accused of misconduct. For these purposes, Wilson argued, a committee was almost useless, the consequence of collective responsibility in a committee being "that things are superficially passed over, without satisfaction to the public, to those who make the enquiry, or him, concerning whom it is made, provided he has been innocent." These mischiefs would, he believed, be avoided if an officer were appointed to "manage enquiries and prosecutions, on behalf of the public." It was the third area of responsibility, however, which he regarded as the most important. This involved the foreign relations of the United States, and he put forward his concept in this way:

> I hope the United States will never be involved far in the maze of European politics; but it is incumbent upon us to know something of them, even to steer clear of them. Every letter from our commissioners at foreign courts, almost every resolution of Congress about foreign affairs, will bring into

view some principle of civil or maritime law, or of the Law of Nations. It is impossible for members of Congress, however enlarged their genius, and however extensive their knowledge may be, accurately to investigate subjects of this kind amidst the hurry of so much other business, which likewise demands their attention. Treaties are considered, in Europe, as a kind of science. In our transactions with European states, it is certainly of importance neither to transgress, nor to fall short of those maxims by which they regulate their conduct towards one another.

An immense influence indeed would have been exercised by Wilson had he achieved the creation of this office and the appointment to it. He asked Morris expressly to propose him, clearly regarding himself as the man in the whole of the United States most fitted for such a post, but at the same time basing his claim also on a desire to serve the nation. "I have not," he wrote, "been so unsuccessful in private life, as to be obliged to obtrude myself upon the public." The fact that Wilson was so eager for this office shows not only where he thought his destiny lay, but is also an early indication at least of his vision of the vital place which the law and the judiciary would come to have in the American system. It is worth alluding to this in this context, though the full implication cannot yet be evident. Wilson, however, failed to achieve his purpose, Morris claiming that although he accepted the idea he was not at that time in a position to urge it on Congress,[12] and perhaps being no more favorably impressed by Wilson's indelicate importuning than Washington was many years later when Wilson sought appointment as chief justice.

As befitted an associate of Robert Morris, Wilson when in Congress took a close interest in economic and financial matters. His ideas in this field are more appropriately treated elsewhere, but in passing it may be said that in Congress he opposed, in 1777, a proposal to regulate prices and wages[13] though remaining at all times opposed to policies he considered dangerously inflationary and, as was to be expected, he strenuously supported Morris' proposals for funding the debts of the Confederation.[14]

It is evident that in many ways Wilson was an active and valuable member of Congress during his terms of office. That he was held in high esteem by his colleagues is very clear from the fact that he was seriously considered in 1777 for appointment as Commissioner to the French Court,[15] and from the number and importance of his committee appointments.[16] As throughout his career, it was unfortunate for his reputation with posterity not merely that he was parsimonious with his correspondence, but that his most important activities took place in secret or at least inadequately reported conclave.

John Adams later in his life observed that because of inadequate knowledge of the proceedings in Congress between 1774 and 1783 a proper history of the American Revolution could never be written; and for the same reason, extending into the post-revolutionary period, a fully satisfactory study cannot be made of James Wilson or many of his contemporaries in Congress and the Federal Convention. With regard to the issue of secrecy of discussion in Congress, many of the difficulties of later historians might have been avoided had Wilson's proposal that the debates be open to the public been adopted. On several occasions then and later Wilson was an advocate of open discussion. According to John Adams, while the Articles of Confederation were being considered Wilson, supported by Adams, urged open debate, though the proposal was rejected mainly, in Adams's cynical view, because delegates "were afraid to let the people see the insignificant figures they made in that assembly."[17] Subsequently, during the discussion in 1783 of the issue of the independent income, Wilson again urged more than once that the debates be open to the public, on the grounds that "it is of importance in every free country that the conduct and sentiments of those to whom the direction of public affairs is committed should be publicly known."[18] Without reflecting on Wilson's sincerity, it can be pointed out that the occasion of the proposal at that particular time was the discussion of an issue in which the public creditors of Philadelphia, where Congress was then meeting, had a particularly close interest, and that contemporaries accused Wilson and his associates of hoping to pack the proposed public galleries with supporters who would intimidate Congress into adopting the measure Wilson was so eager to obtain.[19] It would be totally out of character, however, for Wilson ever to adopt a general principle merely to meet a temporary expediency, and his support of public debate, unless there were compelling reasons against it, was consistent both in theory and in practice throughout his life.

The paucity of the records of Congress makes it impossible to assess with any reliability the part played by Wilson in other important areas. The question of western lands was one that concerned him greatly in his private as well as his public capacity, but the evidence derived from his actions and observations as a member of Congress adds nothing to what we know or can deduce from other evidence. That he regarded the West as national and not state territory was obvious from the start, when in 1776 he attacked Jefferson for opposing the limitation of state boundaries by Congress and suggested that Pennsylvania might not join the proposed confederation unless western claims were first abandoned.[20] At the same time, moreover, he opposed Jefferson's view that each state should control all Indian affairs within its own territory by pointing out, astutely, that Indians could not be expected to recognize state boundaries which might cut across tribal areas,[21] apparently showing a grasp here of an issue, to which Jefferson was blind, which has bedeviled political arrangements in tribal areas elsewhere in the world.

Though there is a wisp of evidence here of Wilson's understanding of the problems of Indians, his obvious primary concern was with the interests of the United States, with which his own were closely identified. The interests of the Illinois and Wabash Land Company, of which he was a leading member and later president, were always a foremost consideration and whenever occasion arose Wilson was the spokesman for the company in Congress. His interest in the West emerged again in relation to the peace treaty with Britain when he praised the peace commissioners for standing firm on the issue of America's western claims. He used the fact that the British cession of western lands was so enormous to undermine the arguments of Virginia over the proposed cession of lands claimed by her, suggesting that the United States ought rather to make cessions to individual states than vice versa, "the extent of the territory ceded by the treaty being larger than all the states put together," and that if state claims were limited according to principles of right then the Alleghenies would be the true boundary, though he qualified this by suggesting that any boundary established should give the Atlantic states "access to the western waters."[22] The effect, either way, would be to augment the area Virginia would cede to Congress. He was careful, however, to ensure that any cession of western land by Connecticut was not interpreted by Congress to include any land in controversy between Connecticut and Pennsylvania[23]—that Pennsylvania, that is, should retain the Wyoming valley and territory on Lake Erie, giving her access to those "western waters." In general, Wilson seemed to regard all land over which any state had not in practice exercised jurisdiction as being properly under the control of Congress. In fact every argument that could be adduced to support the acquisition by the Congress of the United States of all unsettled land was used by him at different times in his effort to prevent state legislatures from dominating western expansion.

It was over the matter of western lands that Wilson displayed a rare instance of inconsistency. Before the Revolution, when control of the West by Britain or the colonies was the crux of the issue, he had staunchly defended the interpretation of the Camden-Yorke opinion[24] which validated direct grants of land by Indian chiefs; now, when the issue was control of the West by Congress or by the states, and the proper organization by Congress of western settlement, he sought, in reversal of his earlier position, to prevent the purchase from Indians of lands outside the clear jurisdiction of the states.[25]

Wilson's remaining known contributions to the work of Congress may be summarized briefly. In 1777 he was one of the committee of three appointed to prepare an address to the people of America on the state of the nation. Wilson's draft of the address emphasized two often repeated themes: "In free states," he declared, "an unreserved communication of sentiments, as well as a union of interest should always subsist between those who direct and those who delegate to them the direction of public affairs." But, he warned his readers, in an expression he used on several occasions, independence could be secured only "if you are not wanting to yourselves," which in this case implied the qualities of "sobriety, vigilance, fortitude, disinterestedness, and firmness."[26] Otherwise, the address was simply a fairly conventional propagandist, morale-building effort, revealing little of Wilson's ideas beyond his commitment to the American cause.

In the years between the Declaration of Independence and the meeting of the Federal Convention, an important contribution to the development of the United States was made by Wilson outside of Congress, and in an area where at other times he had little claim to distinction. Wilson's fame rests mainly on his contributions in the fields of government and law, but in the years 1780 to 1786 he was in the forefront of an effort to put the economy of the United States on a sound basis. In the course of the establishing of the Bank of North America, and the subsequent controversy over the renewal of its charter, Wilson revealed his views not only regarding finance, but of the broad range of economic policy. In addition, he advanced in the process a constitutional principle which became fundamental to the American system of government which subsequently developed.

Wilson's general view of economic policy was largely derived from two distinguished Scottish economists of the eighteenth century—Adam Smith, whose *Wealth of Nations* Wilson thoroughly absorbed and whose influence is frequently evident in his observations on economic matters, and more notably, Sir James Stewart, whose monumental work *An Enquiry into the Principles of Political Economy* had a profound effect on Wilson. Another Scot, David Hume, contributed through his observations on economic matters peripherally to Wilson's attitude. And at the same time there seemed to Wilson striking similarities between the economic needs of his native Scotland in the late seventeenth and early eighteenth centuries and of his adopted America in the later eighteenth century. As in other fields, so in that of economics, many of Wilson's ideas emerged from his Scottish background. It was the view of Stewart that adequate credit facilities were the key to rapid economic development, especially in underdeveloped countries as the United States undoubtedly was at that time. It may well be that Wilson derived from Stewart exaggerated notions concerning the virtues of credit, which led him ultimately to disaster through his imprudence in the manner in which he employed that means of advancing his economic projects. The eagerness with which Wilson seized on the device of credit is evident in his arguments in support of the Bank of North America. It was almost as though he had undergone a religious conversion which had given him the key to success and happiness. Credit on a grand scale was to be the agency of his own as well as his country's advancement.

Wilson's broad imaginative view of the economic function of a bank is revealed in the part he played in the creation of a national banking system, and particularly in his efforts to prevent the revocation by the radical Pennsylvania assembly of the charter of the Bank of North America. Although his connection with the Bank of North America arose in part from his association with Robert Morris (as in fact did other of his economic interests in the 1780s) it was not as a subordinate agent of Morris. Wilson's contribution to the emergence of a more effective economic system was in its own right of major importance, and in a real sense he anticipated, in his economic ideas and their constitutional corollaries, the more enduring work of Alexander Hamilton.

The occasion of Wilson's first approach to matters of banking was his advocacy of, and subsequent participation in, the so-called Bank of Pennsylvania. Rather than a bank in the proper sense, this was simply a means by which men of some substance could channel their financial support of the army, then in a critical situation after the fall of Charleston, by setting up what was in effect a private purchasing agency for supplies for the army. According to Robert Morris,[27] it was termed a bank in order to inspire confidence and thereby attract subscriptions. It lasted only a little over a year, when a far more effective agency for carrying out its patriotic function, as well as others, came into being with the establishment, by the action of Congress at the instigation of Robert Morris, of the Bank of North America. This was the first bank in the modern sense in the United States and Wilson was intimately involved with its creation as well as its operation. The bank was to issue its own notes, the usual form in which money was lent to clients. These notes went into general circulation and, being backed by the bank, were more acceptable than the promissory notes of merchants. The bank would thus provide a more effective circulating medium as well as facilities for raising loans either by private individuals or by the government, which provided the greater part of the initial capital. It appears that the idea of converting the Bank of Pennsylvania into the Bank of North America, though not the plan of the bank itself, may have originated with Wilson or, if not, it is certain that he was the leading advocate of the proposal. In an unpublished paper, headed *Observations on Finance, adapted to the present Conjuncture of Affairs in the United States, and particularly in the Commonwealth of Pennsylvania* Wilson, after affirming that the best hopes of the enemy now depended on America's financial disorder, made proposals for amelioration, including the raising of a loan, and for implementing this proposal he suggested that the Bank of Pennsylvania "be established as an instrument of government for the purpose." Be this as it may, it is clear that Wilson was among the pioneers of a national banking system in the United States.

The creation of an effective banking system was to Wilson closely identified with his expectation of rapid economic and territorial expansion, on which depended his hopes both for his country and for himself. This broad view of financial management emerges most clearly from the arguments he presented in 1785 in defense of the bank against the proposal of the Pennsylvania assembly to abrogate its state charter. The bank, he maintained, was especially important to a new, and therefore undeveloped, country capable of rapid growth, in that it provided an adequate medium of circulation as well as all-important credit facilities. Both domestic and foreign commerce would expand, foreign exchange rates would be stabilized, and a check imposed against an adverse balance of trade. The specific application of these attributes, which Wilson most strongly emphasized and which concerned him personally most deeply, lay in the fields of manufacturing and internal improvements, especially the latter, with its implications regarding investment in land. With the imaginative optimism which was ultimately to contribute to his downfall he envisaged the construction of roads and canals leading to the West, thereby increasing the value of land as well as facilitating settlement with the consequent production of new wealth. In conjunction with the growth of commerce and industry this would create the right environment for a substantial increase in wages, leading to earlier marriages and consequently to a more rapid increase in population, which in turn would help to create new wealth. With the amount of land available the prospect seemed endless, and the key to it all lay in the magical qualities of credit. Throughout his life Wilson was prone to construct chains of fancy in matters in which his knowledge was less than expert and his experience inadequate. On this occasion, as from time to time later, his purpose was partly propagandist; it is therefore possible to accuse him of intellectual dishonesty, but what is far more likely an explanation is an intellectual weakness which led him insufficiently to appreciate the essential time factor in all processes of growth. To Wilson, the culmination of an economic process seemed almost to coincide with its inception.

As well as these positive arguments in support of the bank, Wilson exposed the fallacies in the arguments of its opponents, who had asserted that it would lead to the political domination of Pennsylvania by its directors, that gross social inequalities would develop, that the influence of foreigners in the affairs of the state would become dangerous, and that it would encourage the export of specie to Europe. He pointed out also the dangerous consequences of destroying the bank: its capital would be dispersed and half of it would leave Pennsylvania, mainly to Europe; the international credit of America would be weakened, and in the event of war the United States would find it much more difficult to raise the necessary money.

These specific arguments are, however, of trivial significance in comparison with the broad economic argument to which he gave much greater importance, and with constitutional arguments which he put forward in order to show that, regardless of all other considerations, the bank possessed an immunity against action of the kind then being undertaken by the Pennsylvania assembly. Wilson based this astonishing claim on concepts later defined as the obligation of contracts and the doctrine of implied powers. The importance of this both to an understanding of Wilson himself and to the development of the American constitutional system can hardly be overestimated.

The central government was still the one set up under the Articles of Confederation—in other words a weak government with few effective powers, whether implied or not. There was still, whether at the state or national level, no judicial authority, let alone any abstract legal principle, sufficient to restrain the will of the legislature. Yet Wilson in effect asserted that the legislature of Pennsylvania was inhibited by an abstract legal principle from taking action in an important area, and that in any event it could be overruled by an action based on the authority, not even directly conferred but merely implied, of a feeble national Congress. He could hardly have expected that his arguments would at that time influence many, but it was of importance to the future of the United States that they were put forward, even in such unpromising circumstances.

His arguments on the question of the obligation of contracts anticipated those of John Marshall in suggesting that a corporate charter was a contract between the state and the recipient and therefore was not subject to unilateral annulment by the state. There was as yet no explicit legal basis for this contention, and Wilson had therefore to rely on natural law concepts. This deficiency he subsequently sought to remedy, in the Federal Convention, and the circumstantial evidence is strong not only that Wilson was primarily responsible for the obligation of contracts clause in the Constitution, but that this was directly related to the aim of safeguarding the bank against governmental interference.

Of even greater constitutional importance was the implied powers argument used by Wilson. The Bank of North America existed by virtue of a charter from the Continental Congress, as well as of the confirmatory charter granted by Pennsylvania. It could not be denied that the Articles of Confederation did not explicitly endow Congress with the power to charter a national bank. Wilson's argument was, characteristically, both simple and ingenious. It was that although Congress was not expressly authorized to grant charters of incorporation, neither was it a power reserved to the states. To issue a charter to a national bank was clearly beyond the power of any state, and Wilson accordingly contended that while Congress did not derive from the states any power not expressly delegated, there were other powers possessed by Congress which were derived from a source other than the states. "The United States," he affirmed, "have general rights, general powers and general obligations, not derived from any particular states, taken separately, but resulting from the union of the whole."[28] He went on to point out that the Articles provided for the management by Congress "of the general interests of the United States" and that as these general interests concerned matters lying beyond the competence of the states, then for those purposes the

United States must "be considered as one undivided, independent nation." In other words he was clarifying the concept, later to be expounded more fully in the Federal Convention, of a sovereignty so divided that in their different spheres the states and the national government were respectively supreme. As Wilson saw it, his interpretation of the Articles of Confederation both extended the powers of Congress and emphasized its supremacy in relation to the states within the scope of those powers. Despite the ingenuity of his arguments, Wilson failed to save the bank from the assembly, and though it was before long restored, it was on the basis of a new charter sufficiently modified to repudiate, in effect, the principle of sanctity of contracts. In fact Wilson's intellectual brilliance may have damaged his cause, on this as on other occasions. Those who failed to grasp the significance of his argument often suspected him of cleverly obscuring the truth. Moreover, it was well known and deeply resented that Wilson himself had borrowed large sums from the bank for his land speculations, and it was impossible to dispel the belief that his interest in preserving the bank was largely personal.

In this defense of the Bank of North America, Wilson worked closely with Robert Morris, but no more than in their common advocacy of an independent income was Wilson merely the henchman of Morris. The relationship between them, at least in the field of ideas, was one of equals, though Wilson was Morris's junior in age, experience, and position. In their economic outlook there was close similarity. Wilson's arguments were Morris's arguments, as not long after they were to be Hamilton's. In Congress Wilson, during his periods as a member, strongly supported Morris, especially over the major issue of funding the debts of the Confederation, both as a necessary financial reform and as a means of strengthening the central government. In line with his economic mentors, Stewart and Smith, he advocated antiinflationary policies while accepting their view that to attempt to control wages and prices could not succeed. In all things economic Wilson belonged to the school of Morris and Hamilton and though his real contribution to the United States was in other fields, the part he played in developing what for many years were the policies most appropriate to the economic circumstances of America was of more than minor importance.

CHAPTER 4

*Concerning the Federal Convention of
1787 and the part played therein by
James Wilson, with special reference
to the legislative branch of the
proposed new government.*

On January 3, 1787, the *Pennsylvania Gazette* reported that the General Assembly of Pennsylvania had appointed, among others, James Wilson to represent the state in the forthcoming convention "having for its object an alteration of the Confederation, and the regulation of commerce." Many months later, after the Federal Convention had finished its work, it revealed the distribution of the vote in the assembly. Wilson, it appears, was only narrowly elected to serve in the convention, coming sixth of the seven candidates originally chosen. By only a slim margin did Wilson gain the opportunity to play what turned out to be a decisive part in the formation of the American Constitution, and without this opportunity Wilson could not have risen above the level of the most minor figures of the revolutionary era. Wilson's major achievements, essentially, were compressed into the few years from 1787 to 1790, and all were consequential upon his initial narrow election to the Federal Convention.

Any study of James Wilson must have as its central feature his contribution in this brief period to what he and his contemporaries would have called the science of government, as revealed in his work in the Federal Convention, the Pennsylvania Ratifying Convention, and the Pennsylvania Constitutional Convention. In the second and third of these conventions the records show clearly that Wilson was the dominating influence; in the first, though it could not be claimed that Wilson was dominant, the importance of his contribution relative to that of Madison might well have been enhanced had a less prominent participant, rather than Madison himself, been the chief source of the evidence.

In the Federal Convention Wilson's interests were all-embracing. There was no aspect, however minor, unworthy of his attention, and in the range of his contribution he was unsurpassed. At the same time everything he did was consistent in terms of the broad general principles which guided his every action: that the people, in practice as well as in theory, were the source of all legitimate power; that the future of America depended on the creation of an effective national government; that the spirit diffused through the nation should be broadly liberal. In examining Wilson's contribution to the development of American government it is well to keep these principles firmly in mind.

In the Federal Convention the major issues were the form the three branches of government—legislative, executive, and judicial —should take. To most members of the convention the legislative and executive branches had a measure of predominance over the third; to Wilson, all three were of equal importance to the creation of sound government as he conceived it. But all agreed that fundamental to any effective reform of the system of government was the proper organization of the legislative branch.

There was widespread agreement that any new national legislature should comprise two branches. This was orthodox wisdom, with which Wilson fully concurred, and was based on the grounds that a bicameral legislature was a defense against legislative tyranny, that it provided a corrective to mistakes by one or other of the branches and tended to restrain any disposition in either to act unconstitutionally. When, however, the question was raised of the method of election, controversy arose. Some opposed election of either branch directly by the people, and on a motion of Madison's in favor of the "election of the larger branch by the people," Wilson struck the keynote of what was to be a frequent refrain. "Mr. Wilson," Madison reported, "contended strenuously for drawing the most numerous branch of the legislature immediately from the people." This was not only because of his conviction that "no government could long subsist without the confidence of the people"—especially a republican government—but also because he "was for raising the federal pyramid to a considerable altitude, and for that reason wished to give it as broad a basis as possible." This strong federal government, moreover, was to be as independent as possible of the states, and therefore he "thought it wrong to increase the weight of the state legislatures by making them the electors of the national legislature."[1] Later, Wilson made this point even more trenchantly when he affirmed that he "considered the election of the first branch by the people not only as the cornerstone, but as the foundation of the fabric."[2] What he apparently intended to convey by this double metaphor—it would have been highly uncharacteristic of him to be merely repetitive—was that popular election was both a means of building a strong national government and a means of ensuring that its base was where it ought to be, on the people of the United States. He went on, in the same sentence, to assert that there was an immense difference between indirect and direct election or, as he put it, "between a mediate and immediate election." In his advocacy of direct popular election Wilson revealed a facet of the problem of representation which was for his time highly unconventional. Not only were the people the only legitimate source of all political authority but their views, or at least their interests, should be properly reflected in the legislature. "The legislature," he said, "ought to be the most exact transcript of the whole society. Representation is made necessary only because it is impossible for the people to act collectively."[3] Wilson here seems to be suggesting that the legislature should accurately reflect the views of the electorate and that the will of the majority should always prevail. There are hints here of the concept of the representative as the delegate of his constituents, although elsewhere he modified the position he seems to have taken when, as has already been observed, he asserted that the representatives of the people should vote as in their opinion the majority of their constituents would have voted had they possessed the same degree of information! In order that the lower house should in reality at all times be "an effectual representation of the people at large"[4] he urged that it be elected annually. In his statements in the Federal Convention there is almost always a close identification of popular democracy with the creation of a strong national government. It was, moreover, his firm and often reiterated conviction that the people of America, unlike state politicians, would welcome an effective national government. It was not until later that it clearly emerged that popular democracy was to him much more than merely a means to that end.

Wilson's support of direct popular election for the lower house was uncompromising. He desired also direct popular election to the upper house, though in this he showed, when his cause was clearly lost, a willingness to compromise. However, until this point was reached his advocacy of direct popular election of the Senate was firm. Opposition to direct popular election to the Senate was much stronger than in the case of the House, and the theoretical case for the democratic principle was weaker; therefore in pressing as hard as he did, he showed even more clearly the firmness of his commitment to the cause of popular democracy, whether from reasons of expediency or from principle. Wilson in this matter was ahead of his time, and it took the American nation until 1913 to accept his proposal. This was by no means the only occasion when he was defeated in the convention, only to be posthumously triumphant when a later generation endorsed his view.

On the question of election to the second branch "Mr. Wilson opposed both a nomination by the state legislatures, and an election by the first branch of the national legislature, because the second branch of the latter ought to be independent of both. He thought both branches of the national legislature ought to be chosen by the people. . . ."[5] There were obvious practical difficulties in the way of direct election by the people of a body which all agreed must be considerably smaller than the first branch, and which it was still being assumed would be chosen on the basis of proportional representation—i.e., proportional to the number of inhabitants of each state. This produced mathematical difficulties, since no state could be allotted fewer than one senator, and that would lead, on the basis of strict proportional representation, to an excessively large body. Wilson's solution was to create electoral districts composed of groups of districts for election to the lower house and where a small state was concerned, if necessary, transcending state boundaries[6]—a powerful blow, had it been implemented, in support of the concept of a popular basis of the national government. But as Wilson quickly realized, it was a suggestion far too revolutionary to have any hope of adoption; not only was it incompatible with prevailing concepts of state dignity, it was inconsistent also with the still predominant view that the upper house should differ in its general nature from the lower. Seeing the impossibility of gaining what he really wanted, Wilson before long changed his position and advocated the election of the upper house by electors chosen by the people.[7]

In modifying his original proposal Wilson was endangering a principle to which he had become increasingly attached. This was the concept of what has been called the double representation of the people. Instead of representing different elements in the nation, balance between which was conventionally believed to produce harmony and liberty in government, Wilson was contending that the two branches of the legislature should represent the same democratic element. That this was now possible without the ill consequences usually foretold, was to Wilson a major attribute of the new and unique

American concept of government he was striving to establish, and which after the substantial success of his efforts he extolled at length on later occasions. Part of Wilson's argument was that if the two branches of the legislature represented different elements— particularly, but not only, if one was the states—then they would "rest on different foundations, and dissensions [would] naturally arise between them."[8]

Though Wilson's principle was not at the time adopted in the Federal Convention he continued to advocate it and, as we shall see, succeeded sensationally in introducing it into the Pennsylvania constitution of 1790. He never, however, modified even slightly his other basic principle, that the states as such should not be involved in elections to either branch of the national legislature. The national government should be "separate and distinct" from state governments; every citizen was a citizen both of the United States and of the state in which he lived, and in the former capacity he should consider only the good of the whole nation and ignore "local habits and attachments."[9] "We must not then," he concluded, "refer ourselves to the states or their legislatures, but must proceed on the basis of the people; the Senate should be elected by electors appointed by the people."[10]

So long as election to the Senate, whether directly or indirectly, was based on the people, no principle suffered a fundamental violation. But when it became evident that feeling was growing not only in favor of the election of senators by state legislatures, but in favor of the rejection of proportional representation and its replacement by the principle of equal representation for the states, then indeed Wilson was faced with a crisis of the greatest severity. So strong were his views on this crucial matter, affecting as it did both his belief in popular democracy and his determination to create a powerful national government, that he was willing for a time to contemplate the division of the United States into two political units, one of which would consist of those states willing to unite "on just and proper principles."[11]

It was Wilson who, with the support of Hamilton, introduced in committee on June 11 the formal motion "that the right of suffrage in the second branch ought to be according to the same rule as in the first branch," i.e., according to population—a motion that was passed by six to five. This initial success was the last Wilson achieved on this issue, and it opened the battle which came very close to destroying the convention entirely. This referred only to the principle of proportional representation, Wilson's motion on June 7 for popular election of the Senate having been overwhelmingly rejected in committee, though the issue was not thereby closed entirely.

Whatever the method of election, proportional representation was to Wilson a prerequisite, and the controversy turned primarily on this issue. Paterson's presentation of the New Jersey Plan, providing for equality of representation between the states in a unicameral legislature, confronted Wilson with opposition of a most dangerous kind to three of the principles he was striving to establish: bicameralism; supremacy of the national government; and the people as the source of all legitimate political authority. Proportional representation was the key to all three, and it was to this that Wilson devoted his main attention during the critical period from June 27 to July 16.

As the controversy intensified, Wilson became more and more vehement in his advocacy of proportional representation. One of his contentions was that unless it was so based the government could "be neither solid nor lasting"; and in a veiled threat he asserted that agreement on other matters depended on the adoption of a fair system of representation. At the same time he involved the convention in a maze of statistics designed to show that under the principle of state equality, a minority of the people of the United States could control the majority. If his reasoning was somewhat specious, being based on the assumption that every citizen in a state would hold the same views, it nevertheless did have some validity. His point was that with equality in the Senate, seven states could outvote six. But seven states might comprise only twenty-four ninetieths of the population, thus putting it in the power of less than one-third of the people of the United States to overrule two-thirds.[12] Two days previously, he had ridiculed the state equality argument by drawing a parallel with the much-criticized English electoral system. Wilson's statement illustrates the penetrating wit which on rare occasions he is revealed as displaying. Alluding to a remark by Luther Martin, a leading advocate of state equality, concerning the injustice of a system in which Old Sarum, with one elector, returned two members to the British Parliament, whereas London, with one million inhabitants, was represented by only four, Wilson observed:

> The leading argument of those who contend for equality of votes among the states is that the states as such being equal, and being represented not as districts of individuals, but in their political and corporate capacities, are entitled to an equality of suffrage. According to this mode of reasoning the representation of the boroughs in England which has been allowed on all hands to be the rotten part of the constitution,

is perfectly right and proper. They are like the states represented in their corporate capacity, like the states therefore
they are entitled to equal voices, Old Sarum to as many as
London. And instead of the injury supposed hitherto to be
done to London, the true ground of complaint lies with Old
Sarum: for London instead of two which is her proper share,
sends four representatives to Parliament.[13]

Two weeks later, Wilson indulged in another display of wit,
again at the expense of Luther Martin. This time, however, feeling
was running very high, and there was more than a touch of acerbity in
his comment. Madison, in fact, indicates that Wilson's observations
were prematurely terminated by uproar in the convention. The occasion was the vote on the issue of equal representation, when Wilson
observed that had their constituents voted as their representatives in
the convention had done then the vote would have been two-thirds to
one-third against equality, the reverse of the decision of the convention. Luther Martin, clearly shaken by this argument, replied by de-
nying Wilson's contention and asserting, somewhat inconsequen-
tially perhaps, that "the states that please to call themselves large are
the weakest in the Union. Look at Massachusetts. Look at Virginia.
Are they efficient states?" Madison's version of Wilson's bitterly
sarcastic rejoinder reads: "Mr. Wilson was not surprised that those
who say that a minority does more than the majority should say that
that minority is stronger than the majority. He supposed the next
assertion will be that they are richer also, though he hardly expected it
would be persisted in when the states shall be called on for taxes and
troops. . . . "[14]
    The decisive moment in the struggle over representation in the
Senate came on July 2 when, with the convention deadlocked and in
acute danger of disintegration, a proposal was made to appoint a
committee with the remit to devise a compromise. This committee, it
was suggested, should consist of one member from each state, whereupon Wilson objected, on the grounds that with this composition "it
would decide according to that very rule of voting which was opposed
on one side" and also that "experience in Congress had proved the
inutility of committees consisting of members from each state."[15]
However, the committee as proposed was set up, with Benjamin
Franklin the representative from Pennsylvania.
    Meanwhile the convention, pending the committee's report, ad-
journed until July 5 when the committee submitted a report propos-

ing a package deal by which in the lower house each state should be represented by one member for every forty thousand inhabitants; that all money bills and those fixing the salaries of officers of the national government should originate in the lower house and not be subject to amendment by the Senate; that no money should be drawn from the treasury except in accordance with appropriations originating in the lower house; and that in the second house each state should have an equal vote. Wilson at once objected that the committee had exceeded its powers, and refused to accept the condition that both parts of the report must stand together. He remained resolute in his hostility to equal representation in the Senate, and spurned appeals for concilia-tion and compromise over the issue, declaring that he "was not deficient in a conciliatory temper, but firmness was sometimes a duty of higher obligation,"[16] and again asserted that without the estab-lishment of a fair system of representation agreement on other issues would not be attained.

On July 13 an incidental matter arising from the broad issue of representation provided an opportunity for Wilson to reveal the full depth of his conviction. This was a formal proposal to eliminate the element of wealth from any computation of representation in the House, in order to bring earlier resolutions of the convention in line with the report of the committee regarding representation, and to leave representation based, with periodic adjustments, on the number of free inhabitants and three-fifths of the slaves.

Gouverneur Morris expressed fears that the southern states were attempting to ensure a majority in the new Congress which would involve "a transfer of power from the maritime to the interior and landed interest" and as that might lead to the "oppression" of the commercial interest he would, although until then a firm supporter of proportional representation, "be obliged to vote for the vicious prin-ciple of equality in the second branch in order to provide some defense for the northern states." He foresaw that before long North Carolina, South Carolina, and Georgia would contain a majority of the people of America and would control "the great interior country."

Wilson responded by a firm declaration of his faith in the people. "Conceiving," he is reported as saying, "that all men wherever placed have equal rights and are equally entitled to confidence, he viewed without apprehension the period when a few states should contain the superior number of people. The majority of people wherever found ought in all questions to govern the minority. If the interior country should acquire this majority they will not only have the right, but will avail themselves of it whether we will or no." He went on, in a most revealing assertion, to state that America should be warned by the example of British Western policy: "The fatal maxims espoused by her were that the colonies were growing too fast, and that their growth must be stinted in time. What were the consequences? First, enmity on our part, then actual separation. Like consequences will result on the part of the interior settlements, if like jealousy and policy be pursued on ours." On the question of including the wealth of a state in the assessment of its representation in the House, he agreed with the great majority of his colleagues that it was entirely impracticable and that in any event "the rule of numbers does not differ much from the combined rule of numbers and wealth." But Wilson went further in his support of population as the sole measure of representation. "He could not agree," Madison records, "that property was the sole or the primary object of government and society. The cultivation and improvement of the human mind was the most noble object. With respect to this object, as well as to other *personal* rights, numbers were surely the natural and precise measure of representation." In case anyone drew a false implication from what he was saying he emphasized that "in no point of view . . . could the establishment of numbers as the rule of representation in the first branch vary his opinion as to the impropriety of letting a vicious principle into the second branch."[17]

The next day, however, Wilson ceased to be quite so intransigent on the question of representation in the Senate. On that day it became clear that his cause was lost, but he attempted to salvage what he could by seconding a motion introduced by Charles Pinckney which attempted to achieve a compromise. The principle of full proportional representation was abandoned, but the principle of state equality was not adopted. Instead, the various states were to be represented in the Senate in this way: New Hampshire by 2 members, Massachusetts 4, Rhode Island 1, Connecticut 3, New York 3, New Jersey 2, Pennsylvania 4, Delaware 1, Maryland 3, Virginia 5, North Carolina 3, South Carolina 3, and Georgia 2. Wilson did not consider the proposal a complete abandonment of proportional representation and in his speech in support of the motion he asserted that "the justice of the general principle of proportional representation has not in argument at least yet been contradicted." Equality in the Senate, he reaffirmed, was "a fundamental and a perpetual error." He went on, in one of his most prescient assertions, to give his final warning to the convention, that, "a vice in the representation, like an error in the first concoction, must be followed by disease, convulsions, and finally death itself."[18]

Perhaps he was being too melodramatic, but it is arguable that his predictions came close to fulfillment, if it can be maintained that the power of the South to extend slavery, to the point of civil war, was prolonged disastrously by the rule of equality. In this matter Wilson's principles have not yet been vindicated by the endorsement of a later generation. But many would now maintain, despite the seventeenth amendment providing for direct election, that the provision for equality of the states in the Senate remains the most anachronistic part of the Constitution, and Americans may again have cause to regret that their ancestors did not heed Wilson's warning.

It had been part of the compromise over representation that all money bills should originate in the House, and while the approval of the Senate was necessary, that body was not to amend them. As Wilson was devoted to the principle of proportional representation and popular election, and intensely disappointed that the Senate was to be chosen differently, it might be expected that he would favor a measure which seemed to give greater power to the popularly based proportionally representative House. But he was also a convinced bicameralist, and he believed that the arrangement proposed would be inimical to sound government. He believed that to restrict the initiation of money bills to the House would lead to perpetual conflict between the two branches of Congress. "The House of Representatives," he warned, "will insert other things in money bills, and by making them conditions of each other, destroy the deliberative liberty of the Senate." The Senate should have the right to initiate money bills. In fact, to restrict it in the way proposed would weaken the Senate in relation to the House and so destroy the proper balance between them which was so necessary to sound government. "War, commerce, and revenue," he pointed out, "were the great objects of the general government. All of them are connected with money. The restriction in favor of the House of Representatives would exclude the Senate from originating any important bills whatever."[19] Wilson was fully aware that the proposal in the compromise to restrict the initiation of money bills to the House was intended as a concession to the large states, who would there have greater representation. Although his opposition to the proposal was based on the merit of the case, he denied at the same time that the proposal was of any advantage to the large states. "Where is the difference," he asked, "in which branch it begins if both must concur in the end?"[20] Moreover, two of the large states, Pennsylvania and Virginia, had consistently opposed it on grounds of intrinsic lack of merit, without regard to any compromise of which it was a part. The proposal, whether or not it had any practical importance, was a face-saving formula sufficient to soften the opposition to equality in the Senate of some who were less determined, or less clearsighted, than James Wilson.

It is clear from Wilson's attitude when he perceived the opposite danger of excessive power accruing to the Senate, that his attachment to a balanced relationship between the two branches of the legislature was perfectly genuine. When the convention was nearing its final stages, and the overall relationship of the various branches could be assessed, Wilson expressed misgivings that too much power was falling to the Senate. As things then stood, he maintained, it would have in effect the power to choose the president, it would make treaties and alliances, it would appoint almost all officers, and it would try impeachments. Citing Montesquieu's aphorism that "an officer is the officer of those who appoint him," he went on:

> This power may in a little time render the Senate independent of the people. The different branches should be independent of each other. They are combined and blended in the Senate. The Senate may exercise the powers of legislation, and executive and judicial powers. To make treaties legislative, to appoint officers executive, for the executive has only the nomination, to try impeachments judicial. If this is not aristocracy, I know not what it is.[21]

Wilson was interested primarily in the basic principles of government. Once these had been established, and whether he liked what had been done or not, his interest diminished. Though he contributed to the discussion of various comparatively minor matters and questions of detail concerning the legislative branch, he did not devote to it much energy, which was applied rather to issues of principle concerning the executive branch. It is, however, worthwhile to look at Wilson's views on lesser matters concerning the legislative branch. Some confirm his attachment to the constitutional principles which have already been considered, while others give evidence of a broadly liberal outlook toward political and social questions.

One matter that falls within the former category was a proposal to give the legislature the power to disallow state laws inconsistent with the national interest. This is considered more fully below,[22] in relation to the judiciary. Wilson was in principle much in favor of it, though appreciative also of the practical difficulties its implementation would encounter. The remaining matters concerning the legislative branch on which Wilson made any significant comment can be dealt with briefly. He expressed himself as in favor of as little restriction as possible on eligibility for election to Congress. "Mr. Wilson," Madison reported, "was against abridging the rights of election in any shape. It was the same thing whether this were done by disqualifying the objects of choice, or the persons choosing."[23] He opposed a proposal to make twenty-five the minimum age for eligibility for election to the House, on the grounds that this would tend "to damp the efforts of genius and of laudable ambition." It was as unreasonable, he argued, to disqualify an otherwise acceptable person on the grounds of youth as of age, and cited the younger Pitt and Bolingbroke as examples of men who had held high office with considerable success before they were twenty-five. But, as in so many of his minor liberalisms, Wilson was defeated. The same liberal attitude was displayed in his opposition to restrictions on foreigners.[24] A related issue concerned the residence qualification in the state from which a member of Congress was elected. Discussion turned on whether "inhabitant" was not a more appropriate term in this context than "resident." These were very trivial matters, scarcely worth noticing except as another illustration, however minor, of Wilson's tendency to adopt the liberal side of any question. Resident seemed more restrictive, and might be interpreted to exclude those absent for long periods on business, including even membership of Congress. Wilson, predictably, favored inhabitant.[25]

On the question of voting qualifications, Wilson resisted a proposal by Gouverneur Morris that the right of suffrage be restricted to freeholders.[26] This was in amendment of the report of the Committee of Detail which had interpreted the will of the convention to be that the qualifications for electors in elections to the national legislature should be the same as those for elections to the most numerous branch of the elector's own state. Wilson strongly supported the clause as reported by the committee, pointing out that it "would be very hard and disagreeable for the same persons at the same time to vote for representatives in the state legislature and to be excluded from a vote for those in the national legislature." Wilson's view of the suffrage, which he discusses elsewhere but, strangely, not in the Federal Convention, was that the vote should be extended to every freeman who, by having property or being in a position to acquire property, had a common interest with his fellow citizens. He expressly excluded only a man who was "in such uncomfortable circumstances, as to render him necessarily dependent, for his subsistence, on the will of others."[27]

Reflecting his faith in the people with its corollary of accepting straight majority decisions, Wilson opposed the provision for the concurrence of two-thirds of the Senate to the making of treaties. He wished all treaties to be made subject to confirmation by merely a simple majority of both houses. "If the majority cannot be trusted," he argued, "it was a proof . . . that we were not fit for one society." Moreover, "If two-thirds are necessary to make peace, the minority may perpetuate war, against the sense of the majority."[28] Wilson's confidence in the sound judgment of a simple majority was not shared by many of his fellow delegates, and his suggestion was decisively rejected.

There is in Wilson's view regarding the appropriate term for a senator an uncharacteristic indecisiveness. On the same day he changed his position from support of a six-year term to support of a nine-year term, with one-third retiring triennially. However, as no question of substance was involved, the matter is of trifling importance. Wilson, however, as did most others, regarded the general principle of a long term for senators, with periodic rotation, as of considerable significance. He deliberately did not repeat the arguments put forward by others, concerning mainly the importance of the greater length of experience, the wisdom, the continuity of government which a second chamber could provide, but presented only two, which he claimed had not yet been suggested. One was that the Senate, which probably would have major responsibilities with regard to relations with foreign powers, "ought therefore to be made respectable in the eyes of foreign nations." A Senate in which the term of office was nine years, with a triennial rotation, would provide the government with the qualities of "stability and efficacy" without which the United States would not be treated with respect abroad. A Senate of this kind would be better than a monarchy for conducting foreign policy. "In a monarchy," he said, "much must always depend on the temper of the man," but in the proposed Senate, "the personal character will be lost in the political." His second observation was a refutation of the general belief that public bodies appointed for long terms would tend to extend their powers for life, and then make their position hereditary. He regarded it as a complete answer to this objection that as one-third would go out triennially "there would be always three divisions holding their places for unequal terms, and consequently acting under the influence of different views and different

impulses."[29] Wilson's arguments lost none of their validity when applied to the Senate appointed for six years with a biennial rotation, for which on the same day the convention expressed its preference. The observations regarding foreign policy, though of obvious merit given Wilson's assumptions, never in practice achieved any validity, with the development of that aspect of governmental powers along lines rather different from those then envisaged.

Another example of what appears to be Wilson's genuine attachment to democratic principles, combined with a degree of political astuteness which identified democratic principle with political expediency, is found in his strong advocacy of openness in the proceedings of Congress. He vigorously resisted a proposal that the clause in the draft constitution requiring the House and Senate to keep a journal be struck out.[30] This he regarded as altogether very improper. "The people," said Wilson the democrat, "have a right to know what their agents are doing or have done, and it should not be in the option of the legislature to conceal their proceedings." Then spoke Wilson the political calculator: "Besides, as this is a clause in the existing Confederation, the not retaining it would furnish the adversaries of the reform with a pretext by which weak and suspicious minds may be easily misled." He did not, however, support a proposal that those who dissented from the decisions of House and Senate should be allowed to enter their reasons in the journal, basing his argument on the practical grounds that if this were allowed then others would have an equal right to enter their opinions also, making it excessively voluminous. He does not seem to have seriously contemplated the official reporting of debates, though elsewhere he expressed himself in favor of legislative debates being open to the public and clearly was not thinking in terms of concealment.

A provision of the proposed Constitution which Wilson considered to be potentially damaging to the United States, and on which he had strong feelings, was that which sought to render members of either branch of Congress incapable of holding any office under the authority of the United States, in the case of members of the House during the period of their membership, and in the case of members of the Senate, for an additional year. Wilson's objections to this provision illustrate several aspects of his outlook. He was very conscious that opinion in general, and not only in the convention, would be strongly in favor of such a provision. It was, not surprisingly, regarded as analogous to the British system which it was believed had enabled politics to become corrupted through the misuse of patronage. Wilson, well aware that in opposing the provision he was taking a course of action which, if successful, would be highly unpopular, declared that he would not sacrifice his own judgment to popular prejudices. This he regarded as a betrayal of trust. He was appointed to serve the people according to his own judgment, and they would not respect him were they ever to discover that he had deliberately sacrificed his own judgment "in order to flatter their prejudices." Despite his frequent assertions of democratic attitudes and indeed his positive encouragement of democratic practices, there was always in Wilson something of the patrician. His faith in the people was sincere, but it was often faith in their ability to choose good leaders. And there was certainly in him nothing of the demagogue. To exclude men of ability who were members of the legislature from holding any other office under the national government was to Wilson to restrict unreasonably the opportunities open to talent and to deprive the government of the full benefit of the services of its best citizens. He was anxious at all times not to restrict unnecessarily the opportunities open to men of talent. "He was," he is reported to have said on this occasion, "far from thinking the ambition which aspired to offices of dignity and trust an ignoble or culpable one. He was sure it was not politic to regard it in that light or to withhold from it the prospect of those rewards which might engage it in the career of public service." To emphasize the excessive fears of those who would ban office-holding by legislators he pointed out that Pennsylvania, "which had gone as far as any state into the policy of fettering power, had not rendered the members of the legislature ineligible to offices of government."[31] It is difficult not to suppose that Wilson had his own aspirations and career prospects in mind in taking this position. It is evident also that there was more than a trace in him, whatever the nature of his democratic philosophy, of an elitist outlook. There was a third aspect to Wilson's opposition to the provision which was relevant at the time but which ceased to be so before the convention had finished its work. As things then stood, it appeared that members of the national legislature of whichever branch—and one branch indeed was to be chosen by the state legislatures—would be paid by their states and be eligible for state offices. To a devoted nationalist like Wilson the implication was obvious: "Nothing seemed to be wanting to prostrate the national legislature, but to render its members ineligible to national offices, and by that means take away its power of attracting those talents which were necessary to give weight to the government and to render it useful to the people." Wilson, however, was always conscious that there was real merit in the opposing viewpoint and indeed seemed at times, through the haze of unclear reporting, to be of two minds on the issue. In any event, when several years later he was discussing the merits of the American Constitution, he remarked that the provision for the exclusion of members of Congress, while they remain such, from other offices, "finds with great propriety a place in the Constitution of the United States."[32]

CHAPTER 5

*Continuing consideration of
the Federal Convention,
concerning discussion of the
Executive Branch.*

The question of the form the executive branch of government should take involved fewer fundamental issues, though the technical problems were highly complex. There was general agreement that a government of three branches be set up, so the question of whether or not there should be a separate executive did not arise. Controversy over the executive turned primarily on its nature and composition—whether it should consist of a single person or of more than one; the manner in which it should be appointed—which turned out to be the greatest technical difficulty the convention had to face; and what its powers should be. Wilson played a conspicuous part in all discussions, though at no time with the deep intensity of feeling he brought to the controversy over the legislative branch.

The question at issue in the matter of the nature of the executive branch concerned the dangers and advantages implied in the choice between a single executive or a multiple executive: basically, whether the supposed danger of monarchy implicit in a single executive was sufficient to offset its greater efficiency, and conversely, whether the safeguards of the diffusion of power and balance of interests contained in a multiple executive would be offset by its indecisiveness through divisions of opinion or interest. Wilson on practical grounds strongly advocated a single executive, and on June 1 he formally proposed[1] "that the executive consist of a single person," which, he maintained, would give "most energy dispatch and responsibility to the office." Contrary to the view of many, that a single executive would be "the foetus of monarchy," he argued that it would be an effective safeguard against tyranny. The great extent of the United States required for effective government the vigor of monarchy; but the manners of the people, which were purely republican, would suffice to offset any danger of the rise of a monarchical executive. Basing his argument, as he so often did, on historical experience, he maintained that it was a multiple, not a single, executive which contained the greater danger of a tyranny perhaps "as bad as the thirty Tyrants of Athens, or as the Decemvirs of Rome." More recent experience seemed to bear out his contention. "The people of America," he asserted, "did not oppose the British king, but the Parliament." In other words, the "opposition was not against a unity, but a corrupt multitude."

Later in the convention, when the New Jersey Plan, which provided for a multiple executive, was being discussed, he reiterated this contention even more powerfully. "In order," he said, "to control the legislative authority, you must divide it. In order to control the executive you must unite it. One man will be more responsible than three. Three will contend among themselves till one becomes the master of his colleagues."[2] Drawing again on his extensive knowledge of ancient history he adduced further instances of the danger he feared, adding other examples to those he had already employed. That his fears were well founded can be illustrated as much by subsequent as by previous historical events. The main restraints on the executive power, he declared, were external, and therefore able to be applied most effectively when the object of restraint was clearly evident, which was "when one object only, distinguished and responsible, is conspicuously held up to the view and examination of the public."[3] In this regard it must be clear who is making appointments, an important aspect of the executive function, and better appointments would undoubtedly be made by a single executive. With a multiple executive disputes would occur, leading to horse-trading and the consequent appointment of men of inferior quality. The same danger was inherent in all decisions of a multiple executive, as lack of unanimity produced dissension and weakness, and only when all members of the executive could cooperate harmoniously would decisions be effectively implemented.

In the convention, on June 4, Wilson elaborated his arguments of three days before by adding the quality of tranquillity to the other attributes of a single executive. A triumvirate of equal members would be perpetually torn with animosities, disruptive of the administration of public affairs and contaminating the entire government, both national and state, and indeed spreading to the people themselves. To make the executive consist of an odd number of members, in the belief that this would always produce a majority decision, was based on a fallacy. Unlike a court of justice, where there were only two sides to a question, in both the legislative and executive branches there could be several, and a triumvirate could be divided three ways. On the same occasion in reply to an assertion that to establish a single executive would arouse strong opposition among the people, he maintained that, on the contrary, the people as a whole would regard it as natural and proper. They were accustomed to single executives in the form of governors of their states, and nowhere had a triumvirate been established. This opened another issue, when it was pointed out that governors of the states all had an advisory council, without which they could take no action. This was not quite the same as a multiple executive, though it had some of its defects, but it represented a danger to the kind of executive Wilson had in mind, and it might well attract the support of many who were opposed to the idea of a triumvirate. Wilson was asked directly whether he intended to attach a council to his single executive, and answered unequivocally that he did not, giving as his reason that a council "oftener serves to cover, than prevent malpractices."[4] He did not, however, necessarily oppose a council of any kind, as later in the convention he was willing at least to envisage, as better for this purpose than the Senate, a council whose function it would be to advise the president regarding appointments, but whose advice he need not take.[5] He was, however, strongly opposed to the type of council which would constitutionally fetter the chief executive. These arguments, supported strongly by others, were sufficient to convince the majority, and in the end it was with comparatively little difficulty that his original motion was finally approved.

Wilson believed that the executive branch should be independent; and he did not believe that its powers should be more than commensurate with those of the other two branches. Although he was always more acutely conscious than most of the danger of legislative tyranny, he was not thereby tempted to inflate as a counterbalance the powers of the executive. Whereas in the discussions over the legislative branch he was always pushing hard to achieve a high degree of power and independence for the national government in relation to the states, in the discussions over the executive branch we do not find him displaying the same determination to strengthen the executive at the expense of the legislative branch. But at the same time the executive must be independent, and must have adequate authority to maintain that independence.

In a great many aspects of government, Wilson accepted the theory of the compatibility between the American Constitution and Anglo-Saxon political practices.[6] He believed, for example, that the powers and duties of the president were similar to those of the Anglo-Saxon kings. This view of limited kingship was expressed in Madison's motion, which he seconded, defining the extent of the powers of the executive.[7] The proposal was that a national executive be instituted "with power to carry into execution the national laws, to appoint to offices in cases not otherwise provided for, and to execute such other powers, not legislative or judiciary in their nature, as may from time to time be delegated by the national legislature." This was certainly a limited power, and one considerably less than that wielded by George III by virtue of the royal prerogative over, for instance, questions of war and peace. On a later occasion, however, he acknowledged an executive power in the field of foreign policy by virtue of the treaty-making function.[8] There is, however, no record of his having emphasized this in the convention. In fact he seems to have expressly excluded from executive authority matters relating to war and peace, as being "of legislative nature," and to have emphasized his view that "the only powers . . . strictly executive were those of executing the laws, and appointing officers, not appertaining to and appointed by the legislature."[9]

Wilson's concept of the nature of executive independence, however limited its powers might be, extended to an executive veto on all legislation. When the matter was first discussed he opposed a proposal that the executive should have a power of veto which could be overruled by Congress.[10] Seconded by Hamilton, he proposed that this be amended to give the executive an absolute veto. He contended that the independence of the executive required an absolute veto, as otherwise the legislature could "at any moment sink it into nonexistence." The strongest opposition to Wilson's proposal came from Franklin who, citing the proprietary government of Pennsylvania, argued that an absolute veto would be used by the executive to extract money or concessions from Congress.[11] Wilson's reply to Franklin was that the veto would act as a deterrent by preventing Congress from passing legislation which it knew the executive would oppose and, more significantly, that the proprietary government of Pennsylvania did not provide a relevant example, as "the executive was not then as now to be appointed by the people"—though that had not in fact been firmly decided. And with what seems to be, characteristically, a high degree of foresight, he contended that while to enable the legislature, by a large proportion, to overrule the executive might do no harm in normal times, "there might be tempestuous moments in which animosities may run high between the executive and legislative branches, and in which the former ought to be able to defend itself."[12] Wilson, however, found himself in a minority of three, being supported only by Hamilton and Rufus King.

Thereupon Wilson modified his position, and suggested that the executive and the judiciary be given jointly an absolute negative[13]—a device which would still preserve the independence of the executive against the legislative branch. The overwhelming opinion of the convention was that the legislature should be empowered to overrule an executive veto by a two-thirds majority of both houses. Wilson nevertheless persisted and five weeks later he seconded a proposal of Madison that legislative matters should be submitted both to the executive and to the Supreme Court.[14] Although this was rejected, the issue remained open and Wilson, although obliged to abandon his advocacy of a place for the judicial branch, did achieve a partial though temporary success with the adoption of a proposal he supported for the modification to three-quarters of the proportion of votes in each house necessary to overcome an executive veto.[15]

In the course of the discussion on this day he took the opportunity to reiterate his view regarding the place of the executive in the constitutional structure. The greatest danger to the political stability of the state came, he insisted, "from the legislature swallowing up all the other powers." The prejudices against the executive were, he believed, the result of a misreading of history. Whenever the executive was excessively powerful, monarchy and tyranny tended to be equated in the minds of the people. But if the executive was too weak, then legislature and tyranny could just as readily be associated. This he illustrated by referring to the period of English history which followed the execution of Charles I, when "a more pure and unmixed tyranny sprang up in the Parliament than had been exercised by the monarch." The danger of a similar legislative tyranny in the United States, he maintained, had not been guarded against "by a sufficient self-defensive power either to the executive or judiciary department."[16]

Some years later, in his law lectures, Wilson expressed a view of the presidential veto which was much more in accordance with what the convention had decided than with what he himself had wanted. No matter how hard he had pressed his point on the floor of the convention, be became, after the decision had been taken, a defender of the convention's action, even if he at times indicated that his own view might have differed. In this instance he defended the provision for a two-thirds overriding majority by saying that "if, after all the discussion, investigation, and consideration, which must have been employed upon a bill in its different stages, before its presentment to the president of the United States, and after its return from him with his objections to it, two-thirds of each house are still of sentiment that it ought to be passed into a law, this would be an evidence that the current of public opinion in its favor is so strong that it ought not to be opposed."[17] In defending what he had opposed, he found his justification in the power of the people! Similarly Wilson defended the president's power to pardon, by maintaining that as the supreme power remains with the people, and as every branch of government is derived from the people, the pardoning power is not only a proper function of a democratic government but is "with perfect propriety . . . vested in the president of the United States."[18] In the convention itself, Wilson had not been concerned very much with the question of the pardoning power, his only contribution—though that was a significant one— being successfully to oppose a proposal that the president should be empowered to pardon only after conviction, basing his objection on the grounds that pardon before conviction might be necessary in order to obtain the testimony of accomplices.[19]

The question of the method of choosing the executive turned out to be one of the most difficult the convention had to deal with. Apart from the question of whether there should be a single or a multiple executive, the issue involved the relationship between the executive and legislative branches and between the national executive and the state governments. Many complex issues had to be considered. For example, the questions of the term of office of the executive and of eligibility for reelection concerned closely the relationship between executive and legislative branches, and great issues could turn on matters of apparently minor detail.

Right at the outset of the discussion of the method of selecting the executive, over the proposal to place the appointment in the hands of the national legislature, Wilson made his position abundantly clear. In Madison's version, "Mr. Wilson said he was almost unwilling to declare the mode which he wished to take place, being apprehensive that it might appear chimerical. He would say however at least that in theory he was for an election by the people." Citing New York and Massachusetts as examples of the successful application of this method, he stated as one of its advantages that "the objects of choice in such cases must be persons whose merits have general notoriety";[20]

in other words that only men of wide and established reputation could be chosen, and not men whose nomination and appointment could be engineered by a clique. Later in the discussion, having overcome his initial hesitancy, Wilson reaffirmed his belief in popular election, and revealed what many have regarded as his sole, or at least primary, motive. This was his wish "to derive not only both branches of the legislature from the people, without the intervention of the state legislatures but the executive also; in order to make them as independent as possible of each other, as well as of the states."[21]

He repeated his arguments the next day,[22] adding the point "that this mode would produce more confidence among the people in the first magistrate, than an election by the national legislature." Instead of election by the legislature, he now proposed that the states be divided into a number of districts, and that "the persons qualified to vote in each district for members of the first branch of the national legislature" elect a number of representatives who would then elect the executive by ballot, with the obvious proviso that he should not be a member of the electing body. There is here the origin of the Electoral College system which, after many other possible methods had been explored and rejected, was in a modified form adopted by the convention. It was a feature of Wilson's proposal that the original electorate was to consist of those qualified to elect the lower house of the legislature. In other words, it was to be as broad as it could practically be made, a provision not necessary had his sole purpose been to safeguard the independence of the executive from the states. It seems also that his advocacy of indirect election was not intended to dilute the influence of the people, but arose from the practical difficulties entailed in administering a system of direct election with an electorate extending throughout thirteen states. The proposal was heavily defeated, perhaps largely through fears such as those expressed by Elbridge Gerry that "it would alarm and give a handle to the state partisans, as tending to supersede altogether the state authorities."

Apart from a proposal on June 9, which was quickly disposed of by unanimous opposition, that the national executive be elected by the executives of the states, it was not until July 17 that the question of how to choose the executive again arose. The proposal before the convention was still that the executive be chosen by the legislature, and on this occasion Gouverneur Morris took the lead in vigorously opposing it, and advocated election by the people at large— presumably meaning direct election. Wilson strongly supported Morris, and in the process introduced another idea which, at least in prin-

ciple, was in the end adopted by the convention. First, he disposed of
the example of Poland cited by opponents of popular election, where
elections of the king habitually led to violence, by pointing out that in
Poland all the electors assembled in one place, which would not be the
case in the United States. Wilson seems here to have been assuming
direct election of the executive, as his original proposal for indirect
election contained a provision for the meeting of the electors in one
place. His second point is more interesting. It was in answer to the
argument, which clearly implied direct election, that the people,
spread over the whole of the United States, would not be sufficiently
familiar with all the candidates to enable a majority to be produced for
any one of them. He remarked in passing that a clear majority was not
essential to election, but choosing not to contest this point, he produced an answer to the problem. This was that the legislature, by a
majority, should make the decision whenever popular election did not
produce a clear majority for one of the candidates. "This," he said,
"would restrain the choice to a good nomination at least, and prevent
in a great degree intrigue and cabal." And he went on to emphasize
again his view of the executive as having a close relationship with the
people by stating that "a particular objection with him against an
absolute election by the legislature was that the executive in that case
would be too dependent to stand the mediator between the intrigues
and the sinister views of the representatives and the general liberties
and interests of the people."[23] Legislatures, however admirable their
qualities in relation to other functions, were notoriously corrupt when
given the power of appointment to great offices. Wilson, however,
again suffered defeat on the issue, being supported only by his own
state of Pennsylvania.

When it began to discuss the implications of election of the
executive by the legislature, with which was associated the question of
eligibility for reelection, the convention quickly found itself in serious difficulties. The essence of the problem was that if the executive
were appointed by the legislature he might become dependent on it
for his position, and in order to secure reelection might engage in
improper intrigue. This was related to the question of reeligibility for
election and the term of office of the executive; for instance, a long
term without reeligibility would diminish the influence which the
legislature might otherwise be able to exercise over the executive. Yet
to render the executive ineligible for a second term might deprive the
country of the services of the men best fitted for the position and waste
the valuable experience acquired in the office. Moreover, eligibility for

reelection would be a powerful incentive to good conduct in office; otherwise there might be a temptation to derive the maximum personal advantage from a constitutionally limited period of public service. Men of consuming ambition might be tempted to use unconstitutional means—even violence—to maintain themselves in power.

These and other issues put the convention into a state of great uncertainty concerning the proper method to adopt, and several delegates began to wonder whether the earlier proposal, providing for election by the people, might not after all be the least objectionable alternative available. One thing did become clear, and that was that virtually everyone was agreed that if the executive was to be chosen by the legislature then, whatever its disadvantages, ineligibility for reelection was a necessary safeguard. Wilson, ever alert to opportunities to drive home his arguments, thereupon remarked that "he perceived with pleasure that the idea was gaining ground, of an election mediately or immediately by the people."[24] The ground he gained that day, however, was slight.

The convention did agree that the election of the executive should be by electors, and that he should be eligible for reelection. But it agreed also that the electors should be chosen by state legislatures. This was a step forward as it seemed that the national legislature at least was eliminated from the process. This partial success was overturned a few days later when the question was reconsidered and the motion that the executive be appointed by the national legislature was readopted. This brought up again the question of reeligibility and, in the event of ineligibility being adopted, of the term of office.

The confusion in the convention was now greater than ever, and Wilson was quick to point out that it all sprang from the unfortunate reinstatement of election by the legislature. So fearful was he of the consequences of executive dependence on the legislature that to avoid it he would accept a very long term of office. To restrict unduly the term of office of the executive might easily lead to a man in the prime of life being "cast aside like a useless hulk," and he pointed to examples of the useful services performed in the past by men of great age—popes, for instance, and Venetian doges.[25]

The confusion of mind into which the convention had fallen adversely affected even Wilson's capacity for incisive and lucid presentation of an argument, but when Gerry made the penetrating observation that "we seem to be entirely at a loss on this head," Wilson attempted to break the impasse by producing an entirely new plan.[26] Apparently he had improvised this while sitting in the convention, and admitted when he presented it that it was not "a digested idea and might be liable to strong objections." In any event, he made it clear that he did not regard his proposal as the best means of choosing the executive, declaring that "his opinion remained unshaken that we ought to resort to the people for the election." His scheme was to put the election in the hands of fifteen members of the legislature who would be chosen by lot, whereupon they would withdraw immediately and not emerge until their choice had been made. In this way there could not possibly be any intrigue or corrupt bargaining in connection with the election of the executive, and in no way could he be dependent on the legislature. The term of office he proposed was six years. Wilson however was not greatly enamored of his own proposal, and welcomed a suggestion that the whole matter be postponed. When the discussion was resumed two days later, the convention, though with obvious misgivings, was able to do no more than reinstate its earlier tentative decision that the executive be chosen by the national legislature, for a single seven-year term.

It was not until a month later, when the report of the Committee of Detail was being considered, that another opportunity arose to reintroduce the matter. Wilson then supported a proposal to substitute election by the people for election by the legislature, but opinion in general, however uncertain, was unprepared to accept what still seemed to most a radical suggestion. If Wilson could not yet persuade the convention to admit the people to the process of choosing the executive, at least he could try to ensure that the popular branch of the legislature was given the greater influence in the choice. It was proposed that instead of by ballot of both houses separately, in which each could have a veto on the other, the executive be elected by joint ballot, thus giving the lower house, based on popular election and proportional representation, the bigger share in the appointment. This compromise, if compromise it was, received the agreement of the convention. But when shortly afterward Gouverneur Morris again proposed that the election be "by electors to be chosen by the people of the several states" his motion was defeated by only six to five[27]—an indication that the idea of an election by the people was now indeed gaining ground. In fact partial success was near. The convention failed to come to a final decision on the method of choosing the executive, and on August 31 it was referred to a committee of eleven which was set up to consider parts of the report of the Committee of Detail still outstanding. Wilson was not a member of the committee, though Gouverneur Morris was; yet it reported along lines that closely fol-

lowed Wilson's original proposal of June 2 for the Electoral College
method.[28]

What had produced this change of attitude is not certain,
though undoubtedly the trend of late had been in that direction.
Whether it was simply the view of the committee, or whether it
reflected in some way an unrecorded change of attitude among delegates as a whole matters little. It was clear when the committee's
report was presented to the convention that most delegates were now
ready to accept the principle of the Electoral College. The proposal
put to the convention was essentially that finally accepted as Article
II, Section 1, paragraph 2 of the original Constitution, with the exception that it was originally intended that in the event of a failure to
secure a majority in the Electoral College, expected normally to occur,
the election was to be thrown to the Senate. However, the convention
had severe misgivings, and many objections continued to be raised.
Wilson observed that it was the most difficult question the convention
had had to decide, and confessed that even yet he had himself no firm
view of what the best method was, though he thought the plan now
proposed the best so far. The only modifications he suggested were
that instead of to the Senate, the final choice, when it should become
necessary, ought to be given to the whole legislature—enabling the
House, which was elected by the people on a proportional basis, to
exercise a predominant influence, though this was not the reason Wilson gave in support of his proposal. That was, primarily, that "the
House of Representatives will be so often changed as to be free from
the influence and faction to which the permanence of the Senate may
subject that branch."[29] On the next day Wilson made a formal motion
that the legislature be substituted for the Senate, but it was decisively
defeated. Clearly Wilson was disturbed at this, for he returned to the
convention on September 6 armed with a carefully prepared attack on
what he felt to be the excessive power accruing to the Senate.[30] Power
to select the president, along with the other powers granted to it,
would create in the Senate "a dangerous tendency to aristocracy." His
argument, as others pointed out, was perhaps unduly alarmist, but it
sprang from a clear view of the importance of achieving a proper balance between the various parts of the government, and in this instance, of ensuring that the executive had the necessary degree of
independence. If the Senate could make the appointment, then the
president would be so dependent on it that it would come to have in
practice the power to make other appointments including expressly
appointments to the judiciary, lying constitutionally within the scope

of the presidential prerogative. Along with the influence in the treaty-making power and the power of impeachment, and having the means of manipulating through the influence of senators in their own states the process of electing the president in order to ensure that no clear majority was ever produced in the Electoral College, the Senate could establish permanent domination over the executive branch. Under the plan proposed, Wilson objected that the president would not be "the man of the people as he ought to be, but the minion of the Senate." He did acknowledge, however, that the plan was better than any other that had been considered, and that with suitable amendments it might be made acceptable. The only amendment adopted was that the ultimate choice of the president should be transferred from the Senate not to the legislature as a whole but to the House of Representatives, although in this capacity voting by states and not by individuals. This was at least a partial success for Wilson in that it greatly reduced the danger of a senatorial aristocracy and threw the election to the popularly elected branch. Wilson had to remain satisfied with this; it was not, however, long after his death that the, surprisingly, unanticipated emergence of definable political parties led to the establishment, in fact if not in form, of a system of direct election of the president by the people which revealed in practice the advantages he had claimed for it.[31]

CHAPTER 6

*Further consideration of
the Federal Convention, including
matters concerning the
judicial branch and the general
powers of government.*

Wilson's view of the principle of the separation of powers was not merely that the three branches of government be independent of one another; it was also that their influence should be as nearly equal as it could be made. The position of the judicial branch was one issue toward which he was particularly sensitive—for reasons not entirely free from an element of self-interest—and he strove on every appropriate occasion to ensure for the judiciary the influence to which he thought it entitled. Near the outset of the convention he stated explicitly his opinion "that the judicial, legislative, and executive departments ought to be commensurate,"[1] and on many occasions the assumption that the power of the judicial branch should go beyond the interpretation and application of the laws passed by the legislative branch was implicit in his attitudes. He never, for instance, doubted that one of the primary responsibilities of the judiciary was that of judicial review.[2]

Probably for reasons of expediency he was not explicit on this point in the convention itself, though not long afterward he made abundantly clear what he believed the Constitution in fact meant. In the event of inconsistency between the Constitution and an act of the legislature, he affirmed in his law lectures, "the former is the law of the land; as a necessary consequence, the latter is void, and has no operation." It followed that "it is the right and it is the duty of a court of justice, under the Constitution of the United States, to decide." Wilson was careful to avoid implying that this power of judicial review in any way disparaged the authority of the legislature. "It does not," he contended, "confer upon the judicial department a power superior, in its general nature, to that of the legislature; but it confers upon it, in particular instances, and for particular purposes, the power of declaring and enforcing the superior power of the Constitution, the supreme law of the land." This he regarded as "a noble guard against legislative despotism," the danger he most feared.[3]

The convention was especially sensitive on two issues regarding the judicial branch: the relationship with the legislative branch, in so far as a threat to legislative independence was implied; and the relationship with the states, which might imply a danger of excessive federal influence in state affairs. The first issue was, apparently deliberately, blurred by the nationalists in the convention. On the second it was necessary to be more explicit. The original proposal presented to the convention, in the Virginia Plan, provided for the establishment in the states of inferior federal courts. Some of the delegates from the southern states perceived a threat to their institutions if a federal court, outside their control, could operate within their own boundaries, and accordingly it was proposed that state courts be left to decide all national cases, in the first instance, with an appeal to the supreme national court. They were joined by some New England delegates, ostensibly motivated by a desire for economy in government, and the proposal was narrowly defeated. This was at once seen by nationalists in the convention as a crisis of some magnitude, as it might easily prevent an effective national judiciary from ever coming into being. Madison pointed out that unless inferior national tribunals with final jurisdiction in many cases were set up throughout the United States, the number of appeals from state courts to the supreme national tribunal would become so numerous that the structure would virtually collapse, and to provide for a retrial by the supreme national tribunal would be hopelessly impracticable because of the factor of distance. Wilson concurred with Madison, and added the point that admiralty jurisdiction—a matter in which he had a particular interest —should be wholly within the province of the national courts "as it related to cases not within the jurisdiction of particular states, and to a scene in which controversies with foreigners would be most likely to happen." Because of its nature, federal admiralty jurisdiction would almost of necessity imply federal courts within the states. However, Wilson and Madison thought it wise to avoid pressing the issue directly, as to attempt to do so might well bring a sensitive issue to a head and lead to the explicit exclusion of federal courts from state territories. Accordingly, Wilson and Madison proposed "that the national legislature be empowered to institute inferior tribunals," and they pointed out, perhaps somewhat speciously, "that there was a distinction between establishing such tribunals absolutely, and giving a discretion to the legislature to establish or not establish them."[4] This evasion of the issue, by taking it out of the convention and leaving it for later decision by a different body, was strongly supported by the convention, which no doubt realized that it was thereby side-stepping some explosive issues. Wilson and Madison were certain that the logic of circumstances would oblige the legislature to create the inferior tribunals they regarded as essential. The stratagem worked; a potentially dangerous issue was by-passed in the convention, and the objective achieved by other means. The success of Wilson and Madison made it impossible for the states to undermine the Union by the use of state courts.

Within the convention Wilson's direct influence on the establishment of the judicial branch was no greater than that of many others. Indeed, the question of the judiciary got comparatively little attention. All were agreed that there should be a judicial branch, and the important issue of inferior federal courts in the states was, as we have seen, deliberately put aside. The extent of the jurisdiction of the national judiciary was an issue that aroused little controversy, largely because the most important powers were implied rather than expressly defined—as in the case of judicial review.

Wilson was very cautious in presenting his views in the convention, whether because he realized himself the dangers of raising sensitive issues or, as is much more likely, because the danger was made clear to him by a fellow delegate, and there is tenuous evidence here pointing to Madison. That he did not intend to be so circumspect is indicated in Wilson's papers, from which it appears that he at least contemplated proposing that the jurisdiction of the national courts should explicitly extend to cases involving the collection of the national revenue and the national regulation of trade.

The most far-reaching power he assumed for the national judiciary he made no attempt to assert explicitly in the convention. This was to render governments amenable to the judicial process. His view of the power assigned to the Supreme Court by the Constitution is best illustrated in the majority decision which Wilson wrote in 1793 in the case of *Chisholm* v. *Georgia*, which will be looked at later. The same assumption was revealed in Wilson's law lectures, which reveal just as clearly exactly what he had in mind when he was helping to formulate the clauses of the Constitution relating to the judiciary.

It is also revealed in the Pennsylvania constitution of 1790, which was largely the work of Wilson. The essential issue is well expressed in the law lectures, when Wilson was arguing that governments ought to be amenable to the courts and that this was in fact recognized in the section of the Constitution which declared that the judicial power of the national government "shall extend to controversies to which the United States are a party; and to controversies between two or more states." In amplification he went on to draw a parallel between a man and a state—i.e., in the general sense of a political community. It does not demean a man to be amenable to the courts; no more should a state, the aggregate of free independent men, who are the original sovereigns, feel any loss of dignity in declaring itself amenable to justice. "To be privileged from the awards of equal justice," he went on, "is a disgrace, instead of being an honor; but a state claims a privilege from the awards of equal justice, when she refuses to become a party, unless, in the same case, she becomes a judge."[5] It is not apparent how Wilson was able to maintain a distinction between a state and the chief judicial instrument of that state, but his meaning is clear that the state, no more than the individual, could regard itself as above the law. As so often, Wilson drew an analogy with the government of Anglo-Saxon England, asserting that likewise suits could there be brought against the king.

If democratic principles imply a willingness that the will of the majority should prevail, both in the choice of representatives and in the formulation of policy, then Wilson was no democrat. However, few men in Wilson's day conceived of a system in which the people determined the policy of the state. That Wilson did not do so, great as was his faith in the people as electors, and his concern that their views and interests should be reflected in the government, is indicated by his advocacy of a part for the judiciary in the operation of the power of veto.

Though he was not the initiator of the idea, Wilson was a strong supporter of the establishment of a Council of Revision, comprising the executive and "a convenient number" of the judiciary, and it was his suggestion that the power of veto of this body should be absolute—i.e. not liable to be overriden by the legislature. Just as he had thought a veto on legislative acts necessary to safeguard the independence of the executive, so also he believed a share in the operation of the veto would safeguard the judiciary.[6] The inclusion of the judiciary in the revisionary power was a matter to which he attached considerable importance, and it was therefore one over which he persisted in his advocacy in face of adverse decisions and widespread indifference among the delegates. Late in July he revived the issue, stating that further reflection had convinced him of its importance, and adding the argument that "the judiciary ought to have an opportunity of remonstrating against projected encroachments on the people as well as on themselves." What Wilson was asserting was that the judiciary ought not to be limited to acts it regarded as unconstitutional in the exercise of its revisionary power. "Laws," he argued, "may be unjust, may be unwise, may be dangerous, may be destructive; and yet not be so unconstitutional as to justify the judges in refusing to give them effect. Let them have a share in the revisionary power, and they will have an opportunity of taking notice of these characters of a law, and of counteracting, by the weight of their opinions the improper views of the legislature."[7] What this meant was that in the exercise of the veto an executive in whose election there might be a popular element would be joined collectively as an equal partner by a group of men—one of whom Wilson believed would be himself—whose appointment was only very remotely based on the people.

While this does not vitiate Wilson's democratic principles, it does help to establish the boundaries within which they operated. He was again defeated on the issue, but it was raised once more three weeks later, when Madison and Wilson proposed that every bill passed by both houses of Congress should then be submitted separately to the president and to the Supreme Court.[8] If rejected by either one the measure could become law only if subsequently approved by two-thirds of each house; if rejected by both, only if three-quarters of each house approved. This was the last attempt to give the judiciary a share in the exercise of the veto on congressional legislation. When this, too, failed, Wilson abandoned the struggle, though not without reiterating his fear that neither the executive nor the judicial branch had been sufficiently well safeguarded against the growth of legislative tyranny.[9]

It is hardly necessary to add that Wilson, determined to protect the judiciary from any threat to its security or independence, opposed any proposal that would render judges liable to removal except in the most extreme cases. When, therefore, it was suggested that judges be removable by the executive on application by the Senate and House of Representatives, he was quick to protest that "the judges would be in a bad situation if made to depend on every gust of faction which might prevail in the two branches of our government."[10] Most of the delegates agreed with him, and there was no difficulty in defeating the suggestion, and in replacing it by the much more rigorous process of impeachment.

A constant theme in Wilson's arguments concerning the legislative, executive, and judicial branches of the national government was the importance of creating a national government with extensive powers independent of the states. The relationship of the national government with the states is almost as prominent a concern of Wilson as the popular basis of government. Indeed, as we have seen, the two are intimately related.

A few other matters concerning the relationship between the states on the one hand and the national government on the other remain to be considered. There is nothing, however, which is not fully in accordance with the principles and ideas we have already seen expounded. It is not surprising, for instance, to find Wilson urging that even though one branch of the national legislature might have to be appointed by state legislatures, it would provide some safeguard for the independence of the national legislature if members were paid from the national treasury, and not from state sources.[11] Similarly, it was almost predictable that he would support a proposal to empower the national legislature to veto state legislation "which they should judge to be improper."[12] As either the national or the state government must be supreme, it was clearly in the interests of the people of the United States that the supremacy rest with the national government. "What danger is there," he asked, "that the whole will unnecessarily sacrifice a part? But reverse the case, and leave the whole at the mercy of each part, and will not the general interests be continually sacrificed to local interests?"[13] Though in the end he accepted the more limited power of judicial review, he persisted as long as he could in advocating a more extensive power for the national legislature. On August 23 it was proposed again to give to Congress, subject now to a two-thirds majority in each house, the authority "to negative all laws passed by the several states interfering in the opinion of the legislature with the general interests and harmony of the Union." This Wilson "considered . . . as the keystone wanted to complete the wide arch of government" the convention was erecting. "The firmness of judges," he believed to be an insufficient means of defending the national government from encroachments by the state governments. "It will be better," he declared not unreasonably, "to prevent the passage of an improper law, than to declare it void when passed."[14] The proposal was defeated only narrowly, and for reasons which may have been based mainly on considerations of practicability, but it was the last opportunity that occurred to adopt it. The episode is revealing, however, in that it does provide an indication that Wilson was more deeply concerned with creating an effective, democratic, national government than with augmenting the power of a nondemocratic judiciary. The only aspect of his political ideas that can throw any doubt on the sincerity of his democratic protestations is his effort to augment the judicial power. Yet here we see him preferring the power of review of state legislation to be exercised by the national legislature rather than by any judicial authority.

Wilson was one of the pioneers of the concept of the divisibility of sovereignty, by which state governments and the national government could be recognized as supreme within their separate defined spheres. This was the most effective way of offsetting the widespread belief that as governments tended to become tyrannical the only way of restraining the national government was to leave an undivided ultimate sovereignty with the states. Divided sovereignty, with ultimate power in their respective fields being exercised both by the states and by the national government, made possible the creation of a strong government without the risk of oppression. The question then was, how could power be divided between state and national governments? To most people, danger seemed to lie in excessive power in the hands of the national government. Wilson, however, feared that excessive caution in this matter would put the states in a position to dominate the national government, and in this way to obstruct the general welfare.[15] It was to him more necessary to safeguard the national government against state domination than the opposite. Pointing out that the states would have a direct influence in the national government if the proposal was adopted to entrust the appointment of senators to state legislatures, he argued that the national government should reciprocally be empowered to appoint one branch of each state government. "If a security be necessary on one side," he said, "it would seem reasonable to demand it on the other." It is not certain that Wilson was entirely serious in making this suggestion. What he was more concerned to demonstrate was that state governments had nothing to fear from the granting of ample powers to the national government. His argument was, characteristically, partly pragmatic and partly theoretical. A combination of large states to extend unduly the power of the national government would at once be blocked by the rest. In any event, the large states would not be tempted to take such action. "The states having in general a similar interest, in case of any proposition in the national legislature to encroach on the state legislatures, he conceived a general alarm would take place in the national legislature itself, that it would communicate itself to the state legislatures, and would finally spread among the people at large." Then in a less pragmatic manner he continued: "The general government will be as ready to preserve the rights of the states as the latter are to preserve the rights of individuals, all the members of the former, having a common interest, as representatives of all the people of the latter, to leave the state governments in possession of what the people wish them to retain." Therefore he concluded that the common assumption that the danger of oppression would come from the national government was wholly unfounded. "On the contrary," Madison reported, "he conceived that in spite of every precaution the general government would be in perpetual danger of encroachments from the state governments."[16]

There were those in the convention who believed or suspected that Wilson in reality wished to eliminate the states entirely. While it is not easy to ascertain the precise function Wilson envisaged for the states, there is no doubt that he wished them to continue to exist as an important feature of the government of the United States. Indeed, in a sense he wished to increase the authority of both state and national governments within their respective spheres.

Very early in the convention, on June 6, Wilson went out of his way to repudiate any idea that the states should be abolished, though no one appears in fact to have suggested it, saying that he "saw no incompatibility between the national and state governments provided the latter were restrained to certain local purposes."[17] The following day Wilson denied an assertion by John Dickinson that he wished to destroy the states, but admitted that their existence was made necessary by the great extent of the United States, and that their sphere must be confined to "subordinate purposes" which included "the freedom of the people and their internal good police."[18] Wilson continued to assert the necessity of retaining the states, though without ever clearly defining what he considered their "subordinate purposes" to be. They were necessary, he maintained, for certain purposes which the national government could not reach, and because historical experience showed that "all large governments must be subdivided into lesser jurisdictions"[19] if they are to be effectively administered.

Moreover, in contradiction of Hamilton's belief, Wilson thought a harmonious relationship would exist between state and national governments. Later, outside the convention, he was more direct and explicit in his advocacy of the retention of state governments. It was necessary to preserve both free government and efficient government. "To support, with vigor," he asserted in his law lectures, "a single government over the whole extent of the United States, would, I apprehend, demand a system of the most unqualified and the most unremitted despotism: even despotism herself, extended so far and so wide, would totter under the weight of her own unwieldiness."[20] That he had no emotional attachment to state sovereignty is quite evident. The states were a necessary instrument of sound government. He had not even any real regard for the territorial integrity of the states. Though he knew it to be impracticable, he would have welcomed a redrawing of state boundaries which would have made all states roughly equal in population,[21] thus removing the difficulties over representation in the national government. The desirability of boundary revisions did not, however, extend to the division of states against their own will, and in resisting a suggestion that the national government be allowed to do so, Wilson was guilty of, for him, the rare offense of intellectual inconsistency.

It is fairly clear, though the details are obscure, that he was torn between his political and constitutional principles and his deep personal interest in western lands. Very possibly, it was the implication with regard to the Connecticut Western Reserve, in which he owned land, that was for him the troublesome issue. The controversy began when it was realized that a proposal to prevent states being divided without their own consent might make it impossible to establish new western states without the consent of states which still had claims to jurisdiction over western areas. Wilson declared that "he knew of nothing that would give him greater or juster alarm than the doctrine, that a political society is to be torn asunder without its own consent."[22] He based his position on the doctrine of the majority, arguing that "if the majority of a state wish to divide they can do so," and deploring the implication that the national government "should abet the minority, and by that means, divide a state against its own consent."[23] Here Wilson is in effect asserting that the minority in a state ought not to be allowed to prevail over the majority in that state, even though the minority was supported by the national government— i.e., by the representatives of the majority of the people of the United States. So striking a departure from his otherwise consistent and determined elevation of the people of the United States over the individual states seems explicable only in the light of the existence of an overriding interest. Wilson had laid himself open to Luther Martin's incisive reproof: "He wished Mr. Wilson had thought a little sooner of the value of political bodies. In the beginning, when the rights of the small states were in question, they were phantoms, ideal beings. Now when the great states were to be affected, political societies were of a sacred nature."[24]

Wilson, it is clear enough, did not so regard political societies, least of all the states. His emphasis at all other times was on the sovereign American people—not the states, nor even the national government, as political entities, not the people of the states, but only the people of the United States were the ultimate source of all legitimate authority. Wilson's commitment to this view of sovereignty long preceded the Federal Convention. When the issue arose in the Continental Congress at the end of July 1776 Wilson, according to Thomas Jefferson, insisted that Congress represented not the states but the people of the states and that with regard to the matters within the competence of Congress America was one single large state. He put forward the argument he subsequently used several times, in different forms, in underlining the absurdity of equating for political purposes a large number of people with a small number, "that annexing the name of 'State' to ten thousand men should give them an equal right with forty thousand."[25] It was easy for him to find historical examples of the dangers of such a situation, drawing the conclusion that "the interest of the whole is constantly sacrificed to that of the small states." When it was charged that acceptance of Wilson's argument would put it in the power of four states to govern the other nine as they please, he replied that if his view was not accepted then it would be put in the power of one million people to govern two million. This is the crux of Wilson's contention regarding the tripartite relationship between the states, the national government, and the people, and nothing he said in the Federal Convention modified in any way his basic principle of majority rule.

It was as a corollary of this that Wilson consistently denied that the states, rather than the national government, were the true protectors of the interests of the people. He believed there was no reason at all why the people, as distinct from local politicians, should feel their interests to be better safeguarded by their state than by the national government. "Why," he asked, "should a national government be unpopular? Has it less dignity? Will each citizen enjoy under it less liberty or protection? Will a citizen of Delaware be degraded by becoming a citizen of the United States?"[26] Whenever the opportunity arose Wilson emphasized the artificial nature of states when regarded separately from the people. "Can we forget," he asked, "for whom we are forming a government? Is it for *men*, or for the imaginary beings called *states*?"[27] This concept appears in different forms on many occasions in Wilson's statements and writings, with its unavoidable corollary that so far as the interests of the people were concerned there was no reason whatever for not giving to a national government as much power as effective administration required. Nor, similarly, was there any reason to fear combinations of large states against the smaller. The interests of politicians only, not those of the people, were identified with the exercise of maximum power within defined political limits. The interests of the people of Delaware did not differ from those of the people of Pennsylvania, nor those of the people of Maryland from those of the people of Virginia. Why then should the people fear combinations of large states? In reply to the specific assertion that a combination of the three most powerful states of Pennsylvania, Virginia, and Massachusetts would give rise to a danger of monarchy or of aristocracy he asked simply whether the people of those three states were more aristocratic than those of the rest. Moreover, on purely practical grounds, reflecting their different economic interests, it was most improbable that those states would ever be able to establish a form of cooperation which would be detrimental to the interests of other states.

Though it did not emerge from the reports of Wilson's contributions to the discussions in the convention itself, it appears from some of his subsequent observations that there was an emotional element in his view of the relationship between the United States, its component states, and the people. This arose from his view that it was the nation, not the state, that was the proper focus of patriotic feeling. There are many points at which Wilson emerges as an American nationalist, in the emotional as in the constitutional sense, but nowhere more clearly than in his view of the American nation as a whole as the proper object of the loyalty of the people. "Expanded patriotism," he wrote later, "is a cardinal virtue in the United States." Appealing to his fellow countrymen to cast away narrow-mindedness and local prejudice, he exhorted them to the effort of broadening their outlook in order that they might identify themselves with the expanded community. In one of his finer, because more deeply felt, pieces of literary rhetoric he warned:

> To embrace the whole requires an expansion of mind, of talents, and of temper. To the trouble, though the generous trouble, of expanding their mind, their talents, and their temper, some will be averse from indolence, or what the indolent call moderation; others will be averse from interest, or

what the interested call prudence. The former will encourage a narrow spirit by their example; the latter will encourage it by their exertions also. These last will introduce and recommend the government of their state, as a rival, for social and benevolent affection, to the government of the United States. The simplicity of some, the inexperience of others, the unsuspecting confidence, again, of others will be won by plausible and seducing representations; and in this manner, and by these arts, the patriotic emanations of the soul, which would otherwise be diffused over the whole Union, will be refracted and converged to a very narrow and inconsiderable part of it.

To Wilson, not only the interests, but the enthusiasms of the people should center on the nation. "A union of hearts and affections," he appealed to his compatriots to recognize, "as well as a union of counsels and interests, is the very life and soul of a confederated republic. This is a subject on which it is almost impossible to say too much, or to speak with too much zeal."[28]

If Wilson had had his way, the powers of Congress would not have been enumerated, but instead would have been based on some broad principle ensuring a greater degree of flexibility.[29] The enumerating of powers was a matter that presented many difficulties, and eventually the Committee of Detail, of which Wilson was a member, sought to overcome them by adding to a list of certain specific powers a general welfare clause giving the national government an undefined authority in areas not clearly within the defined spheres of state power. Wilson strongly supported the granting to Congress of general powers,[30] which after some hesitation was accepted by the Committee of Detail, only to be rejected late in the convention by another committee, of which Wilson was not a member. A general welfare clause would have covered two specific powers whose inclusion Wilson unsuccessfully supported. One was the power to establish a university, in which there was to be no discrimination on grounds of religion; the other, proposed by Franklin and seconded by Wilson, would have given Congress the power to construct canals[31]—an authority which, had it been granted, would have prevented much political acrimony in the future. Though it is doubtful whether Wilson was thinking primarily in these terms, both would have enhanced the power of the national government over the states, in the latter case markedly so. Of the powers proposed to be prohibited to Congress, Wilson strongly opposed the decision of the

convention to forbid Congress to impose export duties, arguing that
to deny Congress that power would deprive it of half of its power to
regulate trade and would, moreover, remove a bargaining weapon in
negotiations for commercial treaties.[32] The prohibition on the passage of *ex post facto* laws he condemned contemptuously on the grounds
that it was equivalent to declaring that the legislature should not act
contrary to common sense. "It will," he declared, "bring reflections
on the Constitution and proclaim that we are ignorant of the first
principles of legislation, or are constituting a government which will
be so."[33] Wilson, unlike some of his colleagues, was thinking in
eighteenth-century rather than in seventeenth-century terms.

At many points Wilson revealed in the convention a broadly
liberal democratic outlook, which is illustrated by his consistency in
minor as well as in major matters—for if his democratic protestations
were, as some allege, no more than a means to the end of achieving a
strong centralized government, then there would seem to have been
no need to carry them further than the immediate purpose required.
Yet whenever an opportunity presented itself, Wilson based his argument on liberal principles. It was clearly of no consequence with
regard to the strengthening of the national government whether or
not the proceedings of Congress be made public, yet as we have seen,
Wilson strongly supported the publication of proceedings.[34] Since
the discussions in the convention were secret, Wilson could not have
been merely speaking for the record.

In his support of popular ratification of the Constitution he was
partly motivated by expediency, as he was convinced that reasons of
narrow self-interest would prevent ratification if it were left to the
politicians either of state legislatures or even of the existing Congress.
But in addition he believed not only in the good sense of the people
when faced with an issue of this kind, but also in their right to decide a
matter so important to them. Not that he advocated anything re-
sembling a referendum. What he proposed was that conventions be
chosen by the people of each state, and that the question of ratification
be submitted to these democratically elected bodies. He was convinced that the power of argument would ensure the adoption of the
new Constitution, in itself an indication that he himself was uncon-
scious of anything in it which might be unacceptable to the majority
of the people.

On the question of immigration Wilson took a liberal view.[35] It
was perhaps to be expected that as one himself he would be eager to
give encouragement to immigrants, the more especially as his own

state of Pennsylvania provided the best example in the United States of the beneficial effects of liberal immigration policies. It does not always follow, however, that the beneficiaries of liberal policies favor the extension of these policies to others, and it is not unworthy of note that Wilson took the opportunity in the convention to urge not only that immigration should be encouraged but that no significant restrictions be imposed on new arrivals. They should, in his view, be accorded the rights and privileges, and accept the duties, of citizenship within as short a time as was reasonably possible, and he was willing to admit newcomers to membership in Congress within a very few years of their admission to citizenship. On several occasions he sought to reduce the period of citizenship demanded for eligibility to election. He was emotionally outraged when it was suggested that but for appearances it might be better to confine membership of the Senate to the native-born.[36] With his own situation in mind he looked on the ineligibility of immigrants "as one of the most galling chains which the human mind could experience." He contended that a high proportion of foreigners who came to America were men of superior abilities, and he deplored the loss to the government if such men were debarred from its service. Wilson favored four years' citizenship as a qualification for membership of the House; this, however, was to him a compromise proposal, as he suggested that the Pennsylvania requirement of only two years' citizenship should properly be extended to eligibility for the lower house of the national Congress, and, indeed, then supported Hamilton's proposal that no more than citizenship and inhabitancy be required. Similarly he sought to reduce the period for eligibility for election to the Senate. The fourteen years originally proposed he regarded as outrageous, and even the adopted proposal of nine years he sought to reduce to seven.[37] Wilson's general attitude to the question of eligibility for public office, whether elective or appointive, was invariably liberal; to him, merit was the one essential qualification, and therefore restrictions on eligibility should be minimal.

Though in the Pennsylvania Ratifying Convention Wilson expressed himself unambiguously as being strongly opposed to slavery and the slave trade, in the convention itself he is not recorded as having taken any firm stand on these issues. Indeed, there are some indications that he was motivated by a desire neither to offend his own people in Pennsylvania by equating slaves with free citizens for purposes of representation, nor to alarm southern delegates to the point of opposing adequate federal authority, by taking in these matters a stand on principle.[38] Expediency was clearly his guide, whatever his personal opinions might have been. He was, it is true, willing to support the abolition of the slave trade, but he was certainly not anxious to press the issue beyond the compromise finally agreed by the convention.

Other issues arising in the convention in the discussion of which Wilson participated concerned treason, sanctity of contracts, and the question of paper money. Though the evidence is only circumstantial, there is some reason to suppose that Wilson was largely responsible for the liberal treason clause in the Constitution, with its narrow definition of treason and its requirement for conviction of testimony of two witnesses to the same overt act.[39] Wilson had earlier, in the Pennsylvania treason trials,[40] shown a liberal attitude based on safeguarding the accused. His support of the treason clause, whether or not he helped to initiate it, indicates a limit to his desire to extend the authority of the national government; it was to be a strong government, but it was to be prevented from exploiting a broad law of treason, as arbitrary governments were apt to do, in order to exercise undue authority over the people.

Wilson was at all times a vigorous upholder of orthodox financial principles, and displayed what at times seemed almost an emotional abhorrence of paper money. In the convention he strongly supported Gouverneur Morris in a successful attempt to eliminate a provision which would have expressly empowered the government of the United States to issue paper money.[41] Similarly, it was Wilson who proposed that the prohibitions on the emission of bills of credit by states, and on their making anything other than gold or silver coin legal tender, be made absolute, instead of, as was proposed, making them conditional on the express consent of Congress.[42]

Wilson was an equally vigorous upholder of the principle of the sanctity of contracts. Though there is no clear evidence, it is not unlikely that he was closely involved in the framing of the clause in the Constitution which prohibits a state from passing any law impairing the obligation of contracts. While the actual proposal was made by Rufus King,[43] it was an issue about which Wilson had deep feelings, and it is almost inconceivable that he was not behind this provision. The least that can be said is that if no one else had first made the proposal, Wilson would certainly have done so. The circumstantial evidence derived from Wilson's part in the case of the Bank of North America points clearly in that direction.[44] Moreover, the bank issue was still central to Pennsylvania politics, as the bank, already once abolished and restored, was still in danger, and the sanctity-of-contracts clause would give protection from interference by the Pennsylvania assembly in its affairs.[45] Wilson's interests were closely involved in the bank, and in urging the adoption of the obligation of contracts clause he was undoubtedly seeking to further his own interests. But as so often with Wilson as with other Founding Fathers, there was the conviction that what was in his own interests was equally in those of his country. A stable financial structure, based on strong, stable government, would be most conducive to the expansion of the economy and the prosperity of all the people.

CHAPTER 7

Concerning the
Pennsylvania Ratifying Convention
and the key role therein played
by James Wilson.

The contribution of Wilson to the success of the Federal Convention was known only to his fellow delegates, the rule of secrecy having been strictly observed, and it being many years yet before any of the reports of the proceedings was to become public. Moreover, although there are a few fragments of his prepared contributions to the convention, we depend for the most part on the reports of others—mainly Madison—who while making what we can assume to be reasonably accurate records, could not possibly have made complete ones. Accordingly, some part of Wilson's contribution must have gone unrecorded. The proceedings of the Pennsylvania Ratifying Convention were of a very different nature. Reports were much fuller and were well publicized, and many of Wilson's own speeches are preserved in the form in which he prepared them. Moreover, his efforts in the ratifying convention were in large measure a publicity exercise, and therefore his thoughts are revealed far more fully than they could be at secondhand in the more restricted circumstances of the Federal Convention.

It is very often asserted that it was Wilson who was mainly responsible for the ratification by Pennsylvania of the Constitution. Certainly the part he played in the ratifying convention was a dominant one, but it is doubtful whether it was decisive, as the elections to the convention returned a very clear majority of supporters of the Constitution. This is not necessarily to minimize Wilson's part, as the outcome of the election was undoubtedly affected by a very influential speech which he made before the election took place. This is his State

House Yard speech of October 6, 1787, which was widely publicized not only in Pennsylvania, but throughout the United States.

This speech may well have been crucial to the ratification of the Constitution by enough states to secure its adoption. For as went Pennsylvania, so might go several other states, and the outcome in Pennsylvania, one of the first to elect a ratifying convention, could well prove decisive for the United States. Pennsylvania became the first large state to ratify the Constitution, and while the effect of this cannot be estimated with exactness, it is certain that at the very least it smoothed the way to ratification elsewhere.

There was in Pennsylvania, moreover, a local political factor which created a particular difficulty for the Federalists. This was the fact that the Pennsylvania constitution of 1776, the pride and joy of radicals in the state, and about which more will be said later, was based on principles fundamentally different from those on which the proposed new Constitution for the United States was based. Therefore, it might be that the national Constitution would help to undermine the state constitution, and give encouragement to those, among whom Wilson was conspicuous, who for many years had been trying to replace the 1776 constitution by one based on principles similar to those of the new national Constitution. The ratification process in Pennsylvania, accordingly, was part of a continuing internal political struggle in the state, and victory for the Federalists might have consequences which would be damaging to the group then in power.

From one point of view the controversy lay between Philadelphia, strongly Federalist, and the western counties, believed to be strongly Antifederalist. That they were in general Antifederalist is clear, but one of the surprises in the elections to the convention was that the western counties chose more Federalists than anyone had expected.[1] Whether this was partly the result of Wilson's State House Yard speech can only be surmised, but it is unlikely that it was not influenced by what was the Federalists' biggest propaganda effort before the elections took place. Wilson's main purpose in the October 6 speech was to refute damaging allegations assiduously being spread by opponents of the Constitution in an attempt to arouse popular prejudice against it. There were three elements in the Constitution which were capable of portrayal, whether honestly or dishonestly, in a manner that might arouse a dangerously hostile popular response. These concerned popular rights, the sovereignty of the states, and the supposedly aristocratic nature of the proposed new system.

The alleged threat to the rights of the people arose from both the lack of a bill of rights, which became an important issue everywhere, and from an apparent implication that trial by jury was threatened. The immense importance of the bill of rights issue is very evident, and it is of some significance that to the people in general it quite over-shadowed the state sovereignty issue. Wilson was evidently perfectly sincere in his defense of the lack of a bill of rights, though at one point it may have been made with a mental reservation. His contention was that when the people originally established their governments in accordance with the social contract theory, they gave to their repre-sentatives every power they did not expressly withhold; whereas the proposed new Constitution explicitly defined powers to be delegated to the federal government in "the positive grant expressed in the in-strument of the union,"[2] and powers not thus given were accordingly reserved. Evading the issue of implied powers, which if not strictly relevant to the immediate issue perhaps nevertheless was being left deliberately ambiguous, Wilsón went on to say: "This distinction being recognized will furnish an answer to those who think the omis-sion of a bill of rights a defect in the proposed Constitution; for it would have been superfluous and absurd to have stipulated with a federal body of our own creation, that we should enjoy those privileges of which we are not divested, either by the intention or the act that has brought the body into existence."[3]

If this convoluted reasoning allayed some misgivings, it did not remove them all, and the issue of the lack of a bill of rights continued to play a major part in the struggle for ratification. A closely related issue was that of jury trial in civil cases. The proposed Constitution made proper provision for trial by jury in criminal cases. The lack of any similar provision for civil cases gave opponents of the Constitu-tion the opportunity to attack it on those grounds. This was clearly an appeal to the popular misconception that trial by jury was an essential element in all trials and that without it popular liberties would be endangered. Wilson had no difficulty in refuting so fallacious an alle-gation. The business of the federal government, he pointed out, was not local but general, and as practice in this matter varied considera-bly among the states no general precedent could be followed. The Constitution, therefore, could say nothing on the matter of jury trial in civil cases without involving itself in the enormous difficulty of choosing between the different practices already in being or of estab-lishing a new one. Moreover, he pointed out, jury trial was not al-ways appropriate in civil cases—in admiralty courts, for instance, and courts of equity. The Federal Convention, he informed his audience, had no misgivings over the lack of provision for trial by jury in civil cases as it was fully confident that the omission would not endanger the liberty or rights of the people, as the proceedings of the Supreme Court were to be regulated by the Congress, which was to be "a faithful representation of the people," and, moreover, so long as criminal trials were by jury, oppression of the people by the government would be effectively prevented.

Similarly he dismissed unfounded allegations that because the proposed Constitution did not expressly prohibit it, the government could interfere with freedom of the press, observing that as there was nothing in the new system that would enable the government to do so, it would have been futile to forbid it. Even to raise the issue at all might, he argued, be held to imply that some degree of control of the press lay with the government. It is evident that Wilson's basic attitude toward government differed markedly from that of his opponents. Government to Wilson was a positive instrument for the people's well-being, and effective control of it lay with the people themselves; to Antifederalists it was a negative instrument, potentially oppressive, which would act against the people unless curbed by built-in legal safeguards.

Wilson frequently insisted that the issue of loss of sovereignty by the states in the new Constitution was one which in no way adversely affected the interests of the people in general. Only state politicians, who would have to sacrifice a degree of influence, might suffer any loss. On many occasions he pointed out the advantages to the people of the United States if some power were transferred from state to federal government—a transaction that would involve no sacrifice of "sovereignty" on the part of the individual citizen. He was, however, aware that the sovereignty of the state, though a less important issue with the people than Antifederalists supposed, was important enough to require suspicions to be allayed. As on other occasions, he sought to refute the tendentious allegation that the Constitution was designed "to reduce the state governments to mere corporations, and eventually to annihilate them." This accusation Wilson vigorously countered by drawing attention to the close dependency of the federal electoral system on the existence of states—the election of the president, of the House of Representatives and of the Senate all required the participation, one way or another, of state legislatures, through their power to determine the method of choosing presidential electors, through the provision that electors of the federal House of Representatives be composed in each state of those qualified to vote for the lower house of the state legislature, and through the provision for election of the two senators from each state by the state legislature. It was therefore absurd, he contended, "to suppose that the annihilation of the separate governments will result from their union; or, that having that intention, the authors of the new system would have bound their connection with such indissoluble ties." Moreover, he seized the opportunity to emphasize that under the new system, unlike the old, the people themselves would elect their representatives in the federal lower house.

Wilson did not assert that the powers of the states would be unaffected, only that their existence was not threatened. And though their powers might be diminished, the only group adversely affected consisted of those with a personal interest in the maintenance of state power—namely, state politicians and officials. "It is the interest," he said, "of a very numerous, powerful and respectable body to counteract and destroy the excellent work produced by the late convention. All the officers of government and all the appointments for the administration of justice and the collection of the public revenue, which are transferred from the individual to the aggregate sovereignty of the states, will necessarily turn the stream of influence and emolument into a new channel. Every person, therefore, who enjoys or expects to enjoy a place of profit under the present establishment, will object to the proposed innovation; not, in truth, because it is injurious to the liberties of his country, but because it affects his schemes of wealth and consequence."

The third major criticism of the proposed Constitution which Wilson thought it important to rebut, was the charge that the composition of the Senate would lead to the establishment in the United States of a "baneful aristocracy." If Wilson had had his way in the matter of the election of the Senate this accusation could not have been made. He referred obliquely to this in admitting that the eventual decision of the convention was "a compromise between contending interests," but went on to justify the decision and to defend it against the damaging assertions of the Antifederalists. Acknowledging that the proposed plan of government was not perfect, he observed that "when we reflect how various are the laws, commerce, habits, population, and extent of the confederated states, this evidence of mutual concession and accommodation ought rather to command a generous applause than to excite jealousy and reproach." Moreover, despite the fact that the provisions regarding the Senate were not ideal, there was still no danger that the fears of oligarchy would prove justified. For, he pointed out, both in its legislative and in its executive capacities the Senate was checked by the other branches of government. The exercise of its legislative function required the cooperation of the House of Representatives, and that of its executive functions the concurrence of the president. "Thus fettered," he claimed, "I do not know any act which the Senate can of itself perform, and such dependence necessarily precludes every idea of influence and superiority."

These were the main charges Wilson thought it essential to counter. Others, of lesser importance, were that it was improper to delegate the power of direct taxation to the federal government, and that a potential threat to liberty lay in the power of Congress to raise and support a standing army in time of peace. The first of these criticisms Wilson dismissed by asserting that the great bulk of the national revenue would be raised by impost "for, being at once less obnoxious and more productive, the interest of the government will be best promoted by the accommodation of the people," and that the power to impose direct taxes was really in the main an emergency power—though even if it were widely used he still anticipated no danger that the power would be used oppressively. The supposed danger from a standing army he dismissed almost contemptuously by pointing out that even under the Articles of Confederation the United States possessed this power, and that it was a normal practice with other nations. How, he asked, could an effective foreign policy be carried on if the United States could never be in a state of military preparedness before an actual declaration of war? "No man," he concluded, "who regards the dignity and safety of his country, can deny the necessity of a military force, under the control and with the restrictions which the new Constitution provides."

In conclusion, Wilson again acknowledged the existence of defects in the proposed system, but emphasized that it contained provision for its own reform. His peroration reflected what became the view of virtually all Americans of their Constitution: "I will confess, indeed, that I am not a blind admirer of this plan of government, and that there are some parts of it which, if my wish had prevailed, would certainly have been altered. But, when I reflect how widely men differ in their opinions, and that every man (and the observation applies likewise to every state) has an equal pretension to assert his own, I am satisfied that anything nearer to perfection could not have been accomplished. If there are errors, it should be remembered that the seeds of reformation are sown in the work itself, and the concurrence of two-thirds of the Congress may at any time introduce alterations and amendments. Regarding it then, in every point of view, with a candid and disinterested mind, I am bold to assert that it is the best form of government which has ever been offered to the world."[4]

The report of the event published in the proconstitution *Pennsylvania Gazette* gives an indication of the probable impact: "Mr. Wilson's speech was frequently interrupted with loud and unanimous testimonies of approbation, and the applause which reiterated at the conclusion evinced the general sense of its excellency, and the conviction which it had impressed upon every mind."[5] *The Pennsylvania Gazette* was prejudiced in Wilson's favor; stronger indications of the success of the State House Yard speech came from the Antifederalists, who displayed almost a panic reaction to it. Abuse, ridicule, and appeals to popular prejudices mingled with more reasoned argument in their response. In particular, Wilson was attacked as an aristocrat. "The whole tenor of his political conduct," wrote on opponent, "has always been strongly tainted with the spirit of *high aristocracy;* he has never been known to join in a truly popular measure, and his talents have ever been devoted to the patrician interest." The form of government Wilson was supporting, the writer went on, was admirably contrived to carry his aristocratic ideas into execution, and in order to defend the new Constitution he was obliged to stoop to deceive the people by "mean evasions and pitiful sophistry."[6] Sophistry was a word frequently used by Antifederalists in their condemnation of Wilson. One, in fact, thought it unnecessary to say more. "I pass over," he wrote, "the sophistry of Mr. W————, in his equivocal speech at the State House. His pretended arguments have been echoed and reechoed by every retailer of politics and victoriously refuted by several patriotic pens." Not all the patriotic pens were as irrational as this, but there was a marked tendency to resort to smear tactics rather than to argument. And to assert that Wilson had been victoriously refuted was no more than wishful thinking. Another notable example of this was R.H. Lee's observation to Sam Adams that in response to Wilson "the press has produced such manly and well-reasoned refutations of him and his system, that both have lost ground amazingly in the public estimation."[7]

Whatever loss of ground there may have been was not reflected in the elections to the ratifying convention, and as the leader in that body of the supporters of the Constitution Wilson operated from a position of strength. The outcome, however, was not a foregone conclusion. Complacency, or an error in tactics, might easily give the Antifederalists an opportunity they could successfully exploit. Wilson was aware that in the Pennsylvania Ratifying Convention he was fighting for the adoption of the Constitution by other states as well as by his own. Moreover, he was aware also, as were his opponents, that the outcome of the struggle over ratification of the national Constitution might influence profoundly the domestic political controversy within Pennsylvania over the radical constitution of 1776. The close identification in Pennsylvania of national and local issues gave the controversy there a particular importance. Wilson was deeply committed on both issues, and he approached his task in a spirit of total dedication, devoting his entire energies to it, and displaying the meticulous thoroughness which characterized his approach to every important undertaking.

In the Pennsylvania Ratifying Convention were revealed more clearly than anywhere else the ideas of James Wilson concerning both the principles on which government in and of the United States should be based and the practical devices most appropriate for carrying them into practice. In the convention, Wilson, the only member who had served also in the Federal Convention, carried almost the whole burden of the Federalist cause. According to one of his colleagues nothing was said or done except under his direction.[8] Though this was not quite true, it is clear that Wilson was the dominant, indeed controlling, influence among the Federalists. He was opposed by an able triumvirate composed of three Westerners—William Findley, John Smilie, and Robert Whitehill[9]—all Ulster Presbyterians in origin, and all of whom subsequently served for many years in the United States Congress. These opponents were intellectually formidable, and Wilson could not afford to relax his efforts if the Federalist cause was to prevail.

When the convention began its deliberations, on November 24, Wilson took the initiative, as evidently he was expected to do, in expounding the principles on which the Federal Convention had operated. His exposition reveals more clearly than any statement he made elsewhere his own fundamental attitudes toward government and his view of the extent and nature of the achievement of the Federal Convention. He began by emphasizing the magnitude of the achievement of the convention in producing a sound system of government which could function not merely in the existing territory of the United States, but which could be equally effective in the enormously expanded nation which Wilson saw as the certain destiny of his country. The convention, he pointed out, had to frame a system of government not merely for those states then existing, "several of which contained an extent of territory, and resources of population, equal to those of some of the most respectable kingdoms on the other side of the Atlantic," but also for "numerous states yet unformed" and for "myriads of the human race who will inhabit regions hitherto uncultivated." Wilson, with his characteristic perceptiveness, was underlining at the outset what was subsequently shown in practice to be the most remarkable feature of the new Constitution. The difficulty of achieving such a government, he continued, was "equal to its magnitude" in view of the need "to combine and reconcile the jarring interests that prevail, or seem to prevail, in a single community," especially in one already so extensive. Real, or sometimes imagined, conflicts of interest made compromise a necessary feature of any agreement. No one, in other words, should be deterred from accepting the Constitution because of the inevitable imperfections everyone would see in it. "When the springs of opposition," he argued, "were so numerous and strong, and poured forth their waters in courses so varying, need we be surprised that the stream formed by their conjunction was impelled in a direction somewhat different from that which each of them would have taken separately?"[10]

He then turned to what he knew would be one of the main points of criticism, namely, that the government created by the Constitution would be oppressive and therefore incompatible with the free spirit of the people of America who, in the view of many, "would ill brook the restraints of an efficient government." His answer was that high-spirited though the people of America might be, they also possessed "sound sense" and therefore "would be best pleased with that system of government which would best promote their freedom and happiness."

Wilson was now directly confronted with the issue that pervades so much of his thinking: how to reconcile efficient government with democratic government, especially in a country actually, and even more potentially, so diverse and extensive as the United States. The prevailing idea at the time was, as expressed by Montesquieu, "that the national property of small states is to be governed as a republic; of middling ones, to be subject to a monarch; and of large empires, to be swayed by a despotic prince," and, Wilson pointed out, historical experience seemed fully to confirm it. The problem that the Federal Convention had to solve, therefore, was how to reconcile an extensive territory, which elsewhere had been found to be governable only by methods of despotism, with a people dedicated to the rejection of despotism. Their answer was a new form of government, a "confeder-

WILLIAM FINDLEY

From McMaster, John, and Frederick B. Stone,
Pennsylvania and the Federal Constitution 1787–1788
(New York: Da Capo Press, Inc., 1970), p. 454

By permission of the Historical Society of Pennsylvania

ate republic" which Montesquieu rightly believed to have "all the internal advantages of a republican, together with the external force of a monarchical government."

The way was now opened for Wilson to expound his often emphasized view of the uniqueness of the American system. There had been nothing like it in the history of the world, other confederacies being for various reasons not comparable with it, and therefore there were no precedents to serve as a guide. And above all, the nature of the principle of democracy enshrined in it went far beyond anything before attempted, and was uniquely American. The principle of representation which was an essential element in the Constitution had not ever before been properly applied anywhere. The ancient world did not have any understanding of it, and even the British constitution reflected it only in part. In Britain the executive and judicial branches were not based even indirectly on the principle of representation, and even in the legislative branch "it does not predominate, though it may serve as a check." In the British constitution the principle of representation was therefore confined to "a narrow corner," though it extended further than in any other European government.[11] According to the version of the speech given by McMaster and Stone,[12] Wilson referred to representation as "the basis and the cement of the superstructure." By using the two words *basis* and *cement* Wilson, a concise thinker not given to tautological expressions, may have intended to convey two somewhat different ideas. It was not enough to make representation simply the "basis" of the constitutional system, as that would be consistent with the dilution of the democratic element in practice; it was necessary also that it be the "cement" of the system—in other words (those of Wilson himself using a different metaphor), "representation is the true chain between the people and those to whom they entrust the administration of government; and though it may consist of many links, its strength and brightness never should be impaired," or, as the original draft put it, "in all cases it should be sufficiently strong and discernible."[13]

This concept of representation as a necessary, active ingredient throughout the system as a whole—or at least the legislative and executive branches, it being less conspicuous in the judicial—was fundamental to Wilson's view of government in general and of the proposed Constitution in particular, and its importance was stressed by him at every opportunity. After discussing various other matters he returned to this theme with a resounding reaffirmation of his faith in democracy. "That the supreme power . . ." he proclaimed, "should be vested in the people, is in my judgment the great panacea of human politics. It is a power paramount to every constitution, inalienable in its nature, and indefinite in its extent."[14] But, he emphasized, in a political society like that of America, it was essential that the people act responsibly. If they did, there was nothing to fear, and any defect in the government would ultimately be corrected, but if they did not, then calamity would follow. "There is a remedy," he reasserted, ". . . for every distemper of government, if the people are not wanting to themselves. For a people wanting to themselves, there is no remedy; from their power, as we have seen, there is no appeal; to their error, there is no superior principle of correction."[15] In his peroration Wilson chose to emphasize, not the utility of the Constitution in relation to the needs of the United States, but the fact that it emanated wholly from the people. He repeated:

> In its principles it is purely democratical; varying indeed, in its form, in order to admit all the advantages, and to exclude all the disadvantages which are incidental to the known and established constitutions of government. But when we take an extensive and accurate view of the streams of power that appear through this great and comprehensive plan, when we contemplate the variety of their directions, the force and dignity of their currents, when we behold them intersecting, embracing, and surrounding the vast possessions and interests of the continent, and when we see them distributing on all hands beauty, energy and riches, still, however numerous and wide their courses, however diversified and remote the blessings they diffuse, we shall be able to trace them all to one great and noble source, THE PEOPLE.[16]

The other matters that Wilson felt it appropriate to consider in his opening address to the ratifying convention concerned the relationship between state and federal governments and the miserable condition of the United States under the Articles of Confederation. He made clear his belief that the continued existence of the states was essential as the total centralization of government in so extensive a country would require "despotic power." The recognition of a separate status, however, "would at one time expose the states to foreign insult and depredations, and at another, to internal jealousy, contention and war," and even the less objectionable alternative of dividing the country into two or three confederacies would have, even if in lesser degree, many of the defects of independence for all. He was certain that everyone would reject these alternatives, as the Federal Convention had done, and he chose to regard the idea of a federal republic as noncontroversial.

This still left the question of the division of power between states and the federal government. Acknowledging that in this matter a precise line could not be drawn, he nevertheless openly revealed his preference for entrusting power to the national rather than to the local government, saying that he thought it "more natural to presume that the interest of each would be pursued by the whole, than . . . that the several states would prefer the interest of the confederated body; for in the general government each is represented, but in the separate governments, only the separate states." Arguing on the basis of the social contract theory, by which an individual surrendered part of his natural rights but in fact gained more "by the limitation of the liberty of others," than he lost "by the limitation of his own" he maintained that similarly the surrender of liberty by the states to a national government would in effect increase the aggregate of liberty. The liberty surrendered by the individual was termed civil liberty, and he coined the term federal liberty to describe the similar surrender by the states of part of their freedom of action to the national government, with the same consequence of an effective augmentation of their liberty.

This argument, while sound enough, was not of a kind likely to illuminate the issue convincingly; it is the kind of abstruse argument to which Wilson was somewhat addicted, and it displays him at his least effective. What was far more convincing, and shows Wilson at his most effective, was his appeal to common sense, expressed in simple straightforward terms. In proposing a single, confederated government, he said, the Federal Convention "were necessarily led, not only to consider the situation, circumstances, and interests of one, two, or three states, but of the collective body; and as it is essential to society that the welfare of the whole should be preferred to the accommodation of a part, they followed the same rule in promoting the national advantages of the Union, in preference to the separate advantages of the states. A principle of candor, as well as duty, led to this conduct; for . . . no government, either single or confederated, can exist, unless private and individual rights are subservient to the public and general happiness of the nation."[17]

There were many in the convention who found it difficult to accept the implications of Wilson's assertion that all sovereignty, whether of the nation or of the various states, lay ultimately with the people of the United States. Accordingly, the controversy over the matter of the relationship between federal and state governments persisted throughout the convention, and in its closing stages Wilson felt obliged to expound once more the principle on which he based his view of this fundamental issue. Making a stark distinction between his own attitude and that of the Antifederalists, Wilson declared: "His [Findley's] position is that the supreme power resides in the states, as governments; and mine is that it resides in the PEOPLE as the fountain of government; that the people have not, that the people mean not, and that the people ought not, to part with it to any government whatsoever. In their hands it remains secure. They can delegate it in such proportions, to such bodies, on such terms, and under such limitations, as they think proper."[18] That it was the people of all the states collectively, and not of each state separately, that possessed this power, he maintained was acknowledged implicitly in the opening words of the preamble to the Constitution, "We, the people of the United States." He denied explicitly that the Federal Convention had supposed that it was basing the Constitution on a compact between the states, and expressed his astonishment that after so much discussion one of the basic principles of the Constitution was not yet understood by the Antifederalists. Findley had asserted that in the Federal Convention the state governments had made a bargain with one another. "But far other," Wilson responded emphatically, "were the ideas of this convention, and far other are those conveyed in the system itself."[19] The people, accordingly, may "choose to indulge a part of their sovereign power to be exercised by the state governments," and may also, should circumstances so warrant, resume that power or make a new distribution of it between state and federal governments. "The power," Wilson concluded, "both of the general government, and the state governments, under this system are acknowledged to be so many emanations of power from the people." He exhorted his colleagues in the convention to apply themselves, "instead of disagreeing about who shall possess the supreme power," to considering whether the proposals before them were "well calculated to promote and secure the tranquillity and happiness of our common country."[20]

Associated in the public mind as he was with the aristocratic element in Pennsylvania politics, his emphasis on the sovereignty of the people was naturally suspect. The charge was inevitably made that in taking this position he was merely "cajoling the people." His indignant reply was that he had equally forcefully advocated that principle in the Federal Convention, "when the doors were shut, when it could not be alleged that I cajoled the people."[21] True as this was, it could not be proved until the proceedings of that convention were disclosed, and the time had not yet come when the Antifederalists could accept the sincerity of Wilson's democratic protestations.

Wilson's portrayal of the miseries afflicting the country since the end of the war needs little illustration. "Contention and poverty at home, discredit and disgrace abroad" were his themes. "Devoid of power," he said, "we could neither prevent the excessive importations which lately deluged the country, nor even raise from that excess a contribution to the public revenue; devoid of importance, we were unable to command a sale for our commodities in a foreign market; devoid of credit, our public securities were melting in the hands of their deluded owners, like snow before the sun; devoid of dignity, we were inadequate to perform treaties on our own part, or to compel a performance on the part of a contracting nation." But, he affirmed, "the years of languor are over," and now that the cause, "the weakness and imbecility of the existing Confederation," has been clearly identified, "the loud and concurrent voice of the people proclaims an efficient national government to be the only cure." This the Federal Convention had achieved, in framing a Constitution "by which the peace, freedom, and happiness of the United States should be permanently ensured."[22]

It was natural that Wilson should want to confine the discussion to the broad, general principles of the convention; it was equally natural that opponents of the Constitution should try to concentrate on the criticism of details for, since perfection is unattainable, nothing is easier than to find, and then inflate, issues which in relation to the overall purpose and achievement are trivial. A mass of petty objections in the aggregate can be made to seem to amount to a fundamental criticism. Wilson was aware of the danger, and therefore tried to prevent the detailed examination of the clauses of the Constitution which his opponents demanded. "Shall we," he asked, "while we contemplate a great and magnificent edifice, condescend like a fly, with its microscopic eye, to scrutinize the imperfections of a single brick?"[23] Not surprisingly he was unsuccessful in this. He did, however, succeed in blocking a delaying tactic which might have had damaging consequences to the prospects of ratification, especially outside Pennsylvania. This was a proposal, innocuous enough on the surface, to permit any member to insert in the journals of the convention the reasons for his vote on any issue, a privilege accorded to members of the legislature by the Pennsylvania constitution. Wilson saw at once the danger implicit in this proposal: it might cause the proceedings to be prolonged beyond the point when a favorable result in Pennsylvania would influence the conventions of other states in favor of ratification, and might even, by obfuscating the issues, lead to an unfavorable outcome in Pennsylvania itself. It was a difficult proposal to oppose, as to do so might appear as an attack on the freedom of members to express their opinions fully. Wilson vehemently denied that he had any such intention, saying that he was anxious that the widest possible publicity be given to the proceedings of the convention, but that the press was adequate for this purpose. For everyone to have the right to have his opinion printed at length at the public expense would impose an altogether unreasonable burden on the public revenues. Moreover, it would encourage factional disputes and spread "clamor and dissension not only among our own citizens, but throughout the United States."[24] The unique example produced by the Pennsylvania constitution was not one to be followed: members of the Pennsylvania legislature had the right to express their views in the journals, the consequence being that there were found there "altercations . . . adapted to the meridian of Billingsgate."[25] But the most important objection was the time that would be consumed. He pointed out that if one side expressed in the journals the reasons for its votes, then the other would have the right to reply, and time would have to be given for the preparation of such statements, and with the sarcasm he occasionally exhibited, he then observed that as he was "perhaps more accustomed to composition than other gentlemen" he would "not ask for that purpose more than two or three months." Wilson need not have worried; the Antifederalist proposal was decisively rejected.

In Pennsylvania, as elsewhere, the lack of a bill of rights was the feature of the proposed Constitution which its critics could most effectively exploit. It could with great plausibility be made to seem that there must be something sinister in the failure of the Federal Convention to make express provision for the basic rights of the citizens of America. What reason, it could be asked, could there be for not doing so? In the outcome, Federalists in the United States as a whole were unable to provide a satisfactory answer, and were obliged, though without serious misgiving, to undertake to incorporate in due course a bill of rights into the Constitution. In Pennsylvania Wilson argued vehemently against the inclusion of a bill of rights, and characteristically he took his stand on the democratic principles which pervaded his attitude to all parts of the constitution. Essentially what he argued was that as all power emanated from the people, it would be absurd for the people deliberately to restrict their own power by a device such as a bill of rights. Though he did not express it quite so directly, in effect he asked the counter-question, why should the people safeguard themselves against themselves? This, however, was a highly sophisticated line of thought and it was based on a faith (which not everyone could accept) in the democratic nature of the proposed new government. The great fear was that the new government, like all government, would tend to oppress the people, and that the danger of corruption of the system, if nothing else, required specific safeguards for elementary popular rights. Wilson would have been intellectually disloyal to the democratic principles he was so eagerly expounding had he conceded any validity to the arguments of advocates of a bill of rights. It was entirely in accordance with the democratic spirit of the new Constitution that a bill of rights had been omitted; to have included one would have been an implicit admission that it was not in fact based firmly on the people. Intellectual consistency—a marked feature of Wilson's thought—demanded that the need for a bill of rights be firmly denied.

In the Ratifying Convention Wilson based his defense of the omission of a bill of rights on the general principle "that the supreme power of government was the inalienable and inherent right of the people"[26] and on the precise statement of the preamble to the Constitution that "We, the people of the United States, do ordain, constitute, and establish. . . ." "Those who can ordain and establish," he submitted "may certainly repeal or annul the work of government, which in the hands of the people, is like clay in the hands of the potter, and may be molded into any shape they please." This single phrase in the preamble, he contended, "contains the essence of all the bills of rights that have been or can be devised; for it establishes at once, that in the great article of government, the people have a right to do what they please." Contrasting the Constitution with that other great document of liberty, Magna Carta, he pointed out that as the basis of Magna Carta was no more than the gift of the king the people of Britain would naturally seek "to obtain some evidence of their formal liberties by the concessions of petitions and bills of right." "But here," he went on, "the fee simple of freedom and government is declared to be in the people, and it is an inheritance with which they will not part."

Not surprisingly, the advocates of a bill of rights did not accept a deduction from the words of a phrase in a preamble as having sufficient legal force to render more precise guarantees superfluous, and Wilson was obliged to spend a great deal of time and effort in trying to assuage fears on this matter. He attempted to dismiss the Antifederalist argument as frivolous, choosing to regard an explanation of the omission of a bill of rights as "unnecessary and out of order," and declaring that the onus lay with his opponents to show why it should be included. Of the proceedings in this matter in the Federal Convention he asserted that it "never struck the mind of any member . . . till, I believe, within three days of the dissolution of that body, and even then of so little account was the idea that it passed off in a short conversation, without introducing a formal debate or assuming the shape of a motion." The reason for this apparent neglect was that to have included in the Constitution of the national government a device merely to demonstrate "that any power not mentioned in the Constitution was reserved," would have been thought "an insult to the common understanding of mankind." Wilson went on to assert that in civil government bills of rights were "unnecessary and useless," citing in proof the seven states[27] with no bills of rights where freedom was quite as secure as elsewhere. He then made a point of more practical substance. It was, he said, impracticable to insert a bill of rights, "for who will be bold enough to undertake to enumerate all the rights of the people?" Anything accidentally omitted would be presumed to be purposely omitted, and by implication to have been given to the government, which was not "the principle of the proposed Constitution."

The Antifederalists—notably Smilie and Whitehill—attempted at great length to refute Wilson's contention that the democratic nature of the new government rendered a bill of rights "not only unnecessary, but improper." However sound his logic, if his premises were not understood it was difficult for his arguments to be entirely convincing. His opponents regarded him mistrustfully, and remained, as indeed did most of his fellow citizens throughout the United States, unconvinced that a bill of rights was not a necessary safeguard against governmental tyranny. Smilie and Whitehill in particular attacked Wilson's idea that the people themselves were a sufficient restraint on the government, which they had "a right to alter and abolish." "The truth is," said Smilie, "that unless some criterion is established by which it could be easily and constitutionally ascertained how far our governors may proceed, and by which it might appear when they transgress their jurisdiction, this idea . . . is a mere sound without substance."[28] The Constitution was indeed ratified as it stood, but the controversy over this particular issue probably increased rather than diminished support in Pennsylvania for a bill of rights.

Two matters of detail concerning a bill of rights—jury trial in civil cases and freedom of the press—aroused particular acrimony. Wilson clearly expected both to be important elements in the Antifederalist attack, as he had given them particular attention in his State House Yard speech.[29] The discussion of jury trial in civil cases occupied the whole of one day, when "twice in the course of it the members came to personalities, and once almost to blows."[30] On this occasion Wilson and Findley were involved in a long altercation over the question of jury trial in Sweden. The Antifederalists contended that it was the intention of the framers of the Constitution to abolish juries in all civil cases. This contention Wilson asserted "must proceed from ignorance or something worse." He proclaimed himself sincerely to be devoted to the principle of trial by jury, declaring that "it has excellencies that entitle it to a superiority over any other mode, in cases to which it is applicable."[31] He pointed out, however, that jury trial was not appropriate in all cases and, moreover, that practice in this matter differed among the various states. The fact that the Constitution did not mention jury trial in civil cases did not mean that it wished to abolish it under the Federal government; it was a matter left to the legislature to decide, and the legislature would certainly provide for jury trial in all appropriate circumstances. "Where the people are represented," he argued, "—where the interest of government cannot be separate from that of the people (and this is the case in trial between citizen and citizen), the power of making regulations with respect to the mode of trial may certainly be placed in the legislature; for I apprehend that the legislature will not do wrong in an instance from which they can derive no advantage."[32] It was generally accepted, he maintained, "that there are some cases that should not come before juries; there are others that in some of the states never come before juries, and in those states where they do come before them, appeals are found necessary, the facts reexamined, and the verdict of the jury sometimes is set aside." He went on to assert his opinion that "in all cases, where the cause has come originally before a jury, . . . the last examination ought to be before a jury likewise."[33]

It is easy to understand Wilson's indignation at the assertion that jury trial in all civil cases was deliberately to be suppressed. "It is a charge," he vehemently asserted, "not only unwarrantable, but cruel;

the idea of such a thing, I believe, never entered into the mind of a single member of that convention; and I believe further that they never suspected there would be found within the United States a single person that was capable of making such a charge."[34] Wilson, most reluctantly, was obliged to give a great deal of effort to rebutting what he regarded as trivial, irrelevant, contradictory, distorted, or otherwise misleading arguments, and he was exceedingly irritated especially at the tendency of Antifederalists to criticize clauses of the constitution out of context.

Wilson's dismissal of the contention that liberty of the press and the rights of conscience were threatened was almost contemptuous. Congress was not endowed with the authority to curtail freedom of the press or to attack rights of conscience; consequently "when there is no power to attack, it is idle to prepare the means of defense."[35] Unless his opponents could show in what way Congress could interfere with the liberty of the press or of conscience he refused bluntly "to enter into a minute investigation of the matter."[36] This was a rare, possibly unique, occasion when Wilson showed less prescience than his antagonists.

The issues of the relationship between state and federal governments, and between government and the people as reflected in the controversy over a bill of rights, were both fundamental to Wilson's view of the proper form of political society. Though in both matters he achieved at the time a nominal victory, in that the Constitution as ratified expressed both what Wilson believed was his interpretation of the federal-state relationship, and made no provision for a bill of rights; nevertheless in a sense his was merely a Pyrrhic victory, in that a civil war had yet to be fought to establish clearly the principle that ultimate sovereignty rested with the people of the United States and, somewhat paradoxically, within Wilson's own lifetime there was adopted a bill of rights which in effect was a repudiation of his concept that the people could be the effective source of all political power.

In considering Wilson's approach in the ratifying convention to questions of the structure of government, it is necessary to bear in mind the fact that he had been for many years involved in controversy over the structure of government in Pennsylvania. It was not only the proposed Constitution of the United States that was at issue; also involved was the question of radical reform of the Pennsylvania constitution. But in order to appreciate properly Wilson's arguments in the ratifying convention it must be kept in mind that under the existing constitution of Pennsylvania—that of 1776—a unicameral legislature was almost supreme, without the checks on power contained in the proposed national Constitution. The separation of government into three approximately coequal branches formed no part of the Pennsylvania system, and even the all-powerful popular legislature was not divided into two houses. In defending the Constitution of the United States Wilson was indirectly but transparently attacking the principles of the constitution of Pennsylvania, while conversely his antagonists in the convention were defending the Pennsylvania constitution, to which in fact they often alluded.

On the subject of the division of government into three branches, Wilson was far more explicit than he had needed to be in the Federal Convention. He extolled the manner in which legislative, executive, and judicial powers were kept apart. Though recognizing that the separation was not as complete as he himself would have wished, he maintained that nowhere else in the world was "this great principle so strictly adhered to or marked with so much precision and accuracy as in this." It was superior to the division of powers under the British system, and more perfect than any other government known to him. He emphasized the belief he shared with most other contemporary American political thinkers that this division of powers was essential if tyranny was to be avoided.[37] Moreover, again expounding a conventional view, he emphasized the positive virtues of a proper division of powers; vigor and responsibility in a single executive; experience in a Senate elected in rotation for six years; and benevolence and attachment to the people from a House of Representatives biennially chosen by them. In praising the virtues of a bicameral legislature Wilson equally clearly had in mind the deficiencies of the Pennsylvania constitution. He began his remarks on the subject by expressing his belief that they "will apply to mankind in every situation." The gist of them was that all men will act "with more caution, and perhaps more integrity," if what they do is "under the inspection and control of another, than when they are not." Accordingly the bicameral Congress of the United States would conduct itself "with a degree of circumspection not common in single bodies, where nothing more is necessary to be done than to carry the business through among themselves, whether it be right or wrong." Wilson believed the quality of legislation would be greatly improved by the checks provided by a bicameral legislature as well as by the executive veto. "In compound legislatures," he contended, "every object must be submitted to a distinct body, not influenced by the arguments, or warped by the prejudices of the other. . . . As there will be more circumspection in forming the laws, so there will be more stability in the laws when made. . . . Though two bodies may not possess more wisdom or patriotism than what may be found in a single body, yet they will necessarily introduce a greater degree of precision. An undigested and inaccurate code of laws is one of the most dangerous things that can be introduced into any government." Then in a rare direct reference to the Pennsylvania constitution he went on, "The force of this observation is well known by every gentleman that has attended to the laws of this state."[38]

In defending the decision of the Federal Convention with regard to the Senate, Wilson was faced with a particular difficulty in that two of the main criticisms leveled against it—that it was in general too powerful, and that its treaty-making power in particular was inappropriate to it—reflected views he shared with the Antifederalists, and which he had expressed in the Federal Convention. The Senate, with regard to the method of its election, its balance of representation, and the powers it was to exercise, was the part of the proposed Constitution with which he was least happy. Yet he was obviously obliged to defend it against its detractors in the ratifying convention. In doing so he did not attempt to conceal the fact that if he had had his way the Senate would have taken a somewhat different form, and that with regard to its powers, if not its composition, the criticisms of the Antifederalists would largely have been met. It was, however, part of a package, and if not the best possible arrangement, at least it was a reasonably good one, and in any event the best that could be obtained. Wilson explained his attitude succinctly and precisely. "I am not," he said, "a blind admirer of this system. Some of the powers of the senators are not with me the favorite parts of it, but as they stand connected with other parts, there is still security against the efforts of that body: It was with great difficulty that security was obtained, and I may risk the conjecture that if it is not now accepted, it never will be obtained again from the same states. Though the Senate was not a favorite of mine, as to some of its powers, yet it was a favorite with a majority in the Union, and we must submit to that majority, or we must break up the Union."[39] On the particular issue of the power of senators, Wilson could point out that to believe that they had been given powers "better . . . distributed in other parts of the system," was by no means the same as to believe, as some did, that the Senate had been given the opportunity of acquiring tyrannical power. The check provided by the House of Representatives and the president would be enough to prevent this; the danger of tyranny from the existing unicameral national Congress was obviously much greater, and accordingly objections that the Senate would have excessive power "came with a bad grace from . . . those who prefer the present Confederation, and who wish only to increase the powers of the present Congress."[40] Moreover, he asserted "though in this system, the distinction and independence of power is not adhered to with entire theoretical precision, yet it is more strictly adhered to than in any other system of government in the world."[41]

In attempting to justify the treaty-making power of the Senate, Wilson acknowledged that he was presenting a case which he did not fully believe in.[42] In the Federal Convention he had regarded treaty-making as essentially a legislative act, and therefore one requiring the participation of both houses of Congress, as well as of the president. Now, however, he had to expound fairly an argument he had recently rejected. This he did, though both implicitly and explicitly he revealed his real views:[43]

> Some gentlemen are of opinion that the power of making treaties should have been placed in the legislature at large; there are, however, reasons that operate with a great force on the other side. Treaties are frequently (especially in time of war) of such a nature that it would be extremely improper to publish them, or even commit the secret of their negotiation to any great number of persons. For my part I am not an advocate for secrecy in transactions relating to the public; not generally even in forming treaties, because I think that the history of the diplomatic corps will evince, even in that great department of politics, the truth of an old adage, that "honesty is the best policy," and this is the conduct of the most able negotiators; yet sometimes secrecy may be necessary, and therefore it becomes an argument against committing the knowledge of these transactions to too many persons.

He was, of course, making what was the general assumption at that time, that the legislative branch would be actively involved in the negotiation of treaties; but even if that were not to happen it would still be a violation of principle if the legislative act of ratification were performed by one branch only of the Congress. Wilson was always well aware of this, and his attempts to obscure it were not very effective. "It well deserves to be remarked," he averred, straining his argumentative ingenuity to the limit of plausibility, "that though the

House of Representatives possess no active part in making treaties, yet their legislative authority will be found to have strong restraining influence upon both president and Senate. In England, if the king and his ministers find themselves, during their negotiation, to be embarrassed because an existing law is not repealed, or a new law is not enacted, they give notice to the legislature of their situation, and inform them that it will be necessary, before the treaty can operate, that some law be repealed, or some be made. And will not the same thing take place here? Shall less prudence, less caution, less moderation, take place among those who negotiate treaties for the United States than among those who negotiate them for the other nations of the earth?" That he should be forced to adopt an argument so unworthy of him is perhaps the measure of his uneasiness. Equally lacking in conviction was another contention, that negotiations with foreign nations were often prolonged, especially when the other party was three thousand miles away, and it was unreasonable to expect "that the legislature should be in session during this whole time." The most plausible of his arguments, bearing in mind the principle involved, was that the Senate represented both the states and the people, the one immediately, the other mediately, and that as the president also must concur, there did in fact exist a system of checks sufficient "to produce a security to the people."

Wilson did not expect the treaty-making function—the United States being "happily removed from the vortex of European politics"[44]—to engage the Senate more than very infrequently, and therefore the charge made by the Antifederalists that the Senate would have to be constantly in session, at the public expense, had no foundation. With the only other powers apart from legislating being those of trying impeachments and concurring in presidential appointments where in any event there was provision for the filling of vacancies, subject to later confirmation, during its recess, the Senate would rarely have to sit longer than the House of Representatives. Nor did he regard seriously the allegation that senators would be able to enrich themselves, since they could not under the constitution receive any money not paid to them out of the public treasury, and could not "vote to themselves a single penny, unless the proposition originates from the other house."[45]

He could not resist the opportunity to reaffirm his objection, in which he was now supported by some Antifederalists, to the unequal representation in the Senate. The states, he again remarked, "ought to be represented according to their importance," but, he emphasized, "in this system there is considerable improvement; for the true principle of representation is carried into the House of Representatives, and into the choice of the president; and without the assistance of one or the other of these, the Senate is inactive, and can do neither good nor evil."[46]

The issue of the presidency appears to have aroused comparatively little controversy. Wilson began his defense of the presidency by stressing its importance, through the presidential veto, as a further restraint on the legislature, and he emphasized that the significance of the veto was enhanced by the fact that by the manner of his election the president represented the people of all the United States, and would be free from sectional prejudices. Moreover, the president was likely to have fuller information than Congress, having immediate access to all foreign and domestic records and official communications, and to "the advice of the executive officers in the different departments of the general government."[47] There was little to dispute here; nor was there any significant objection to the method of electing the president.

Nevertheless, Wilson wanted to say something about an important issue in which he had played a significant part and which, he declared, had caused the Federal Convention more difficulty and perplexity than any other feature of the system. Accordingly he expounded to the convention the problems which had confronted the Federal Convention in this matter. He discussed the alternative of selection by the legislature, the length of a presidential term, and the question of reeligibility, in a manner entirely in accordance with the position he had taken in the Federal Convention. He emphasized, naturally, the essentially democratic nature of the method of choosing a president. "The choice of this officer," he said, "is brought as nearly home to the people as is practicable; with the approbation of the state legislatures, the people may elect with only one remove. . . ." The consequential advantages, he claimed, were avoidance of corruption, and less exposure "to the lesser evils of party and intrigue," which in fact the government when organized would undoubtedly take steps to counteract![48]

There seems to have been some slight controversy over the question of a multiple executive, or association with the president of a council, sufficient at least for Wilson to feel obliged to stress the conventional arguments against multiple executives—notably the facts that a single executive must bear full responsibility for his actions and cannot shift the blame for any shortcomings or misdeeds on to others, and that single command tends to produce vigor in the conduct of government. "We well know," he said, "what numerous executives are; we know there is neither vigor, decision, nor responsibility in them."[49]

The most serious criticism leveled against the proposals regarding the executive branch was that the powers of the president "are so trifling that the president is no more than the tool of the Senate." Wilson seems to have been surprised by this argument; what he had been expecting was an attack on the president as a monarchical power. He contended that had the powers of the president been extended in a way the opposition in the ratifying convention seemed to want—by giving him an exclusive treaty-making power and the authority to make appointments with the advice only of a Council of State—then some members of the Federal Convention would have contended that Congress was the tool of the President. His refutation of the criticism seems to have been improvised, in that it lacks the thorough, vigorous, and polished qualities of most of his prepared statements. "I do not apprehend this to be the case," he responded, "because I see that he may do a great many things independent of the Senate; and with respect to the executive powers of government in which the Senate participates, they can do nothing without him. Now I would ask, which is most likely to be the tool of the other? Clearly, Sir, he holds the helm, and the vessel can proceed neither in one direction nor another without his concurrence." Wilson, however, was on the whole well pleased with the attitude shown by his opponents to the issue of the presidency. "Upon the whole of the executive," he said, "it appears that the gentlemen in opposition state nothing as exceptionable but the deficiency of powers in the president, but rather seem to allow some degree of political merit in this department of government."[50]

The Pennsylvania Ratifying Convention gave Wilson his first opportunity other than that offered very inadequately by the Federal Convention of expressing his far-reaching views about the nature and powers of the judicial branch of the federal government. His reply to the Antifederalist objection that under the constitution judicial powers were coextensive with legislative powers was forthright and unequivocal. They were, and so they should be. The complaint of Whitehill that laws passed by Congress may be inconsistent with the Constitution, and "that therefore the powers given to the judges are dangerous," he answered by asserting that it was the opposite inference that was the true one. "If a law," he said, "should be made inconsistent with those powers vested by this instrument in Congress, the judges, as a consequence of their independence, and the particular powers of government being defined, will declare such law to be null and void. For the power of the Constitution predominates. Anything, therefore, that shall be enacted by Congress contrary thereto, will not have the force of law."[51]

He had already a few days earlier expressed his view of judicial supremacy in constitutional interpretation in a more sophisticated if less politically effective form. He had then argued:

> In order to give permanency, stability, and security to any government, I conceive it of essential importance that its legislature should be restrained; that there should not only be what we call a passive, but an active power over it; for of all kinds of despotism, this is the most dreadful and the most difficult to be corrected. . . . I say, under this Constitution, the legislature may be restrained and kept within its prescribed bounds by the interposition of the judicial department. . . . I had occasion on a former day to state that the power of the Constitution was paramount to the power of the legislature acting under that Constitution. For it is possible that the legislature, when acting in that capacity, may transgress the bounds assigned to it, and an act may pass in the usual mode notwithstanding that transgression; but when it comes to be discussed before the judges, when they consider its principles, and find it to be incompatible with the superior powers of the Constitution, it is their duty to pronounce it void; and judges independent, and not obliged to look to every session for a continuance of their salaries, will behave with intrepidity and refuse to the act the sanction of judicial authority.[52]

The issue of the judicial power remained in controversy throughout the process of ratification, and in the closing stages Wilson felt it necessary to reemphasize his point, "that the judicial were commensurate with the legislative powers; that they went no further, and that they ought to go so far."[53]

On one issue involving the judicial branch, Wilson was outwitted, or nearly so, by his opponents. Wilson emphasized the importance of the independence of judges, appointed during good behavior, on which he believed to depend "public happiness, personal liberty, and private property."[54] Findley, to Wilson's evident embarrassment, argued late in the convention that under the Constitution the judges would not be sufficiently independent because they may hold other offices, and though independent as judges may depend for their other offices on the legislature. This was a damaging attack, as Wilson, very probably partly for reasons of personal aspiration, strongly favored permitting judges to hold additional posts, and the Constitution admittedly deliberately avoided any prohibition. Similarly, Wilson pointed out, many states, though not Pennsylvania, did not preclude judges from other appointments as they did not wish to "limit the usefulness of their best men, or exclude them from rendering such services to their country, for which they are found eminently qualified." But he clearly had to find a constitutional answer to Findley's criticism. He admitted the point was one that had never occurred to him, and asserted that it had not occurred to Findley either until a few days previously. The best answer he could make, after suggesting that Findley's argument was a "little wiredrawn," was that "the legislature can appoint to no office; therefore the dependence could not be on them for the office, but rather on the president and Senate;" but, he continued, "these cannot add the salary, because no money can be appropriated but in consequence of a law of the United States. No sinecure can be bestowed on any judge, but by the concurrence of the whole legislature and of the president," and he "could not think this an event that will probably happen."[55]

On the subject of the jurisdiction of federal courts, Wilson gave especial attention to the issues of jurisdiction in cases arising under treaties, or involving controversies between a state and citizens of another state, or concerning states or their citizens in controversy with a foreign state or its citizens. On the issue of treaties, he emphasized the supreme importance of their scrupulous observation, citing and justifying the British refusal to evacuate the Northwest posts because of treaty violations on the debt issue by various states. "This clause," he claimed, "will show the world that we make the faith of treaties a constitutional part of the character of the United States; that we secure its performance no longer nominally, for the judges of the United States will be enabled to carry them into effect, let the legislatures of the different states do what they may." Whatever the economic or political objections no one could seriously criticize Wilson's position on legal grounds.

On the issue of controversies between a state and citizens of another state, however, Wilson was on much more highly controversial ground. The issue involved will be considered later, in dealing with the case of *Chisholm* v. *Georgia,* in which Wilson played a major part. It is interesting here, however, to observe that he tried in the Pennsylvania Ratifying Convention to dismiss the matter as though it were of only minor importance. His comment was simply, "When this power is attended to, it will be found to be a necessary one. Impartiality is the leading feature in this Constitution; it pervades the whole. When a citizen has a controversy with another state, there ought to be a tribunal where both parties may stand on a just and equal footing." While he may be thought evasive in saying no more about what eventually emerged as an issue of fundamental importance, it should nevertheless be borne in mind that the implications seem to have passed largely unobserved until he himself made them explicit several years later, in the majority opinion in *Chisholm* v. *Georgia.*

The jurisdiction of the federal courts in cases "between citizens of different states," and "between a state, or the citizens thereof, and foreign states, citizens or subjects," Wilson chose to discuss together in that they involved the same issues, those of the restoration and maintenance of public and private credit and the consequential growth of industry and commerce. He expected opposition to these provisions, and to moderate it he pointed out that in those cases there was no compulsion to resort to federal rather than to state courts, the provision being merely permissive. In any event, implicitly assuming that impartial justice was everyone's desire, he felt that so long as men of ability and integrity were appointed as federal judges, no one need feel any apprehension as "the government can have no interest in injuring the citizens." His basic defense of the provisions was that otherwise public and private credit could not be restored. Foreigners, as well as Americans, needed to "have a just and impartial tribunal to which they may resort." Imagine, for instance, the feelings of a merchant whose property was "at the mercy of the laws of Rhode Island," or of a creditor whose debts were at the mercy of tender laws of certain other states. Though under the Constitution major iniquities could be restrained, not every means of avoiding payment of debts could be safeguarded against; there could be instalment acts, and similar measures which might "destroy the very sources of credit." "Is it not," he went on, "an important object to extend our manufactures and our commerce? This cannot be done unless a proper security is provided for the regular discharge of contracts. This security cannot be obtained, unless we give the power of deciding upon those contracts to the general governments." Without such security, an object he regarded as particularly desirable could not be obtained. This was "the improvement of our domestic navigation, the instrument of trade between the several states." "That decay of private credit," he asserted, "which arose from the destruction of public credit by a too inefficient general government will be restored, and this valuable intercourse among ourselves must give an increase to those useful improvements that will astonish the world."

The security afforded American citizens through access to the federal courts ought in justice, Wilson maintained, to be extended to foreigners. Moreover, the advantage thereby accruing to the United States would be considerable, through the good will it would engender. It might even be a means of preserving peace, as otherwise a foreign creditor might find himself with no redress except an appeal to his own government which, unable to intervene with the particular state, might feel obliged to resort to war. "If," he observed, "the United States are answerable for the injury, ought they not to possess the means of compelling the faulty state to repair it? They ought, and this is what is done here. For now, if complaint is made in consequence of such injustice, Congress can answer, 'Why did not your subject apply to the general court, where the unequal and partial laws of a particular state would have had no force?' "[56]

As well as expounding the general principles of the Constitution and replying in advance to anticipated objections, Wilson had to answer specific criticisms on a number of points. Taxation, as was to be expected, was a particularly sensitive issue, and he found it necessary to go to some trouble to allay the fears the Antifederalists were seeking to arouse. According to the opposition, the people of the United States were facing the threat of "hosts of tax gatherers that will swarm through the land," perhaps backed by military force. Wilson forecast that direct taxation would be reduced, "at least in proportion to the increase of the other objects of revenue," and stressed the importance of the power granted to Congress to impose and collect imposts, which would become the major source of revenue. This he argued was "the easiest, most just, and most productive mode of raising revenue,"[57] and moreover, it was one that would arouse little discontent as it was in effect voluntary, in that no one was compelled to buy more than he wanted, and since the tax was included in the price of the commodity it might be effectively concealed. Furthermore, much of the revenue from imposts would in effect come from foreigners. He did not believe that the consumer always ultimately paid the import duty on a commodity; sometimes it was effectively paid by the importer, and sometimes even by the foreign exporter. However, Wilson envisaged that Congress would find it necessary to impose taxes in addition to an impost. But he refuted vigorously the argument that a swarm of officials would need to be appointed to collect the revenue, asserting that fewer officials than were at present employed to collect taxes by the various states would be needed by state and federal governments combined when, as he seemed to envisage, the federal government should become the main revenue collecting agency. The cost of government would also be reduced in another way, in that state legislatures would no longer have to spend the vast amount of time at present spent on discussing requisitions from Congress, and no one acquainted "with the expense of long and frequent sessions of assembly" would doubt that a considerable saving of public money would result. "There will be," said Wilson in conclusion, "many sources of revenue, and many opportunities for economy, when the business of finance shall be administered under one government; the funds will be more productive, and the taxes, in all probability, less burthensome than they are now."

Wilson's answer to the objection to the power given to the federal government to raise and maintain standing armies was that Congress was not *required* to do this, and that Congress, being based on the same source of authority—the people—as the state legislatures, would no more be likely to want to do so unnecessarily than they were. "We must not," he reminded his hearers on this, as on so many other occasions, "lose sight of the great principle upon which this work is founded. The authority here given to the general government flows from the same source as that placed in the legislatures of the several states." For purely practical reasons he considered that the power to raise and keep an army in peacetime was vitally necessary to any national government. Only in that way could the people be safeguarded against internal and external dangers. "When we consider," he declared, "the situation of the United States, we must be satisfied that it will be necessary to keep up some troops for the protection of the western frontiers and to secure our interest in the internal navigation of that country." Moreover, in providing a deterrent against foreign aggression, a small standing army would in fact be a measure of economy as it would "prevent the occasion for larger standing armies." No government in the world, he asserted after what he said had been careful investigation, was without the power to raise and maintain a standing army. "A government without the power of defense! —It is a solecism!"[58]

The clause in the proposed Constitution that empowered Con-

gress "to make all laws which shall be necessary and proper" for carrying its assigned powers into execution caused Wilson some little
difficulty, and he avoided any lengthy discussion of its implications.
He denied the charge that the clause gave Congress a general power to
legislate, but emphasized that it was essential that Congress have the
power to carry into effect the laws made under the powers constitutionally vested in it. When it was pointed out that Congress itself
would be the judge of what was necessary and proper he was even more
evasive, asserting simply but emphatically that the powers of Congress were limited to those defined in the Constitution and that the
effect of the "necessary and proper" clause was clearly limited to carrying into effect those defined powers. "It is," he said, "saying no more
than that the powers we have already particularly given, shall be effec-
tually carried into execution."[59] It is difficult to suppose that Wilson
did not perceive that the implications of the clause might carry the
legislative power of Congress beyond the limit acceptable to many
members of the ratifying convention, but for him to have revealed this
might well have had damaging consequences.

The treason clause of the Constitution was one in which Wilson
had a very particular interest. It was a matter that had given him
concern ever since the Carlisle treason trial in 1778.[60] It is in fact
likely that it was Wilson who was primarily responsible for the treason
clause in the Constitution, the effect of which was to safeguard the
citizen against oppressive action by a government exploiting, as had
frequently happened elsewhere, a broadly defined law of treason.
Treason in the Constitution was defined narrowly, and the accused
safeguarded against improper conviction. Wilson did not need to
convince his opponents of the merits of the case, but he clearly was
anxious to expound a matter so important to him. "You will find," he
said, "the current running strong in favor of humanity. For this is the
first instance in which it has not been left to the legislature to extend
the crime and punishment of treason so far as they thought proper.
This punishment, and the description of this crime, are the great
sources of danger and persecution on the part of government against
the citizen. Crimes against the state! and against the officers of the
state! History informs us that more wrong may be done on this subject
than on any other whatsoever." He then stated, with evident pride,
the unique safeguards in the Constitution against oppressive use by
the government of the law of treason. "But," he continued, "under
this Constitution, there can be no treason against the United States,
except such as is defined in this Constitution. The manner of trial is

clearly pointed out; the positive testimony of two witnesses to the same overt act, or a confession in open court, is required to convict any person of treason. And after all, the consequence of the crime shall extend no further than the life of the criminal; for no attainder of treason shall work corruption of blood, or forfeiture, except during the life of the person attainted."[61]

The provisions of the Constitution that touched on the slavery issue gave rise to some confusion and misunderstanding, which Wilson was able quickly to dispel. The importance of the discussion of this issue in the ratifying convention lies rather in the revelation of Wilson's own attitude toward slavery. He rarely committed himself on this issue, which does not seem to have concerned him deeply, but when he did he took a strong antislavery line. He was at least a convinced theoretical opponent of slavery, though there is no clear evidence that he was ever emotionally aroused over the issue. In the ratifying convention he took a very optimistic view containing some unwarranted assumptions of the impending disappearance of slavery from every part of the United States. He expressed his regret that the Federal Convention was unable to go further at this time toward eliminating the "reproachful" slave trade,[62] but asserted his belief that within a few years Congress would "have the power to exterminate slavery from within our borders."[63] The provision for the elimination of the slave trade after 1808 would, he was sure, quickly lead to the disappearance of slavery itself. Pending total prohibition, he pointed out that slavery could not be introduced into the new states created under the terms of the Northwest Ordinance, and it was undoubtedly inconceivable to him that slavery would not have disappeared long before the creation of any new states outside the terms of the Northwest Ordinance. There is no doubt, despite the fact that for a time he owned a slave, that Wilson was a convinced opponent of slavery, but there was no fervor in his conviction.

Whatever point he was making, whatever feature of the Constitution he was elucidating, Wilson had constantly in mind his basic principle that all political authority emanated from the people. Never did he miss an opportunity of stressing this point. "A chain of connection with the people,"[64] throughout every part of the government was fundamental to the proposed system, in which, he asserted with the greatest possible emphasis, "all authority of every kind *is derived by* REPRESENTATION *from the* PEOPLE *and the* DEMOCRATIC *principle is carried into every part of the government,*" and it was one of the great virtues of the Constitution that "*it secures in the strongest manner the right*

of suffrage," which is fundamental to a republican form of government.[65] At the same time he believed, unlike many of his contemporaries, that everyone elected to Congress represented not just his
own district, but the community as a whole. This, however, was not a
point to which any great emphasis was given, and it is not certain that
Wilson regarded it as essential to the proper functioning of the new
system. Undoubtedly, however, he regarded it as a valuable attribute
in a member of Congress to be "one whose mind and heart are enlarged; who possesses a general knowledge of the interests of America,
and a disposition to make use of that knowledge for the advantage and
welfare of his country."[66]

In his general observations on the merits of the Constitution
Wilson put the greatest stress on the positive advantages to be gained
from its adoption, and gave comparatively little attention to the evil
consequences of rejection. He did, however, warn that rejection
would be followed by the certainty of economic decay in agriculture,
commerce, and industry and, in a reference to Shays' rebellion, by the
probability of "a return of those insurrections and tumults to which a
sister state was lately exposed."[67] Also, though he expressed it in the
positive form of strengthening American defenses, he warned of the
likelihood in course of time of attack by a foreign power if the Constitution were rejected and the opportunity of providing for effective
defense therefore lost. Moreover, the rejection of the Constitution
would leave the country exposed to the danger of serious conflict between various states, like that which had occurred between Pennsylvania and Connecticut over the question of the Wyoming valley.[68]

The glorious future of the United States, not the overcoming of
present difficulties, was the main theme of Wilson's peroration. But
apart from the interesting exception of internal improvements, which
clearly he envisaged as a federal function,[69] his emphasis was on the
nonmaterial, spiritual virtues that would arise from the adoption of
the new system. His vision was of the future, and more than once he
had urged his colleagues to "think not only of themselves, not only of
the present age, but of other, and of future times."[70] He looked to a
vast and rapid expansion of both population and territory, and in order
that the people of this enlarged society, reinforced by immigration as
well as by natural increase, should "live happy, free and secure," internal harmony and international respect were required, which only
the adoption of the Constitution could guarantee.

Wilson, moreover, had become a nationalist in the emotional as
well as in the political sense. He wished the United States to become a

true nation, which he believed the adoption of the Constitution would ensure. "This system," he said, "will at least make us a nation, and put it in the power of the Union to act as such. We will be considered as such by every nation in the world. We will regain the confidence of our own citizens and command the respect of others." Nationhood, however, was far more than a political convenience. It implied, ideally at least, a distinctive national character. "As we shall become a nation," said Wilson, "I trust that we shall also form a national character; and that this character will be adapted to the principles and genius of our system of government; as yet we possess none—our language, manners, customs, habits and dress, depend too much upon those of other countries. Every nation in these respects should possess originality." Americans, he went on to assert, possessed qualities unsurpassed elsewhere out of which a national character could be formed—energy, perseverance, industriousness, ambition, eagerness for knowledge, determination in adversity, and endurance under hardship. "From these materials," he continued, "what a respectable national character may be raised!" The language of Americans, he forecast, would become the "most generally known in the civilized world," and the prestige and influence of the United States would be greatly enhanced. Especially the great contributions made, and yet to be made, by Americans in "the science of government" would be read and absorbed by "the patriots and literati of every nation" and the United States in consequence would "take the lead in political knowledge."

Declaring that the probability of the United States attaining a position of moral leadership in the world was a subject in which he felt himself "lost in the contemplation of its magnitude," he expanded his theme into that of a world mission for America. "By adopting this system," he pronounced in conclusion, "we shall probably lay a foundation for erecting temples of liberty in every part of the earth. It has been thought by many that on the success of the struggle America has made for freedom will depend the exertions of the brave and enlightened of other nations. The advantages resulting from this system will not be confined to the United States; it will draw from Europe many worthy characters who pant for the enjoyment of freedom. It will induce princes, in order to preserve their subjects, to restore to them a portion of that liberty of which they have for so many ages been deprived. It will be subservient to the great designs of providence, with regard to this globe; the multiplication of mankind, their improvement in knowledge, and their advancement in happiness."[71]

The Federalists achieved in Pennsylvania a decisive victory, the

Constitution being ratified by a margin of exactly two to one. Disappointed Antifederalists in Wilson's former home town of Carlisle
thereupon burned him in effigy, an episode immediately followed by a
celebration by Carlisle Federalists at Mr. Joseph Postlethwaite's
tavern where, among many others, a toast to James Wilson was
drunk.[72]

Wilson's final act in the process of framing and inaugurating the
Constitution came on July 4, 1788, when there took place in
Philadelphia the Great Federal Procession.[73] It was a most elaborate,
highly organized affair. The procession contained an item composed of
ten gentlemen, walking arm in arm, representing the ten states which
had so far ratified the Constitution. To Wilson fell the honor of representing Pennsylvania. The central feature of the celebration was an
oration, also delivered by Wilson. Packed with erudite classical allu-
sions, it did not add any new dimension to his political thought, but
in the main repeated, in a more general and popular form, arguments
he had already often used. He made a point, however, of emphasizing
what he had always said was crucial to the success of the new
system—the duty of the citizens to participate responsibly in the
process of government. No one should feel that he can be of no value to
his country. Every citizen has a fundamental service to offer. "Allow
me," he exhorted the people of Philadelphia, "to direct your attention, in a very particular manner, to a momentous part, which by this
Constitution, every citizen will frequently be called to act. All those
in places of power and trust will be elected either immediately by the
people, or in such a manner that their appointment will depend ultimately on such immediate election. All the derivative movements of
government must spring from the original movement of the people
at large. If to this they give a sufficient force and a just direction, all the
others will be governed by its controlling power. To speak without a
metaphor, if the people, at their elections, take care to choose none
but representatives that are wise and good, their representatives will
take care, in their turn, to choose or appoint none but such as are wise
and good also. The remark applies to every succeeding election and
appointment. Thus the characters proper for public officers will be
diffused from the immediate elections of the people over the remotest
parts of administration." The importance of the "faithful and skilful"
discharge of this awesome responsibility could not be overstressed.
This duty, he said, "is the first concoction in politics; and if an error is
committed here, it can never be corrected in any subsequent process,"
with disease in the body politic the certain outcome. One vote, he

urged his audience to remember, may turn an election, and while in battle every soldier should consider the safety of the state to depend on him, so, "at an election, every citizen should consider the public happiness as depending on his single vote."

Wilson's last words in public on the subject of the Constitution, crudely flamboyant as they are in their description of that day's procession, nevertheless reflected the vision he had of the future of his country:

> The commencement of our government has been eminently glorious; let our progress in every excellence be proportionately great. It will—it must be so. What an enrapturing prospect opens on the United States! Placid husbandry walks in front, attended by the venerable plough. Lowing herds adorn our vallies; bleating flocks spread over our hills; verdant meadows, enamelled pastures, yellow harvests, bending orchards, rise in rapid succession from east to west. Plenty, with her copious horn, sits easy smiling, and in conscious complacency enjoys and presides over the scenes. Commerce next advances in all her splendid and embellished forms. The rivers, and lakes, and seas, are crowded with ships. Their shores are covered with cities. The cities are filled with inhabitants. The arts, decked with elegance, yet with simplicity, appear in beautiful variety, and well-adjusted arrangement. Around them are diffused, in rich abundance, the necessaries, the decencies, and the ornaments of life. With heartfelt contentment, industry beholds his honest labors flourishing and secure. Peace walks serene and unalarmed over all the unmolested regions—while liberty, virtue, and religion go hand in hand, harmoniously, protecting, enlivening, and exalting all! Happy country! May thy happiness be perpetual![74]

CHAPTER 8

*Concerning the
Pennsylvania constitution of
1790 and the fulfillment of
James Wilson's democratic
aspirations.*

The principles on which the Pennsylvania constitution of 1790 was based are even closer to those of Wilson than are those of the federal Constitution, and it is at least arguable that this document, for which he was unquestionably primarily responsible, represents his finest achievement. Widely acclaimed as the most liberal as well as the most effective of state constitutions, it became subsequently the model for others and was admired in Europe as representing the nearest approximation then attained to the ideal liberal political system.[1]

Yet at the time Wilson's adamant opposition to the ostensibly even more liberal constitution which that of 1790 replaced was regarded by many as clear evidence of his supposedly aristocratic prejudices. The constitution of 1776[2] was a center of fierce political controversy in Pennsylvania. While reflecting to an extreme degree the concept of power to the people it violated almost every principle of sound government which men like Wilson, Madison, and indeed the great majority of politically conscious Americans regarded as axiomatic. The 1776 constitution was narrowly doctrinaire in conception; it was based on a belief in the efficacy of pure democracy, and therefore elevated the power of the single-chamber legislature to a point which denied the validity of the principle of the separation of powers.

Despite the fact that Franklin, on doctrinaire grounds, gave the constitution his support, it would not be an exaggeration to claim that it tended toward the creation of a system based on an all-powerful legislature with an entrenched radical majority, which while ostensibly liberal and democratic reflected purposes that were decidedly illiberal. It was the view of most contemporary political thinkers, Wilson among them, that uncontrolled power, whether exercised by a single individual or a numerous legislature, inevitably produced tyranny, and this was the principal charge against the constitution of 1776. Commenting on the system of government, the *Pennsylvania Gazette*, reflecting probably directly the view of Wilson, declared in 1787: "All single governments are tyrannies—whether they be lodged in one man—a few men—or a large body of the people."[3] From the moment of the adoption of this constitution it became one of Wilson's major objectives to secure its replacement by one based on what to him were sound principles of government. After years of struggle in which considerable bitterness was aroused, the outcome was the adoption, in a spirit of general harmony, of the very different but equally democratic constitution which became so much admired. For this achievement Wilson was primarily responsible. It brought him, for the only time in his life, the esteem of the people of Pennsylvania whose interests and privileges, with those of the people of all America, he had consistently labored to advance and safeguard.

Almost from the moment of the inception of the 1776 constitution the Anticonstitutionalists, or Republicans as they later called themselves, began their effort to bring about its repeal, for a system of government so much at variance with sound principles could hardly be ameliorated by mere amendment. Moreover, a great many leading Republicans declared their unwillingness to accept any office under the constitution, and though it is unlikely that many would have been offered appointment they thereby became scapegoats, both with contemporaries and some historians of a later generation, for the evident failure of the system of government and the political chaos which Pennsylvania had to endure. The first attack on the constitution came soon after its adoption, when in October 1776 a protest meeting held in the Philosophical Society Hall unanimously condemned it.[4] The reasons put forward were that the power of the convention that framed it had not been derived from the people, that it did not treat the Christian religion "with proper respect," that it "unnecessarily" deviated from the former system in Pennsylvania, that it introduced "strange innovations" not desired by the people, that it differed in many important respects from every other form of government set up in America as a result of the Revolution, notably in defying the principle of the separation of powers by creating a single legislative body on which both the executive and the judiciary were dependent. The meeting went on to consider means of rendering the constitution inoperative and securing its replacement.

Wilson quickly emerged as a recognized leader of the opponents of this constitution. An attempt in April 1777, with Wilson clearly involved, to establish a new form of government was frustrated partly, it seems, by the threat of force.[5] In May a more determined effort was made, when Wilson led a group of forty-two prominent citizens who had refused to take office under the 1776 constitution in petitioning the president of Pennsylvania and the Board of War for urgent reforms in face of imminent invasion.[6]

Exploiting the threatened advance into the state of Howe's army, the petitioners blamed the alleged extreme weakness of Pennsylvania on the bitter controversy aroused by the constitution, and suggested that the only remedy was the summoning of a new convention to draft a new constitution. "Weakness and languor" throughout the administration, and monetary inflation to an excessive degree in the economy, were the consequences of constitutional controversy, and only through the "election of a new convention for the purpose of altering and amending the constitution agreeable to the sentiments of a majority of the people" could Pennsylvania be put in a fit state to repel the enemy. Given this, they naively asserted, "unanimity and strength, the consequence of unanimity, will soon be restored to Pennsylvania."

The key to the proposal, and its political subtlety, lay in its demand for the *election* of this convention, unlike its predecessor, thereby in typical Wilsonian fashion making the people, not a band of radical politicians, the ultimate source of constitutional authority. The scheme failed, according to Wilson, through the public-spiritedness of his group in suspending their pressure on two occasions when the advance of Howe's forces produced a military crisis, but in the end, somewhat paradoxically, through the failure of the people to support the plan for a convention when their views were eventually solicited by an assembly dominated by supporters of the constitution.[7]

Wilson persisted with his campaign and in 1777 he claimed that most of the newly elected members of the assembly were disposed in favor of constitutional reform, and urged his friend Anthony Wayne to leave the army for the time being and return to Philadelphia, on the grounds that his presence there "during this important conjuncture, will be of signal service, in many respects, which we forbear to mention in a letter."[8] "Matters," he went on, "are now approaching to a crisis; and in a few weeks it will be determined whether the state of Pennsylvania shall be happy under a good constitution; or be oppressed by one, the most detestable that ever was formed. We need say no more to induce you to be with us." Wilson's hopes again were unrealized.

Early in the following year, however, he was actively engaged in organizing support for a constitutional referendum authorized by the assembly toward the end of 1778, only to be thwarted by the reversal of their previous decision by an assembly dominated by radicals becoming fearful of the outcome of the project.[9]

In 1780, however, signs began to appear that the Constitutionalist ascendancy in the assembly might be coming to an end. The Republicans gained many seats in the election of that year, and from this time the distrust with which they had been regarded by the people seems greatly to have diminished.[10] This was due partly to the success of the Bank of North America, with which Republicans were closely identified, and which discredited Constitutionalist accusations of corruption and inefficiency. But in the main it was the outcome of a change in tactics by the Republicans, who abandoned their uncompromising hostility to the constitution in favor of a policy based on expediency, which aimed at cautiously working from within the framework of the constitution in order to prepare the ground for its reform.[11]

The election of 1782 gave the Republicans for the first time a majority—though not a decisive one—in the assembly, and John Dickinson, with Wilson's support, was elected president of the Executive Council. The alarm of the Constitutionalists was reflected in the vehemence of their attacks in the press on Wilson and his colleagues, but nevertheless the Republican success was repeated in the election in 1783. This was a year of critical importance, as the constitution of 1776 provided for the election after seven years, and every seven years thereafter, of a Council of Censors whose function it was "to enquire whether the constitution has been preserved inviolate in every part," but which also had the power, provided two-thirds of those elected agreed, to summon a convention "if there appear to them an absolute necessity of amending any article of the constitution which may be defective, explaining such as may be thought not clearly expressed, and of adding such as are necessary for the preservation of the rights and happiness of the people." Even if not abused, this was a considerable power, and with the election to the Council of Censors coming in a year of Republican upsurge there was cause for Constitutionalist anxiety.

When it met, the Council of Censors appointed a committee "to report those articles of the constitution which are materially defective, and absolutely require alteration and amendment." To this committee was nominated Arthur St. Clair, one of Wilson's few close friends and one whose political views reflected his own. It would not be unwarrantable to regard Arthur St. Clair as the spokesman in the Council of Censors for James Wilson. The report of the committee was drafted mainly by St. Clair, and it contains nothing inconsistent with the views expressed on other occasions by Wilson. It criticized the constitution for vesting the supreme legislative authority in a unicameral legislature which, being unchecked, could enact unjust and tyrannous laws and could usurp both the executive and the judicial authority; for assigning the executive authority to a council rather than to an individual, for the reasons which Wilson later adduced in the Federal Convention; for restricting the tenure of office of judges of the Supreme Court and rendering them liable to removal at any time by the assembly, thus violating the principle of judicial independence; and for applying to various posts the principle of rotation in office, thus depriving the people of the right to choose the men they want and the state of efficient public servants.

All these objections could well have been made by Wilson, as could the proposals which followed from them. These were that the existing assembly be replaced by a bicameral legislature in which the Senate would be elected by freeholders and the lower house by freemen, with apparently no property qualification; that a governor be elected annually by those qualified to vote in elections to the lower house of the legislature; and that Supreme Court judges and judges of the Courts of Common Pleas be appointed by the governor to hold office during good behavior. The recommendations of the committee were accepted by a majority of the Council of Censors, but not by the two-thirds whose agreement was required before a constitutional convention could be summoned.[12]

After 1783 Pennsylvania reverted for a while to radical ascendancy, but in 1786 the Republicans recovered, and in the following year events in Philadelphia outside the assembly enormously increased the probability of an early reform of the political system. The Federal Convention, and the ratification of the national constitution by the state ratifying convention made it difficult for Pennsylvania to adhere to one system of government for the state, while endorsing a very different one for the nation. Federalists and Republicans were essentially the same group, and they immediately followed up their triumph in the federal and ratifying conventions by a renewed onslaught on the despised and now anachronistic constitution of 1776. To many this was at least as important as the establishment of a sound national constitution.

Wilson was in the forefront of what turned out to be the final attack on the old constitution, and he quickly established himself both in the public view and in the eyes of politicians directly involved in the matter as the leading protagonist of major constitutional reform. The intrigues and negotiations which culminated directly in reform seem to have begun in March 1789 when Wilson met with a few associates in the house of his friend Benjamin Rush and among them they organized a public campaign which helped to induce the assembly to summon a new constitutional convention.[13] It seems likely that, concurrently with this, Wilson entered into informal discussions with leading Constitutionalists in order to bring about the desired constitutional change without arousing acrimony. Certainly when the convention met, in November 1789, mutual forbearance marked the attitude of many on both sides.

A rapprochement between the erstwhile arch-opponents, James Wilson and William Findley, was the key to the success of the Pennsylvania Constitutional Convention. It was based on the discovery by Constitutionalist leaders that Wilson's association with the conservative element in Pennsylvania politics did not necessarily imply that he was antidemocratic or in general illiberal in his political views. This would have been evident to anyone who had been present in the Federal Convention. But the Constitutionalists in Pennsylvania had not been represented there, and as its proceedings were secret no means existed of ascertaining the opinions therein expressed by its members. Wilson's views were not revealed to the world until after the Federal Convention had ended, when they were given full publicity, especially in the ratifying convention where he was confronted by the men—notably Whitehill, Findley, and Smilie—who were ostensibly the leading adherents of the 1776 constitution. But in that assembly, and in his public speeches elsewhere on the federal Constitution, Wilson's sincerity was suspect, as it was supposed by many that his sole concern was with securing the adoption of a constitution believed by its opponents to be autocratic and excessively centralized, by arguments designed rather to allay misgivings by obscuring the truth than by disclosing forthrightly Wilson's real political principles.

How much preparation for the impending rapprochement had been made before November 1789 it is impossible to ascertain. It is unlikely that the process was complete by then, and very probably the conclusive stage was the disclosure by Wilson of his draft of a proposed new constitution—a draft which on several crucial issues revealed Wilson as the liberal democrat he professed to be, and which was compatible with the basic political ideas of the leading radicals. At the same time, for constructive harmony to be attained it was necessary also for Wilson to become convinced that the radical leaders were not so dedicated to the principles of the existing constitution that no others would be acceptable to them. The needed assurance was provided by Findley,[14] and it was the agreement between Wilson and Findley, based on mutual confidence and respect, that made possible the speedy adoption of a new constitution based on Wilsonian principles. There was created, essentially, a coalition of the center, designed either to conciliate or out-maneuver both the extreme radicals and the extreme conservatives, and though over one important issue intense conflict developed, in the end it achieved its purpose. The convention experienced the strange phenomenon of extreme forbearance by Wilson in his observations on the 1776 constitution—a prearranged tactic necessary to conciliate Constitutionalists—and the remarkable spectacle of Wilson voting with his recent enemies—Findley, Smilie, and Whitehill—on almost every issue.

That Wilson was well pleased with the constitution that emerged from the convention in 1790 he made abundantly clear in the lectures on the subject in the following year in the College of Philadelphia. It was, he believed, in many ways an improvement on the Constitution of the United States, and in the fundamental matter of the "correct distribution of the powers of government," he declared that it "approaches, if it does not reach, theoretic perfection."[15] Not only was it an improvement on the American Constitution; it approached what many political theorists in America had come to regard as a nearly ideal system—that of Anglo-Saxon England before the Norman Conquest. Wilson frequently extolled the Pennsylvania constitution as reflecting Anglo-Saxon concepts of government, notably in relation to democratic practices, though the comparison was based more on myth than on reality, and fallaciously identified Wilson's own ideals of government with those of pre-conquest England.

After the formal preliminaries, serious discussion of the principles on which the new constitution should be based began in the Committee of the Whole on December 2, when Wilson moved "that the legislature of this state should consist of more than one branch." On the following day, after inconsequential amendment, it was agreed almost unanimously. On December 4 Wilson moved that "the supreme executive power be vested in a single person" and obtained the unanimous endorsement of the committee. Also on December 4 Wilson moved "that the judges of the Supreme Court hold their commissions during good behavior and be independent as to their salaries," and this was adopted, with minor amendment, on the next day. Thus the theoretical basis of the constitution of 1776 had been totally rejected almost without dissent, and the way prepared for the adoption of a new system founded on very different principles. Retaining the initiative, Wilson then proposed "that the supreme executive department should have a qualified negative on the legislature," a proposal again overwhelmingly carried. The Committee of the Whole then unanimously resolved that there should be some revision of the Declaration of Rights contained in the 1776 constitution in order that "the rights of the people . . . may be more accurately defined and secured." In concurring with this resolution Wilson showed that his opposition to a bill of rights in the federal Constitution did not reflect opposition to bills of rights in general, but merely that, as he had at the time asserted, such guarantees in the federal Constitution were inappropriate.

When these five propositions had been formally endorsed by the convention a Committee of Nine was chosen to draft a detailed constitution in accordance with the principles laid down. The leading members of this committee were James Wilson, William Findley, and the man who on the central issue of representation became Wilson's most vigorous opponent, William Lewis.[16]

With general agreement on the structure of the new government, little occurred to arouse serious controversy until the question of the method of electing the Senate came before the convention. There was widespread agreement, whether on grounds of principle or expediency, that the very liberal franchise under the 1776 constitution, which amounted in effect to manhood suffrage, should be retained. A matter of minor controversy was over the residence qualification for eligibility for election as representative, when for what evidently were narrow political reasons the conservative faction led by Lewis wished ostensibly to liberalize the provision by requiring as a condition of eligibility merely residence in the electoral district at the time of the election, rather than for one year previously. Wilson, perhaps from principle rather than political expediency, supported Lewis and was opposed in this instance by his new allies, Findley, Smilie, and Whitehill. Lewis's amendment, which was overwhelmingly defeated, presumably was designed to facilitate the election of certain conservatives; hence the voting alignment on the issue. But Wilson could not have done other than support it, in line with two of his basic principles, that the best men should be available for election with the minimum of restriction, and likewise that the people should be able to choose with minimal restriction the men they want.

Some discussion of a point of detail took place over a clause which reflected another of Wilson's basic principles—that of "one man, one vote" illustrated by his concern that electoral districts should be as nearly as possible equal. Wilson's original draft provided for districts based on the number of taxable inhabitants—in practice the number of voters—and this was accepted without demur by the convention. An enumeration of taxable inhabitants was to be made periodically, and boundaries adjusted accordingly, and it was only over the length of this period that any controversy arose. After an initial enumeration in three years, Wilson had proposed ten-year intervals. It was proposed unsuccessfully to reduce this to five, with Wilson in opposition, and he thereupon proposed the uncharacteristically impractical compromise of a maximum of ten and a minimum of five years. Predictably, the compromise reached, with Wilson's support, was for seven-year intervals. This was not a matter of much consequence. Rather more important was an attempt made to limit the number of consecutive terms of service of representatives—a violation of the two Wilsonian principles just referred to—but this was comfortably if not overwhelmingly defeated.

The crucial issue in the Pennsylvania convention was the method of choosing senators—whether by direct or indirect election. Alexander Graydon, who was a member of the convention, records that this was "the subject of the warmest controversy," as it was regarded as representing a confrontation between "the principles of democracy and aristocracy" and it was believed "that great advantages would be gained to either that might prevail." Clearly the controversy in the convention was intense; Graydon reported that "a considerable degree of heat was engendered," and William Bradford reported that over this issue "very bitter feuds have taken place between [Wilson] and Lewis who have been personally abusive of each other."[17] Graydon was one of the very few conservatives who supported Wilson in this matter; he reports that "Wilson, hitherto deemed an aristocrat, a monarchist, and a despot, as all the Federalists were, found his adherents on this occasion, with a few exceptions, on the democratic or Antifederal side of the house."[18] This was the issue that was at the core of the Wilson-Findley pact, and which was central to the nature of the new constitution. Moreover, through it is revealed more clearly than any other episode in his career Wilson's view of the essentially democratic nature of sound government.

The Committee of Nine recommended a system of indirect election to the Senate, which was to be appointed by electors chosen by those eligible to vote for representatives. Defeated in the Committee of Nine Wilson carried the fight to the convention where on December 31 he made one of the most important speeches of his career. It is notable mainly for two reasons: first, as the fullest expression of Wilson's democratic principles; and secondly, as the clearest enunciation yet of the principle which Benjamin Rush called the "double representation of the people."

The relationship between the two houses of a bicameral legislature had been a troublesome theoretic problem underlying the constitution making of the revolutionary period. From the concept of separate organs of government to reflect aristocratic and democratic qualities there had emerged the idea of representation in one branch of property, in the other of "the people." Now in typically Wilsonian fashion was emerging a very different concept—that both houses represented the people, with each a check on the other to prevent the abuse of power so feared in unchecked legislatures and of which Pennsylvania had had recent experience. That two bodies chosen by the same people would in fact perform this function he did not doubt. This, he said in the convention, according to Graydon, would result from "the circumstances of their different spheres of election; of their sitting in different chambers, which would produce . . . an *esprit du corps* in each; and their being chosen for different periods, the representatives for one year, the senators for four years."[19] Later, in his law lectures, he made a similar point when he suggested that "the Senate will consider itself, and will be considered by the people, as the balance wheel in the great machine of government, calculated and designed to retard its movements, when they shall be too rapid, and to accelerate them, when they shall be too slow."[20] With their *esprit de corps* and their sense of public responsibility sharpened by the existence of another house, "they will be rivals in duty, rivals in fame, rivals for the good graces of their common constituents."[21] When more practical constitutional devices to ensure sound government could not be invented, Wilson from time to time resorted to metaphysical interpretations of human nature.

This concept of the double representation of the people rested on Wilson's view of the people as the proper source of all authority, not only as of right, but also as conducive to good government. This view he expounded at length in his speech of December 31. Pointing out that as the composition of the electorate was not in dispute, whether the election was to be for electors or directly for representatives, the only question at issue was "whether an intermediate grade of persons, called electors, should be introduced between the senators and the people," Wilson went on to expound his view of the nature of representation. Stressing, as he had on previous occasions, the mystical bond which ought to exist between voters and those they elected, and the nature of representation as a trust, he contended, irrefutably, that this trust could not properly exist unless legislators were elected directly by those they were to serve. Moreover, he went on, indirect election implied the choice of men other than those whom the voters would have elected without electors as intermediaries—"because, if the people and the electors would choose the same senators, there cannot be even a shadow of pretense for acting by the nugatory intervention of electors."[22]

In a passage that reveals him at his best as a political thinker, Wilson argued that progress in the development of better forms of government must necessarily be slow, especially with regard to "the discovery and improvement of the interesting doctrines and rules of election and representation," an aspect of government still only in its childhood. "And yet," he went on, "this is the subject which must form the basis of every government that is at once efficient, respectable, and free. The pyramid of government—and a republican government may well receive that beautiful and solid form—should be raised to a dignified altitude, but its foundations must, of consequence, be broad, and strong, and deep. The authority, the interests, and the affections of the people at large are the only basis on which a superstructure, proposed to be at once durable and magnificent, can be rationally erected." Wilson here used his favorite metaphor of the pyramid to support, not as in 1787 a strong federal government, but to support a strong and democratic state government, an indication at least that his desire was not, as some believe, to enhance the power of federal at the expense of state government, but rather to construct within their proper spheres strong government at both the federal and the state level and in both to provide the solid democratic basis on which he believed maximum efficiency to depend.

The right of suffrage, above all else, can "impart the true republican luster to freemen," and he wished the value of that right to be enhanced as much as possible. Deploring its neglect, and attributing that to the fact that in the colonial era only the lower house was elected—with the upper house and the governor having a veto—he now had cause to expect that the enhancement of the right, through direct election of senators, would "secure, in future, the merited attention to the exercise of it."[23] Proper appreciation of "the dignity and value" of the right of suffrage would have a "benign influence" on society. Men conscious of its importance would exercise it responsibly by, for instance, taking a close interest in "public men and public measures," which would be stimulating to the mind. Not every citizen would take an enthusiastic interest in politics, but even those with only a moderate interest would thereby derive greater pleasure from the reading of newspapers or from conversation. It is better, he affirmed, to discuss politics than to talk about local trivialities or "the frailties or the involuntary imperfections of a neighbor." Useful as even a casual interest would be in uplifting the moral tone of society, Wilson clearly hoped that most voters would take a more profound interest in public affairs, and would study carefully both the issues at stake in elections and the qualifications of candidates—something that would benefit the voter by endowing him with a consciousness of the interests of his country and benefit the candidate by inculcating in him a desire for "honest and well-earned fame" reflected in the votes of his constituents. The conclusions Wilson drew from his observations were "that the right of suffrage, properly understood, properly valued, properly cultivated, and properly exercised is a rich mine of intelligence and patriotism; that it is an abundant source of the most rational, the most improving, and the most endearing connection among the citizens; and that it is a most powerful and, at the same time, a most pleasing bond of union between the citizens and those whom they select for the different offices and departments of government." This being so, he concluded emphatically, there was no case for weakening the right of suffrage by the "interjection of electors."

Enumerating other advantages of direct election: that the choice of the people could not be less valid than that of electors since the latter derived all their authority from the people; that in direct election the interest of the whole people would be reflected, the choice therefore being more impartial and more certainly providing for the common advantage; and that, if all this were true, the choice of the people could not be less wise than the choice of the electors. He maintained that unless the advocates of indirect election could show a clear balance of advantage to that method, then "the predilection . . . will certainly be in favor of a choice by the people themselves." But this could not be shown, as in addition to the advantages inherent in direct election there were positive "inconveniences" associated with indirect election. These inconveniences were, briefly, the breaking of the emotional bond which ought to bind "those who impart power and those to whom power is imparted" which was "the brightest gem in the diadem of a republic."

Wilson then moved into a peroration that reflected the essence of his political thinking. "The great desideratum in politics is," he said, "to form a government, that will, at the same time, deserve the seemingly opposite epithets—efficient and free. I am sanguine enough to think that this can be done. But, I think, it can be done only by forming a popular government. To render government efficient, powers must be given liberally; to render it free as well as efficient, those powers must be drawn from the people, as directly and as immediately as possible." Accordingly, while in the executive and judicial branches it might be necessary in many instances to remove direct appointment one stage, though one only, from the people, even there such removals from the people should be kept to the minimum, and there was no case for introducing them into the election of the legislative branch, "the most powerful and, if ill constituted, the most dangerous of all." "Corruption and putridity," he asserted, "are more to be dreaded from the length, than from the strength, of the streams of authority."[24]

Wilson's attutude toward the remaining parts of the provisions for the legislative branch was predictable in the light of the attitudes he had displayed previously. On the question of the payment of representatives and senators, he adhered to the position he had taken in the Federal Convention by opposing a proposal that they be paid out of the revenues of the districts from which they were elected[25]—at the state level, as at the national level, resisting the view that representatives should be simply the dependent agents of their constituents. He concurred in the largely uncontroversial proposal that money bills originate in the lower house, and approved the provision for the keeping and publishing by each house of a journal of its proceedings, though as in the ratifying convention he resisted the proposal that if they have their votes revealed, members should have the right to have printed in the journal a full explanation of the reasons why they voted as they did.

The openness of the proceedings of the Pennsylvania legislature was a feature he particularly extolled in his exposition of the constitution in his law lectures. This openness was not limited to the publication of journals; it extended to public discussion in both houses, including committees of the whole, except when secrecy was necessary. "That the conduct and proceedings of representatives," he maintained, "should be as open as possible to the inspection of those whom they represent, seems to be, in republican government, a maxim of whose truth or importance the smallest doubt cannot be entertained."[26] This provision of the Pennsylvania constitution he cited as one of the several instances where it was an improvement on the Constitution of the United States.

Over the method of choosing the executive Wilson had little difficulty in securing the acceptance of the principle he had long favored, that of direct election of the governor by the same broad electorate responsible for the election of both houses of the legislature. The draft presented by the Committee of Nine recommended this method, and there is no evidence of any serious opposition to it. There was, however, an attempt made on doctrinaire grounds to dilute it, by associating with the governor a council which, whatever method of appointment might be chosen, could hardly be directly elected by the people. It was Findley who proposed the addition of a council as a check on the governor, and the issue produced the only instance of conflict between him and Wilson on a matter of major principle. Wilson thought the threat sufficiently serious to warrant a carefully prepared defense of the principle of the unity of a democratically elected executive branch.[27] Citing the view of Selden and Bacon that an executive authority shared by two wise men produces an unwise collective authority, he sought to allay the widespread prejudice against the executive branch derived from experience during the colonial era by contrasting a nonelected executive with one chosen directly by the people. The executive, as much as the legislative branch, should be thought of as representing the people. "The executive authority," he urged the convention to realize, "is now drawn from the same source, is now animated with the same principles, and is now directed to the same ends with the legislative authority. He who is to execute the laws will be as much the choice, as much the servant and, therefore, as much the friend of the people as he who is to make them. The character and interest and glory of the former will be as intimately and as necessarily connected with your happiness and prosperity as the character and interest and glory of the latter will be." Moreover, the impact on the people was greater in the execution than in the formulation of the laws, and the man entrusted with this responsibility ought not to be thought of as being "unconnected with the people," nor should he "be treated with a chilling indifference, or with a disgusting jealousy."

Defining the qualities of a well-constituted executive branch as energy, stability, economy, impartiality, responsibility, and patriotism, Wilson chose to discuss impartiality as the one most relevant in this instance. The question was whether impartiality would be best achieved by a governor with, or without, a council. With a characteristic rhetorical flourish he said of a governor with no council: "*By* the whole state this single executive magistrate will be chosen; *For* the whole state he will be appointed; *To* the whole state he will be responsible." Hence "toward the whole state he will be impartial." With the political naiveté he occasionally revealed he went on to affirm that no one could be elected governor unless the people were confident he would "promote the interests of the whole state," and that once elected, a governor would have an "irresistible" inducement not to disappoint the expectations of the electorate, not only for the sake of his future political interests, but also for—what always carried great weight with Wilson—his reputation with contemporaries and posterity. To promote the interest of the whole state was the "very quintessence of impartiality," while to sacrifice the whole to a part, or one part to another, was "the very quintessence of partiality."

Wilson then proceeded to consider the consequences of associating a council with the governor. The record of his arguments has not survived, but it is unlikely that they would differ significantly from those on the same theme enunciated in the federal and ratifying conventions. Who would compose this council, and the method of their appointment, were the main issues he discussed, leading to the inevitable conclusion that a single executive, untrammeled by a council, was the most reliable way of ensuring objectivity in this branch of government, by maintaining "the chain of connection" with the people.

Nothing else of any great consequence arose in the discussion of the executive branch. The original draft of the Committee of Nine had recommended that a three-fifths majority of each house be necessary to override the governor's veto of legislation. When it was proposed to amend this to a mere majority, Wilson made a counterproposal, which was carried, that it be amended to two-thirds. There was no issue of principle here, unless the slight increase in the influence of the governor be so regarded. Nor was of much consequence Wilson's opposition to a successful amendment that the governor "shall not be capable of holding his office longer than nine years in any term of twelve years" in place of the original proposal that he be forbidden to serve longer than nine years successively and be rendered ineligible thereafter to serve again until three years have elapsed—unless, that is, Wilson's attitude was intended to show his opposition, attested elsewhere, to any limitation on eligibility. Of some importance was an afterthought, to repair a possible oversight in the original draft, when Wilson successfully proposed the insertion of an additional clause, empowering the governor "to remit fines, and grant reprieves and pardons for crimes and offenses, except in cases of impeachment."[28]

There was one feature of the Pennsylvania constitution of 1790 which, while not arousing any controversy in the convention, was nevertheless subsequently deemed by Wilson worthy of special commendation as another instance of the superiority of that constitution over the Constitution of the United States.[29] This was the granting to the governor of the power to appoint all officers "whose appointments are not . . . otherwise provided for," without the need for confirmation by the Senate. In other words the constitution of Pennsylvania retained the purity of the principle of the separation of powers, whereas the Constitution of the United States on this point violated it.

Article III of the draft constitution concerned the extent of the franchise in general. There was no controversy over the broad issue, that freemen over the age of twenty-one who have paid a state or county tax, and the sons of such persons between the ages of twenty-one and twenty-two, even if they have not paid taxes, should be entitled to vote. Nor was there any dispute over the matter of election by ballot. There was some discussion, however, over the residence qualification. The original draft had proposed a requirement of two years' residence in the state; it was proposed by Wilson, unsuccessfully, that this be reduced to one year. Compulsory voting, "if elections are not properly attended," was provided for in the proposals of the Committee of Nine. This was rejected by the convention with Wilson supporting retention of the clause. These two instances—two among many —are revealing of the extent to which Wilson carried his democratic predilections. The proof of Wilson's sincerity lies not so much in his often grandiloquent advocacy of democratic ideas, nor in his support for the major democratic devices, as in his support of democratic principles on small issues in which democracy could not have been simply a means to an end, nor indifference toward them regarded as a mark of hypocrisy.

The extent of Wilson's concern with the question of the proper relationship between state and federal governments has already been amply illustrated. It was not to be expected that the issue would emerge again in consideration simply of a state constitution. Yet it did emerge, unexpectedly, in what appears to be a final attempt by Antifederalists to resist the onslaught of federal power. Wilson chose not to see it this way, preferring to regard it as a naive attempt, conceived in ignorance of the implications, to establish a fallacious principle. The occasion was a proposal that "No member of Congress from this state nor any person holding or exercising any office of trust or profit under the United States, shall, at the same time, hold or exercise any office whatever in this state," a motion that was at once amended by the insertion of the inconsequential proviso "otherwise than in the militia." Innocent or not as the motives of the supporters of this proposal may have been, Wilson saw it as a challenge to his whole concept of federal-state relations. Moreover, he admitted frankly that he was exceedingly disturbed by the fact that he himself, as a justice of the Supreme Court of the United States, would be unable to hold simultaneously any office whatever in Pennsylvania. Right of appointment to office he considered "the most valuable right of citizenship," and to be deprived of it arbitrarily was "mortifying." But what alarmed Wilson most was the implication that the interests of the United States were so different from those of Pennsylvania that by appointing to its own service officials of Pennsylvania the government of the United States would be able to "attach them to the measures, the interests, and the counsels of the United States, in opposition to the measures, the interests, and the counsels of Pennsylvania." Wilson had consistently endeavored to refute any suggestion of conflict between national and state interests, and to imply, as the motion did, that the people of the United States could have a basically different set of interests from those of the people of Pennsylvania was to challenge one of his most fundamental principles. The proposal was, he said, based on a "principle of political hostility" between state and national governments, and he defied his adversaries to explain how this hostility could arise. If it was adopted, he warned, Pennsylvania "may become as infamous for her antifederal, as she has hitherto been renowned for her federal principles" and "may hereafter be as much dishonored by the littleness, as she has heretofore been admired for the liberality, of her politics."[30]

Wilson did not deny the impropriety of allowing certain offices to be held under different governments, and he recognized the need to check pluralism; but he pointed out, rightly, that the motion the convention was discussing was not designed to prevent this. It was designed simply to reduce the influence of the federal government in the affairs of Pennsylvania. It would remain possible to hold office under, for example, the governments of New Jersey and Pennsylvania, or even France and Pennsylvania, as well as to hold an indefinite number of offices in Pennsylvania; only the simultaneous holding of offices under the United States and Pennsylvania was forbidden. In any event plural office holding, he maintained, can often be advantageous to the public interest, whether under the same or different governments. And by depriving its officers of the right to serve the United States government, Pennsylvania would deprive herself of the services of her best citizens, who might well prefer national to state office. That Wilson was deeply disturbed over the issue is shown not only by the fact that he made it the occasion for a lengthy prepared statement, but also in the almost emotional tone of that statement. Whether he need have gone to all this trouble is doubtful; the motion, as he expected, was rejected.

Unlike the Constitution of the United States, that of Pennsylvania made elaborate provision for the setting up of a proper judicial system. This was very much in line with Wilson's ideas. The only matter of real substance on which he was defeated was over the establishment of a Court of Chancery. Wilson desired a Court of Chancery in order to facilitate foreign commerce,[31] but the convention thought constitutional provision for such a court to be inappropriate, and provided instead for its creation by act of the legislature. At many points the judicial and legal clauses of the constitution directly reflected Wilson's liberal views: in its prohibition of any secret proceedings in any court; in its provision that in indictments for libels juries may determine both the law and the facts; and in other minor provisions where, at least partly through his influence, the more liberal view prevailed.

Various general provisions or proposals for which Wilson was wholly, or in part, responsible illustrate other facets of his mind and personality. A most interesting one, which unfortunately must remain in isolation, was an unsuccessful proposal to amend the clause regarding religious qualifications for office-holding by eliminating the words "of rewards and punishments" from "That no person who acknowledges the being of a God and a future state of rewards and punishments, shall, on account of his religious sentiments, be disqualified. . . . "[32] Clearly Wilson had strong and, for the time, somewhat unorthodox views concerning the nature of the afterlife. Another, revealing of his meticulously logical mind—and in this case also his attachment to a state bill of rights—was his successful proposal to amend the first clause "To guard against transgressions of the high powers which we have delegated, we declare, that everything in this article expressed, is excepted out of the general powers of legislation, and shall forever remain inviolate" by substituting "government" for "legislation"[33]—thus ensuring that the executive as well as the legislature was brought unequivocally within its scope. He also displayed the interest he showed elsewhere in encouraging education by providing for the establishment of schools available to all, and for the support of higher education.[34]

The convention adopted the new constitution on February 26. This was not the end of the matter, as on Wilson's proposal it was thereupon agreed unanimously that it now "be published for the consideration of the good people of Pennsylvania." The convention adjourned until August 9, when it reconvened in order to consider the good people's views. Evidently the people were well content. No major innovations were suggested, and the changes that were made seem to have been more the result of afterthoughts among members of the convention than of ideas emanating from outside it. One amendment which is of considerable interest in view of Wilson's subsequent career is the express provision made at his instigation for bringing suits against the Commonwealth of Pennsylvania.[35] Another proposal made by him, this time successfully, was that no one should be deprived through the new constitution "of any right or privilege of electing or being elected into any office for the same to which he is entitled by the present constitution."[36] The only other feature of the second session of the convention that warrants any comment is the defeat of a final attempt by conservatives to restore the provision for the indirect election of senators. The extent to which Wilson had imprinted his view on the minds of the members of the convention is shown in the overwhelming nature of the defeat, by a vote of fifty-one to thirteen.[37]

On September 2 the new constitution was finally approved, with only one opposing vote.[38] The views of the people having already been ascertained, it was not thought necessary to submit it to popular ratification. Wilson received the accolade of being appointed chairman of the committee to arrange the order of procession at the proclamation of the constitution.[39]

Wilson's sense of satisfaction with his achievement in the Pennsylvania convention was soundly based. Mainly through his efforts, the constitution it produced was probably the best of all the constitutions of the period, not excepting that of the United States. It portrays the political thinking of the revolutionary period in its most profound and most enlightened aspects.

CHAPTER 9

Concerning James Wilson in his capacities as associate justice of the Supreme Court of the United States and professor of law in the College of Philadelphia.

Wilson expected that after the adoption of the federal Constitution he would be appointed to one of the major offices in the new government. The office to which he aspired was that of chief justice of the United States—one which, in view of his belief that "the judicial should be commensurate to the legislative and executive authority,"[1] could hardly be surpassed in the influence it might wield. Wilson asked Washington to consider him for the appointment, though in terms which would reduce rather than enhance his chances.[2] The president's response was unsympathetic, though he did make him an associate justice. On two other occasions Wilson was passed over for the chief justiceship, in each case to his own bitter disappointment, though even his friends by then realized that his financial embarrassments in effect precluded him from consideration for the post.

Wilson's activities as an associate justice of the Supreme Court are of importance to the extent that they are a projection of his work in the Federal Convention. Of particular importance was the part he played in the suppression of the Whisky Rebellion, and in the decision of the Court in *Chisholm* v. *Georgia*.

Wilson's opinion in *Chisholm* v. *Georgia*[3] was the culmination and the epitome of his thinking on the political issues of democratic government and the relationship between state and federal governments. Indeed, had this been the sole survivor of Wilson's contributions to the theory and practice of government it would almost have been possible to deduce from it the essential features of his outlook. The case arose from a suit brought against the state of Georgia by two citizens of South Carolina, acting in the capacity of executors for a British creditor, for the recovery of confiscated property. Sensitive political issues, as well as fundamental constitutional issues were raised by the case—as, for instance, the still active issue of loyalist debts which might, if indirectly, come before the Supreme Court should the decision of the Court go against Georgia.

Wilson described the case as one of "uncommon magnitude" raising as it did the question whether a state, "claiming to be sovereign," was amenable to the the jurisdiction of the Supreme Court of the United States or, expressed more fully and more fundamentally, "Do the people of the United States form a nation?" To examine the question, Wilson adopted three different lines of approach. First he considered the issue in relation to the principles of general jurisprudence; secondly, in relation to the laws and practice of foreign countries; and thirdly "and chiefly" in relation to the Constitution of the United States.

Wilson began with a semantic approach, in which he examined the meaning of the terms state and sovereign and redefined them in a way he believed appropriate to the circumstances of the United States in 1793. Sovereign, he pointed out, was a term totally unknown to the Constitution of the United States; in fact the only place where its insertion would have been appropriate was as a descriptive adjective in the phrase "We, the people"; its omission, so he said, being due to a desire by the convention to avoid an "ostentatious declaration" of what was self-evident. The state, he again asserted, had as one of its attributes subordination to the people. Everything else, by which he meant the government, should be subordinate to the state. This was not often recognized. "The government," he declared, "has often claimed precedence of the state; and to this perversion, . . . many of the volumes of confusion concerning sovereignty owe their existence" with the consequence that "The ministers . . . have wished, and have succeeded in the wish, to be considered as the sovereign of the state." This was prevalent in Europe, though not in the United States; but even there, however, there remained a tendency to elevate the state above the people. He then proceeded to define what he meant by a state:

> By a state I mean a complete body of free persons, united together for their common benefit to enjoy peaceably what is their own, and to do justice to others. It is an artificial person. It has its affairs and its interests; it has its rules; it has its

rights; and it has its obligations. It may acquire property distinct from that of its members; it may incur debts, to be discharged out of the public stock, not out of the private fortunes of individuals; it may be bound by contracts; and for damages arising from the breach of those contracts.

Asserting somewhat naively that this definition was uncontroversial, he went on to deduce the obligation of a state, as of an individual, "to do justice and fulfill engagements," and in the case of a state which did not fulfill these obligations, as with an individual, it was entirely proper "to secure by compulsion that which will not be voluntarily performed." If an individual, "an original sovereign," did not feel demeaned by being amenable to the courts, why should "a collection of original sovereigns" feel differently. "If the dignity of each of them singly is undiminished, the dignity of all jointly must be unimpaired."

Following a slightly different, though related, line of argument, Wilson pointed out that if a state claimed immunity from the jurisdiction of a court on the ground that it is a sovereign, then it was under the necessity of explaining what sovereignty is. In an argument that was emotionally evocative rather than logically coherent he claimed that "in one sense, the term sovereign has for its correlative, subject," which was a term having no application in the American Constitution under which, except in the single reference to foreign subjects, "there are citizens but no subjects." In this sense, Georgia had no claim even on her own citizens, let alone those of other states of the Union. By another definition sovereignty implied a lack of any dependence on any other power, but whether the people of Georgia had "surrendered the supreme power to the state or government, and retained nothing to themselves" or whether, like the people of the other states "and of the United States" they had kept in their own hands the supreme power, it was not proper for him in his capacity as a justice of the federal Supreme Court to inquire into, though as a citizen he knew what the answer was. But as a justice of the Supreme Court he could recognize that the people of Georgia, "when they acted upon the large scale of the Union, and as a part of the people of the United States, did not surrender the supreme or sovereign power to that state, but, as to the purpose of the Union, retained it to themselves." Accordingly, Wilson concluded that "as to the purposes of the Union," Georgia was not a sovereign state, though it remained for him to consider whether "the judicial decision of this cause forms one of those purposes." A third definition of sovereignty was derived from feudal concepts, and now took the form of the belief that all human law must be prescribed by a superior, an assumption he disdained to examine, merely asserting his acceptance of the very different principle that "the basis of sound and genuine jurisprudence" was that "laws . . . must be founded on the consent of those whose obedience they require." "The sovereign," he concluded, "when traced to this source, is found Man."

Examination of the issue in the light of principles of general jurisprudence having produced strong indication that Georgia was indeed subject to the jurisdiction of the Court, Wilson then went on to consider the question by analogy with the practice of states in different times and places, in order to show that the denial to Georgia of immunity from the Court's jurisdiction was historically perfectly reasonable. He cited examples from Spain, Greece, Prussia, and Saxon England of subjects prosecuting successfully suits against those deemed their sovereign. Accordingly, in the practice of other states was to be found "nothing against, but much in favor of the jurisdiction of this Court over the state of Georgia."

The last, and essential, line of inquiry concerned directly the Constitution of the United States and what Wilson termed "the legitimate result," by which he meant the implications, of that document. The two simple questions to be answered were, first, could the Constitution of the United States vest in the Supreme Court a jurisdiction over the state of Georgia, and secondly and consequentially, had it in fact done so? Remarking that "in political practice, and even in the science of politics, there has been very frequently a strong current against the natural order of things and an inconsiderate or an interested disposition to sacrifice the end to the means," he observed that even in nations regarded as "free," "the state has assumed a supercilious preeminence above the people who have formed it." From this had arisen the "haughty notions of state-independence, state-sovereignty, and state-supremacy." In despotic governments, moreover, "the government has usurped in a similar manner both upon the state and the people. In every case, Man is degraded from the rank which he ought to hold in human affairs." A prime example was the reputed assertion of Louis XIV: "*L'état, c'est moi.*" Even Britain was similarly tainted, though to a lesser degree. In Britain sovereignty was the attribute solely of Parliament—king, lords, and commoners who "together form the great corporation or body politic of the kingdom," with the people, having "entirely delegated their power to their representatives," excluded altogether.

Although the United States does not go so far as France and Britain in limiting the source of political authority, nevertheless even there there is distortion of the natural order of things. "The states," he charged, "rather than the people for whose sake the states exist, seem frequently the objects which attract and arrest our principal attention," and this has given rise to a great deal of intellectual confusion. Revealing what was a sincere religious basis for much of his thinking on the nature of man and of society he declared: "A state, I cheerfully admit, is the noblest work of Man. But Man himself, free and honest, is, I speak as to this world, the noblest work of God."

"The people of the United States" were, Wilson emphasized, "the first personages introduced" by the Constitution. Wilson, indeed, was the member of the Federal Convention who had ensured that they were. These "people," he went on, "were the citizens of thirteen states, each of which had a separate constitution and government, and all of which were connected together by Articles of Confederation." As "that Confederacy was totally inadequate" to the achievement of strength and happiness for the nation, "those people, among whom were the people of Georgia, ordained and established the present Constitution," for the reasons adumbrated in that document, and vested in the new government legislative, executive, and judicial power. To the question whether these people, among them the people of Georgia, could bind the states, including Georgia, by the power so vested, Wilson replied positively on the basis of the principles he had already expounded. In amplification of this he declared:

> If those states were the work of those people; those people, and—that I may apply the case closely—the people of Georgia, in particular, could alter, as they pleased, their former work. To any given degree they could diminish as well as enlarge it. Any or all of the former state powers, legislative, executive, or judicial, they could extinguish or transfer. The inference which necessarily results, is that the Constitution, ordained and established by those people, and—still closely to apply the case—in particular by the people of Georgia, could vest jurisdiction or judicial power over those states and over the state of Georgia in particular.

The question then became: Had the Constitution in fact vested in the federal government jurisdiction over the states? If, Wilson argued, the people intended, as they surely did, "to bind the several states by the legislative power of the national government," it followed that they must have had the same intention regarding the executive power, since it would be useless to make laws without the power also to enforce them. But did it follow further from this that the people intended the judicial power similarly to be binding on the states. Wilson employed a more sophisticated argument to support this contention, one which revealed his elevated view of the judicial power. "When," he said, "laws are plain, and the application of them is uncontroverted, they are enforced immediately by the executive authority of the government. When the application of them is doubtful or intricate, the interposition of the judicial authority becomes necessary." Accordingly, it did follow that the people of the United States had vested the Supreme Court with jurisiction over Georgia.

"The declared objects and the general texture of the Constitution" also pointed in the same direction. One purpose of the Constitution was to form a Union more powerful than that then existing, in which the legislative power of Congress had been unenforceable on the states. "Nothing," Wilson deduced, "could be more natural than to intend that the legislative power should be enforced by powers executive and judicial." Another purpose was "to establish justice." In conjunction with the declaration "that no state shall pass a law impairing the obligation of contracts" this would seem to establish the jurisdiction of the Court over the several states as, he asked, "What good purpose could this constitutional provision secure, if a state might pass a law impairing an obligation of its own and be amenable for such a violation of right to no controlling judiciary power?" His conclusion from the general texture of the Constitution was "that the people of the United States intended to form themselves into a nation, for national purposes," and therefore created a government with legislative, executive, and judicial powers "extending over the whole nation." It was, he contended, inconsistent with these purposes that "any man or body of men—any person natural or artificial—should be permitted to claim, successfully, an entire exemption from the jurisdiction of the national government." Such claims, if substantiated, would "be repugnant to our very existence as a nation." Many trains of deduction, he concluded, established that "as the legitimate result of this Constitution . . . the state of Georgia is amenable to the jurisidiction of this Court."

Deduction, moreover, was not the only way by which the Court's jurisdiction could be ascertained. It was confirmed beyond all doubt, in Wilson's view, "by the direct and explicit declaration of the constitution itself." This explicit declaration was the provision that the judicial power of the United States shall extend to controversies between two states. How, he asked, "can the most consummate degree of professional ingenuity devise a mode by which this controversy between two states can be brought before a court of law, and yet neither of those states be a defendant." Moreover, he regarded as describing with complete accuracy the case before the Court, the provision extending the judicial power of the United States to controversies "between a state and citizens of another state." Observing, finally, that "causes, and not the parties to causes, are weighed by Justice in her equal scales," he concluded that the combined inference from "the principles of general jurisprudence . . . the laws and practice of states and kingdoms, and . . . the Constitution of the United States" was that in the case before the Court Georgia was subject to its jurisdiction. With only one dissenting opinion, the Supreme Court concurred with Wilson's judgment.

The outcry that followed the judgment shows how far ahead of public opinion were Wilson and the colleagues who thought like him. Assurances given by many Federalists, though not by Wilson, during the ratification process had conveyed the impression that the Constitution did not enable a private citizen to sue a state in the federal courts. The Supreme Court had now decided otherwise, and so strong was the feeling against it, at least among politicians, that the decision was reversed by constitutional amendment.[4] It was left to John Marshall, many years later, to restore, substantially, the authority of the Supreme Court over the states which Wilson believed he had established in 1793.[5]

While *Chisholm* v. *Georgia* was by far the most important case with which Wilson was concerned as a justice of the Supreme Court, there were others in which issues were raised that gave him further opportunities to express his belief in the parity of the Supreme Court with the other two branches of government and in the supremacy of the federal government over the states.[6] It may be said, briefly, that John Marshall was a worthy inheritor of the political and judicial concepts of James Wilson.

Wilson's contribution as a member of the Supreme Court to the strengthening of the federal government in relation to the states was not confined to the judicial proceedings before the Court in which he was involved. As a Supreme Court justice he became directly involved in the suppression of disaffection which imposed a serious threat to the credibility of the federal government. Ever since 1791 when Congress imposed an excise on whisky there had been unrest in the Appalachian regions of Pennsylvania and the states to the south, whisky being important to the economy of the frontier as a means of disposing of surplus grain. Worried by these signs of discontent, Congress, in 1792, implementing their constitutional authority "to provide for calling forth the militia to execute the laws of the Union, suppress insurrections, and repel invasions," enacted a measure giving the president power to call out the militia in the event of an insurrection against the federal government, or if a state asked for federal aid in suppressing internal disorder it was unable itself to control. However, before the president could act he had to be formally notified by "an associate justice or the district judge" that normal judicial proceedings were inadequate to the task of enforcing the law.

In 1794 the situation in the frontier areas became, or seemed to become, still more critical, when in western Pennsylvania excise officers were intimidated, the mail was robbed, and Pittsburgh was threatened with attack by a force of "rebels"—an attack apparently averted only by the decision of the people of Pittsburgh to join their prospective assailants. In the administration Washington and Hamilton were deeply worried about these events—though not Jefferson, who regarded the rebellion as existing mainly in Hamilton's imagination—and regarded them as a threat both to the unity of the United States, there being a suspicion that some of the western leaders were considering attempting to detach the region, and to the stability and strength of the federal government, whose authority was being defied. After the event, Washington and Hamilton attempted to implicate the Democratic Societies—products of the French Revolution and the activities of Edmond Genêt—in the rebellion, in order to discredit them, but it is very doubtful whether this was a factor in their initial reaction. The threat to the federal government was in itself sufficient to cause great alarm among those who believed in strong central government. Federal law must be upheld, and whether or not the danger was a very serious one, it still presented an admirable opportunity to demonstrate what federal authority implied, and what the Constitution meant. This, it may be assumed, was the basis of Wilson's interest in the matter. Whether or not there was prior collusion is uncertain, though it is probable that there was. Clearly, no one more suitable than Wilson for fulfilling the necessary legal function could be found. He responded at once to the report, drafted by Hamilton and sent to him by Washington,[7] replying on August 4: "From evidence which has been laid before me, I hereby notify to you, that, in the counties of Washington and Allegheny in Pennsylvania laws of the United States are opposed, and the execution thereof obstructed by combinations too powerful to be suppressed by the ordinary course of judicial proceedings, or by the powers vested in the marshal of that district." Washington thereupon at once issued the proclamation required of him by law and then called out the militia.

The response was far greater than the exigencies of the situation were found to require. An army of over twelve thousand men, larger than any Washington had commanded during the Revolutionary War, was quickly assembled, and accompanied by Hamilton, Washington, and Governor Thomas Mifflin of Pennsylvania—whose massive consumption of whisky on the expedition became an embarrassment, despite the consequential benefit to the Treasury—set out to defeat the rebel forces. This was a task that presented few problems, as there was no rebel army to be found. A few men reputedly disaffected were rounded up, and treated with leniency, there being no executions or even sentences of imprisonment. Like many apparently trivial episodes, the Whisky Rebellion had an importance far exceeding its dimensions. The authority of the federal government was vindicated in a manner which displayed its power to act directly on individuals and consequently avoided a confrontation, which might have produced great bitterness, between federal and state governments. That Wilson's part in it, technical as it might appear to be, was regarded by contemporaries as important is indicated by the congratulations of his colleague, Justice Iredell. "I warmly congratulate you," he wrote, "on the great success of the Western expedition. I am persuaded it has added strength and dignity to the government."[8]

Despite his very great services to the Supreme Court, Wilson through sheer pertinacity so characteristic of him, came close to inflicting on it a damaging blow. It is not improbable that only his death saved him from impeachment with the consequence, if he were convicted by the Senate, of removal from the Court, an event which would have seriously damaged its prestige at a critical stage in its development. As early as 1792, Wilson's effectiveness on the Court was being adversely affected by the need, when on circuit, to return to Philadelphia as soon as possible to deal with urgent personal business there.[9] As his fortunes declined, the danger of his imprisonment for debt so increased that there were several states he did not dare to enter,[10] and by 1797 he could not appear even in Philadelphia, whence, according to Iredell, he was "in a manner absconding from his creditors" in order "to wait until he can make a more favorable adjustment of his affairs than he could in a state of arrest."[11] It was

expected by many of his associates that he would resign from the
Court if only through the implied rebuke of his rejection as chief
justice; as early as 1795 the attorney general believed Wilson's resig-
nation imminent.[12] By July 1798 the situation was clearly desperate.
"Surely," wrote Governor Samuel Johnston to Iredell, "if his feelings
are not rendered altogether callous by his misfortunes, he will not
suffer himself to be disgraced by a conviction on an impeachment."[13]
Wilson, ever hopeful, did not resign, and was saved only by death
from what would have been the ultimate humiliation. It would have
been some consolation to him to have known that he would be succeeded by his former pupil Bushrod Washington, who though over-
shadowed by John Marshall helped to continue the tradition begun by
his mentor.

Wilson's practical accomplishments or endeavors were often
supported by a theoretical base consisting of his deep knowledge of
philosophy and law. It is impossible to appreciate adequately his contribution in the field of government without at least some knowledge
of the law lectures which he prepared for delivery in 1790–91 to the
law school of the College of Philadelphia. After his failure to become
chief justice of the United States, he derived some consolation from
his appointment as professor of law in the college, a post he held
concurrently with the associate justiceship of the Supreme Court, a
case of plural office-holding he defended on the grounds that each
would benefit the other. He did not, however, actually deliver more
than half of the lectures, the growth of other pressures, especially in
the work of the Supreme Court, forcing him to abandon them in the
winter of 1791–92. All of them, even if not delivered, were at least
written, though some of them are little more than drafts, and they
provide additional reinforcement of the views and attitudes of Wilson
in the arena of practical politics.

The introductory lecture, delivered in the college hall on December 15, was almost a state occasion. Present were "the president of
the United States, with his lady—also the vice-president, and both
houses of Congress, the president and both houses of the legislature of
Pennsylvania, together with a great number of ladies and gentlemen
. . .; the whole comprising a most brilliant and respectable audience."[14] The presence of a number of distinguished ladies gave Wilson the opportunity to expound his views on the proper place of
women in society. His praise of feminine qualities was perhaps excessively effusive, but it did reflect what for his day was a fairly liberal if
not advanced view of the position of women. Asserting that women

were as honest, as virtuous, and as wise as men, he nevertheless warned the ladies of his audience against using these talents to the detriment of their feminine charm. They cannot, he declared, follow "masculine employments" without sacrificing "the lovely and accomplished woman." Though they ought not, for instance, "undertake the management of public affairs," this did not mean that their place in society was inferior to that of men. Government and law were not made for themselves; "they were made for something better;" and of that "something better," he flattered his female listeners, "you form the better part." "To protect and improve social life is," he assured them, ". . . the end of government and law. If, therefore, you have no share in the formation, you have a most intimate connection with the effects of a good system of law and government." They might even, as well as training their daughters, have a share in the education of their sons—in, for instance, the art of eloquence![15] Wilson had great respect and admiration for women, but within the context of the eighteenth century.

Praise of women was not the prime object of Wilson's introductory lecture. Its main purpose was to announce his intention of trying to establish a system of law which was distinctively American. Though it would be derived in part from the common law of England, it would move steadily toward an American common law, based on American needs and circumstances. Moreover, its base would be different from that of law in England, as it would reflect "the vital principle . . . that the supreme or sovereign power of the society resides in the citizens at large." For this reason, above all others, "the principles of our constitutions and governments and laws are materially better than the principles of the constitution and government and laws of England."[16] The law, along with other aspects of government in the United States, was to be based on Wilsonian principles, and Wilson was to be immortalized as the creator of a system of uniquely American jurisprudence.

The common law, being based whether in England or in America on custom, which in turn was based on "free and voluntary consent,"[17] was central to Wilson's concept of law in a republic. It revealed, moreover, something of Wilson's innate religious spirit: in rejecting the authority of a human superior as the source of law, he acknowledged God as the ultimate source since it followed from the fundamental moral and social nature of man that popular consent as revealed in the common law would reflect the will of God.[18] If God was the source of the common law, it was the Saxons of preconquest

England who were its earliest exponents. As with so many aspects of law and government, Wilson believed that the system established, or emerging, in the United States was closely similar to that of Saxon England. So with the common law which, he argued, "as now received in America, bears, in its principles, and in many of its more minute particulars, a stronger and a fairer resemblance to the common law as it was improved under the Saxon, than to that law as it was disfigured under the Norman government."[19] This disfigurement was the result mainly of the injection of feudal concepts, particularly those relating to land tenure. With regard especially to the common law relating to crimes and punishments, the practice of the Saxons bore to some of the constitutions recently framed in America "a degree of resemblance which will strike and surprise those who compare them together."

Whether or not Wilson's view of Saxon institutions was historically accurate, it is clear that his view of the common law eliminated many of the impurities which he believed had crept into it since 1066. An essential quality of the common law was its ability to adjust to the changing needs of society. This Wilson called "the accommodating principle" which "in some eras" would bring about extensive changes and improvements in the common law commensurate with rapidly changing circumstances. The United States, he suggested, was entering "one of those happy eras" of improvement in the common law. The common law he regarded as a great corrective of human error and an antidote to evil. "When," he said, "through the errors, or distempers, or iniquities of men or times, the peace of the nation, or the right order of government have received interruption, the common law has wrought out those errors, distempers, and iniquities and has reinstated the nation in its natural and peaceful state and temperament." Above all, through the operation of the common law, whether through its flexibility or, in other parts, its wise stability, "the great ends of liberty are kept steadily and constantly in view." Even invasions or revolutions have not undermined it because "it contains the common dictates of nature, refined by wisdom and experience, as occasions offer, and cases arise."[20]

In administering the common law, the function of judges, Wilson emphasized, was that of a "skillful guide" rather than an authority. Nevertheless, he regarded judges as of crucial importance, and though he expressly denied it, it is evident that their function of interpreting the common law would at times amount to the power to create it. "In certain sciences," he said, "a peculiar degree of regard should be paid to authority. The common law is one of those sciences. Judicial decisions are the principal and most authentic evidence which can be given of the existence of such a custom as is entitled to form a part of the common law. Those who gave such decisions were selected for that employment, on account of their learning and experience in the common law." But, he warned, "every prudent and cautious judge . . . will remember that his duty and his business is, not to make the law, but to interpret and apply it."[21]

Though obviously Wilson would give full weight to authority in the sense of expertise, he totally repudiated the concept of the law as the province of a closed community of lawyers. The people, he urged, should be encouraged to acquire some knowledge of the law, since without it they could not fulfill properly some of the duties of citizenship. "The science of law should, " he said, "in some measure and in some degree, be the study of every free citizen and of every free man. Every free citizen and every free man has duties to perform and rights to claim. Unless, in some measure and in some degree, he knows those duties and those rights, he can never act a just and an independent part."[22] He asserted that "the general and most important principles of the law are not removed to a very great distance from common apprehension" and hoped that law would retain its comparative simplicity.

It was largely for this reason that he wished to undertake the enormous task of preparing digests both of the laws of the United States and of Pennsylvania. Knowledge at least of the broad outlines of the law would assist a citizen in the exercise of the vital function of choosing those who would represent him in the various legislative bodies, and would be of immense value to those called to serve on juries. He placed great stress on the importance of juries in the administration of justice, going so far, for instance, as insisting that in libel cases juries must have the right to determine the law as well as the facts.[23] In particular, those who sought election to legislative bodies ought of necessity to have a knowledge of the basic principles of law, as otherwise they could hardly assess properly the legislative proposals laid before them.[24] Law, originating from the people, was to remain inherent in the life of the people, and must never become a barrier between them and those they had chosen to administer the affairs of the state.

Wilson believed sincerely that in government and law the United States was creating a new system markedly superior to any that had previously existed anywhere in the world. He also believed that ideas emanating from America, and her example, would make it possible to create a better world order. The concept of the city upon a hill was as real to Wilson as to the early Puritans, but he gave it a new dimension which they had not envisaged. Wilson regarded all civilized nations as forming a single natural society, governed, as with a single community, by a moral law based on human nature.[25] All nations, as all men, were equal, and each had a duty toward the others. The law of nations, he maintained, was simply "the law of nature, when applied to states or political societies," and, like it, was "of obligation indispensable . . . of origin divine."[26] Neglect of the law of nations was, therefore, thoroughly to be deplored, especially in the United States where the sovereign power lay with the people, and the law of nations, being the law of sovereigns, was there "the law of the people." Americans were "under the most sacred obligations" to exercise the sovereign power "in a manner agreeable to those rules and maxims, which the law of nature prescribes to every state, for the happiness of each, and for the happiness of all." They should also be aware of their obligations under the law of nations, as "the laws of morality are equally strict with regard to societies, as to the individuals of whom the societies are composed." With nations as with individuals "integrity and sound policy go hand in hand," and general acceptance of this maxim "would diffuse far and wide the most salutary and benign effects."[27] Obviously, therefore, promises must be kept—an obligation of more importance in the case of states than of individuals because of the more serious consequences of nonfulfillment. Treaties must be honored in full, as "among states and princes, good faith is both respectability and power."[28] The obligations of states to one another, however, went far beyond adherence to formal commitments. He stressed the importance of amity and benevolence among nations, to the extent that they should actively seek one another's good. Certainly they should do no wrong to one another, justice being "a sacred law of nations." But they must also do good to one another, since "the duties of humanity are incumbent upon nations as well as upon individuals," and "the law of that great and universal society requires that each nation should contribute to the perfection and happiness of the others." "Nations," he averred, "ought to love one another."[29] Influenced perhaps as much by the French Revolution, with which in 1790 he greatly sympathized, as by the example of his own country he asserted that by civilized nations "at last it is acknowledged that mankind are all brothers" and that there was reason to hope that the time was approaching "when the acknowledgment will be substantiated by a uniform corresponding conduct."[30]

Wilson, however, was always at bottom the practical statesman. International benevolence was highly desirable, but it should not be forgotten that every nation's first duty was to itself, and to its own people. The preservation of its own existence and that of its members was of prime importance, and a nation had the right to do everything necessary, without injury to others, to achieve these objects.[31] Moreover, he did not expect a nation to sacrifice its own interests for the sake of others. "If," he said, "a nation, in the necessary prosecution of its own duties and rights, does what is disagreeable or even inconvenient to another, this is not to be considered as an injury; it ought to be viewed as the unavoidable result, and not as the governing principle of its conduct. If, at such conduct, offense is taken, it is the fault of that nation which takes, not of that nation which occasions it."[32] Clearly there were limits to Wilson's international benevolence.

Friendly collaboration between nations was what Wilson hoped to achieve. Anything that fostered intercourse among them should be encouraged, and anything that obstructed it discouraged. As with individuals the "natural state" of nations was "a state of society and peace," and this every nation had a duty "to preserve and improve."[33] Disputes between nations would certainly occur from time to time, and he was much concerned to find a way of resolving such disputes without recourse to war. Mediation with a veiw to conciliation was one method. Arbitration, with an obligation generally to accept the verdict of arbitrators, was another. An international congress, in which disputes might be settled by those nations not involved in them, was a third. Here, however, Wilson went much further, in suggesting that an international congress might devise an effective method "for compelling nations at war to conclude a peace upon fair and equitable conditions."[34] If a solution acceptable to both parties could not be found then, he suggested, economic action might be an alternative to military action. However, in a civilized international society better methods could surely be found of settling disputes. It would be helpful, for instance, in restraining improper action by a citizen of one state against another state, if the example were followed of England, where the law of nations was regarded as part of the law of England and violations of it could be brought before the courts. His most forward-looking idea was for an international court to adjudicate in international controversies. "Must," he pleaded, "the alternatives in disputes and differences between the dignified assemblages of men,

known by the name of nations, be the same which are the prerogatives of savages in the rudest and most deformed state of society—
voluntary accommodation, or open war, or violent reprisals, inferior,
in odium, only to war? Individuals unite in civil society, and institute
judges with authority to decide, and with authority also to carry their
decisions into full and adequate execution, that justice may be done
and war may be prevented. Are states too wise or too proud to receive a
lesson from individuals? Is the idea of a common judge between nations less admissible than that of a common judge between men? If
admissible in idea, would it not be desirable to have an opportunity of
trying whether the idea may not be reduced to practice?"[35]

The model Wilson had in mind for this enlightened and ambitious project was to be found in the Constitution of the United States,
though he refrained from defining in detail the plan he contemplated.
Indeed it is doubtful whether he really considered it practicable. But
what was immediately attainable was the extension to the federal
courts of the United States of a vast volume of jurisdiction involving
the law of nations—matters of private international law involving, in
the main, merchant and mercantile law and the law regarding contracts. English courts exercised such jurisdiction, and the Constitution of the United States might be regarded, in Article III, Section 2,
as extending the same power to the federal courts of the United States.
Yet to Wilson this was merely a by-product, though an important
one, of an idealistic concept of an international order which would
produce peace, harmony, and prosperity among all nations.

In the less exalted and more practical field of domestic jurisdiction, Wilson took a very close interest in the reform of the criminal
law. His ideas were closely similar to those of other advanced legal
thinkers of the time—notably Jeremy Bentham—but Wilson was
afforded a better opportunity than they had of putting these ideas into
practice. The law relating to crimes and punishments which he expounded to his law students, he expounded also to a grand jury in
Virginia in 1791, in expressed accordance with his belief that a citizen
should know the laws. "I deem it," he told the grand jury, "my duty
to embrace every proper opportunity of disseminating the knowledge
of them far and speedily."[36] The view of criminal law that Wilson
expounded was a humane one, having as its aim both the protection of society and the reformation of the criminal, and seeking above
all the prevention of crimes. He specified three qualities in punishments which would render them effective preventives of crimes—
moderation, speediness, and certainty. Rejecting the widespread be-

lief that severity of punishment was an effective deterrent, he maintained rather that excessive severity of the law would incline juries to acquit, thereby encouraging a repetition of the crime. Moreover, aversion to laws providing for barbarous punishments would tend to encourage among the people at large a disrespect for the law in general.[37] Or, should aversion be replaced by acceptance, such punishments would damage the character of the people. "A nation broke to cruel punishments," he declared, "becomes dastardly and contemptible."[38] Moderate punishments would check crime in another way. "When," he asserted, ". . . punishments are moderate and mild, everyone will, from a sense of interest and of duty, take his proper part in detecting, in exposing, in trying, and in passing sentence on crimes. The consequence will be that criminals will seldom elude the vigilance, or baffle the energy of public justice."[39] It follows almost of necessity that Wilson considered capital punishments to be only rarely appropriate, believing "that nothing but the most absolute necessity can authorize them."[40]

Speediness first of trial and then of infliction of punishment was the second of the qualities Wilson looked for in a sound system of criminal jurisprudence. Avoidance of delay in bringing an accused person to trial was a measure of humanity, especially if the accused were innocent, as it would keep to the minimum the mental torment he would certainly have to endure, a degree of torment that Wilson, with characteristic sensitivity, realized would be proportionate "to the delicacy of sentiment and the strength of imagination possessed by him." Only in rare cases—for example to allow prejudice against an accused person to subside—should trial be delayed. With the exception of the death sentence, "the speedy punishment of crimes should form a part in every system of criminal jurisprudence."[41]

Of supreme importance in Wilson's view of criminal jurisprudence was the certainty of punishment. It was this, more than any other quality, that would prevent crime. Faced with the near certainty of punishment, prospective criminals would often be deterred from carrying out criminal acts, and thereby be prevented from embarking on a life of crime. "The strict execution of every criminal law," Wilson emphasized, "is the dictate of humanity as well as of wisdom."[42]

Adherence to the three virtues of moderation, speediness, and certainty would, Wilson believed, greatly reduce the amount of crime in the United States, and this should be the prime aim of the criminal law. He also advocated less essential measures. One was that, in accordance with Saxon practice, provision be made for reparation for injuries inflicted as a consequence of criminal acts—a deficiency in contemporary English law he described as "both gross and cruel."[43] Another was that punishment as far as possible should be related directly to the crime. "To a scale of crimes," he argued in one of his less realistic moods, "a corresponding scale of punishments should be added, each of which ought to be modified, as far as possible, according to the nature, the kind, and the degree of the crime to which it is annexed. To select, where it can be done, a punishment analogous to the crime, is an excellent method to strengthen that association of ideas, which it is very important to establish between them."[44]

Altogether, Wilson took a very humane view of criminal law, and to the Virginia grand jury he gave high praise to that of the United States as much superior to that of England, which previously was regarded as the most humane in the world. Though it was not a feature he emphasized, Wilson was not unmindful of the welfare of the criminal as well as of society. "Let the reformation," he told the Virginia grand jury, "as well as the punishment of offenders be kept constantly and steadily in view."[45] Much remained to be done, but in the United States "the seeds of reformation are sown" and, he entreated his law students, "the tender plants which from some of them are now beginning to spring, let it be our care to discover and to cultivate."[46]

The importance of property to the stability, progress, and happiness of society is a matter which was often in Wilson's mind. And yet, though he was a very firm upholder of the obligation of contracts, Wilson did not give the protection of property a central place in his view of government and law. "Property, highly deserving security, is," he declared in his introductory lecture, ". . . not an end, but a means. How miserable and how contemptible is that man who inverts the order of nature, and makes his property, not a means, but an end!"[47] The happiness of the people, not primarily the defense of property, was to Wilson the main purpose of government. Often, of course, the happiness of the people depended on the defense of property, but there is no strong reason to doubt the sincerity of his contention that the highest purposes of government were nonmaterialistic.[48] His view of property was rather that it was expedient for society to permit it to be held, rather than that individuals had a right to property independently of society. "The right of separate property," he wrote in his brief paper *On the History of Property,*[49] "seems to be founded in the nature of men and things; and when societies become numerous, the establishment of that right is highly important to the existence, to the tranquillity, to the elegancies, to the refinements, and to some of the virtues of civilized life." Property was the reward for industry, "for of useful and active industry, property is the natural result." That it was expedient for society to allow, or even encourage, exclusive ownership of property was a consequence of human nature. "Who," he asked, "would cultivate the soil, and sow the grain, if he had no peculiar interest in the harvest?" The community as a whole would accordingly benefit from the greater production which exclusive property would stimulate. The alternative would be disorder and disharmony, the result of "fierce and ungovernable competitions for the possession and enjoyment of things, insufficient to satisfy all, and by no rules of adjustment distributed to each."

The conveniences and the elegancies and refinements of life likewise depended on exclusive property ownership. In an argument lacking his usual clarity of thought Wilson maintained that economic growth depended on the division of labor, including separate professions, and that "labor cannot be divided, nor can distinct professions be pursued, unless the productions of one profession and of one kind of labor can be exchanged for those of another," and that "this exchange implies a separate property in those who make it." But however opaque his argument, Wilson's emphasis was, characteristically, on the needs of a free society rather than on the rights of the individual. "The establishment of exclusive property," he concluded, "may justly be considered as essential to the interests of civilized society." This was notably true with regard to land. Attachment to private landed property he wrote, "has, in some parts of the globe, covered barren heaths and inhospitable mountains with fair cities and populous villages; while, in other parts, the most inviting climates and soils remain destitute of inhabitants, because the rights of private property in land are not established or regarded."

CHAPTER 10

*Concerning James Wilson's
enterprise in the extension of
settlement and the expansion of
the American economy.*

In the Continental Congress and in the three conventions in which he
took so major a part, Wilson was concerned first and foremost with the
future political development of the United States. In his activities
outside these bodies, land featured very prominently, and while it
is clear that material ambition was a primary motive, it is apparent that
he was concerned also about the territorial expansion of the United
States as a means to the growth of its power and to the advancement of the welfare of its people. Wilson was much more than merely
a speculator in land. While he coveted the personal fortune he might
in that way acquire—indeed he came to be regarded as one of the
richest men in America—he desired also to be identified with something he believed essential to the future well-being of his country.

Wilson's business activities illustrate one of the contradictions in
his character and conduct. There is ample evidence that he was exceedingly hard in his business dealings, and at times acted in ways which
contemporaries regarded as less than honorable.[1] Indeed, his unsavory
reputation in business sometimes affected adversely his credibility in
other spheres. Moreover, he lacked in business the judicious attitude
he displayed elsewhere. One historian has in fact suggested that in his
land enterprises he displayed the characteristics of a compulsive gam-
bler,[2] and certainly his whole approach showed a lack of caution which
is entirely compatible with this view. The charitable view—which
might well be the right one—is that he was so convinced that the
United States could not fail to expand and develop rapidly and steadily that western lands were the safest as well as the most lucrative of

investments. His method was to buy, usually with borrowed money, a warrant which for a small down payment on the ultimate price would entitle him to have a survey made of the tract so preempted and to buy it when the survey was done. Before this process was finished he would buy more warrants, again with borrowed money, in the expectation that the first transaction would be complete, and the land, or enough of it, sold at a sufficiently high price to pay the cost of the second transaction.[3] This was a process that could be carried on as long as his credit was good, and Wilson did in fact borrow enormous sums in order to keep his empire in being. He was most reluctant ever to disgorge any land, for he always believed that very soon it would become a source of great profit to him. Moreover, like many others, he contracted to pay the balance of the cost of his purchases in public securities at a future date at their then face value, expecting that he would be able to buy them on the open market at a price lower than would prevail when payment was due.

It appears, ironically, that one effect of the adoption of the Constitution was to increase the price of public securities, with the prospect of the funding of the national debts. In addition, growing competition among speculators for depreciated public securities in itself forced the price upward. Though this was a contributory factor to the disaster that eventually struck him, it was clearly not the main one, which was his gross overestimation of the speed of expansion and settlement, aggravated by the economic depression of the mid-1790s which dried up all sources of funds. Had he been able to hold on just a very few more years his calculations and his methods would have appeared justified, as what remained of his holdings after the collapse soon produced wealth for his heirs.

Wilson's land interests were extensive. He was an active member of the Illinois-Wabash Company as well as of smaller groups like the Canaan Company, and had holdings amounting to millions of acres spread throughout an extensive area stretching from New York through present-day Ohio, Pennsylvania, West Virginia, Virginia, Kentucky, and North Carolina to the Yazoo lands of Georgia.

Of much greater interest than the misfortunes of an unsuccessful, unscrupulous businessman is the aspiration of a visionary who perceived and expounded a method of settlement which would in the near future create in the West contented, flourishing communities. Wilson was the most dedicated of continental expansionists, believing it to be the destiny as well as the duty of the United States to populate and civilize the whole of North America. Believing that the attainment of perfection should be the object of a nation, he contended that this conveyed "the right of acquiring everything, without which its perfection cannot be promoted or obtained."[4] He was not unmindful of the welfare of the Indians who inhabited the regions in which white settlement was now imminent. But he believed that their interests lay in adaptation to the higher civilization represented by the white inhabitants of America. In what is one of the earliest, as well as one of the clearest justifications of cultural supremacy, Wilson wrote:

> If a nation establish itself, or extend its establishment in a country already inhabited by others, it ought to observe strict justice, in both instances, with the former inhabitants. This is a part of the law of nations that very nearly concerns the United States. It ought, therefore, to be well understood. The whole earth is allotted for the nourishment of its inhabitants, but it is not sufficient for this purpose, unless they aid it by labor and culture. The cultivation of the earth, therefore, is a duty incumbent on man by the order of nature. Those nations that live by hunting, and have more land than is necessary even for the purposes of hunting, should transfer it to those who will make a more advantageous use of it; those who will make this use of it ought to pay, for they can afford to pay, a reasonable equivalent. Even when the lands are no more than sufficient for the purposes of hunting, it is the duty of the new inhabitants, if advanced in society, to teach, and it is the duty of the original inhabitants, if less advanced in society, to learn, the arts and uses of agriculture. This will enable the latter gradually to contract, and the former gradually to extend their settlements, till the science of agriculture is equally improved in both. By these means, these intentions of nature will be fulfilled; the old and the new inhabitants will be reciprocally useful; peace will be preserved; and justice will be done.[5]

Though Wilson's conscience was satisfied by the assumptions and implications of this outlook, there is no evidence of any practical provision either for a reasonable equivalent or for instruction other than by example in his western projects.

As a citizen of a state without western claims, and as a member of the Illinois-Wabash Land Company which tenuously held lands acquired directly from the Indians, Wilson sought vigorously to secure the establishment of congressional authority over western lands. His hope was that Congress would then validate purchases made from Indians, to the great advantage especially of the Illinois–Wabash Company. In this he was disappointed; congressional jurisdiction over western lands was secured, but not the validation of the claims of land companies. Wilson, however, while continuing to press the claims of the Illinois-Wabash Company, was well pleased with what he regarded as the more important gain, the assumption by Congress of control of the West. Accordingly he took a close interest in the organizing of the western territories, and in response to the resolution of a committee of Congress to which had been submitted Jefferson's proposals of 1784 for the organization of the Northwest Territories he put forward supplementary proposals of his own.[6] His main concern was to strengthen congressional authority over the new territories, believing that the unity of the new nation might come to depend on it. An expression of attachment—he did not say oath of loyalty—to the United States should be required from all existing residents in the area, and future residents should have no right to any land except under a grant or license from the United States government. "This regulation," he contended, "is of fundamental importance: Every person who shall settle under the sanction of the United States may be considered their friend; every person who shall settle without that sanction may be considered as their enemy. The former will think his fortune connected with their establishment; the latter will view it as depending on their destruction." To reinforce this policy, he urged Congress to authorize settlements in those areas—which included lands in which he himself had an interest—where squatting was most likely to occur. The lands he had particularly in mind were those along the Ohio, to which he believed, "emigration will be rapid and strong." Accordingly, land offices should be opened as soon as possible, enabling orderly settlement to take place and helping to prevent the trouble and indeed danger which can be the consequences of unauthorized settlement. Moreover, he admitted in perhaps conscious acknowledgment of the merits of prerevolutionary imperial policy that "after the most mature reflection" he had now come to the "clear and decided" opinion "that with regard to the back lands, nothing more baneful to the United States can happen than to suffer the range of settlements to extend beyond the habits and influence of law, order, and government."

The firm establishment of federal authority as the basis of all land titles was the first rule; the second was ease of acquiring title to land.

"When," he wisely pointed out, "titles can be procured on reasonable conditions, and when it will be useless and dangerous to make settlements without titles, the two rules will mutually fortify each other." Supplementing this argument, but motivated clearly by self-interest, he urged Congress "to satisfy such as have reasonable claims upon the public for lands by virtue of purchase from Indians, or of any other contract or engagement, which the United States are bound, in justice, to ratify or perform." This, he asserted with the naiveté he occasionally displayed when arguing a weak case, was in the interests of the nation, as "to prevent or remove the uneasiness and discontent of citizens is the interest of every wise government."

The remainder of Wilson's comments concern primarily matters of detail involving the appointment of surveyors general and registrars and their functions. It is notable that he extended even to this comparatively minor matter the two principles of national authority and democratic government with which he was to become so closely involved. Each surveyor general and his deputies should reside in the district for which they were appointed, partly because "it will accustom the settlers to look up to the officers of the United States and to respect the authority from which their appointments flow." Moreover, he went on, "those officers will also, in all probability, be chosen by the people to fill the places of greatest trust and importance in the country; and, by this means, a chain of communication and of confidence will be formed between the United States and the new settlements."

There was one major proposal put forward by Wilson for the administration of the Northwest Territories. This was that Congress appoint a minister for the new settlements and for Indian affairs. He did not expect that new states would be established soon, as according to the resolution of Congress they could not be represented in Congress until they "have, of free inhabitants, as many as shall then be in any one of the least numerous of the thirteen original states." As these original states would also be growing rapidly in population, he believed a considerable time would pass before new western states emerged. In the meantime, the proposed minister would have a vitally important function as the principal administrative link between Congress and the new territories—this being of the greatest importance as henceforth the western territories would be as important as any other part of the world to the United States. The powers of the minister would be great and extensive, and "every part of his duty and business should have a reference to this great object—to preserve the closest and most intimate intercourse and connection between the head and those distant members of the Union."

In the following year Wilson began a protracted and ultimately abortive negotiation with Dutch financial interests in order to secure their support for elaborate schemes he was then beginning to develop for settlement on his lands in the West. In March 1785, he submitted to the Dutch ambassador a comprehensive proposal which he claimed would be mutually advantageous to both the Netherlands and the United States.[7] It was based on the fact that the Netherlands had abundant capital but no land for development, whereas the United States, and Wilson, had an abundance of land and insufficient capital. Prospects, he assured the ambassador, had never been better. Depreciation of the currency in America had reduced the availability of capital there, yet the scope for investment had been increased, with the demand for money so great that a return of 6 percent could easily be obtained with little risk. Offering his services in the management of capital provided by Dutch investors, Wilson defined three ways in which it might advantageously be employed: by buying unsettled and unimproved land; by buying settled land partly improved; and by lending money with land as security.

Pride of place was given, not surprisingly, to the purchase of unsettled and unimproved lands, especially, again not surprisingly as Wilson had an interest in them, "those near the frontiers of Pennsylvania and New York, . . . having an easy communication with the rivers in those two states, whose navigation leads to the Atlantic." These lands would shortly be available for public sale, at a rate low enough, especially as payment could be made in depreciated public securities, to enable a private owner soon to make a considerable capital gain. Wilson expressed his willingness to manage transactions of this kind, on terms which would enable him to acquire for himself under highly advantageous conditions one-third of the lands purchased. The second method of investing capital, in partly improved land, he regarded as offering less chance of large and rapid profits, though presumably the risk would be less, and it needed more capital. The area Wilson suggested for an enterprise of this kind was on the Delaware, near the Falls of Trenton, where, he misleadingly informed the ambassador, Congress had decided to build the federal capital. Accordingly land values would rise rapidly, and it was therefore important to act quickly if the chance was not to be lost. For his services in this transaction Wilson requested, because of its greater complexity, an even higher fee than for purchases of unimproved lands.

The great object in buying and improving lands, Wilson pointed out, was "a rapid accumulation of the capital, beyond any rate of interest," which while difficult for those from long-settled communities to understand, was the way in which "the foundations of by far the greatest number of large fortunes in North America had been laid." Payment of annual interest was not therefore guaranteed in the first type of scheme, though it might occur. The second type would produce both an annual profit and an increase in the capital, though of course less than with totally unimproved lands.

The third method of investing Dutch capital, lending the money on the security of land, Wilson asserted would bring in at least 6 percent. He was willing to act as agent in this type of business also, and it is not an unreasonable supposition that had his schemes matured a significant part of the money lent would have been put, directly or indirectly, to the support of his own projects.

Wilson realized that his demands for remuneration for his services might be thought excessive. He admitted that the gain to him would be very great, but contended that his services would entitle him to high rewards. The work involved, he maintained, would be so onerous that he would have to abandon a good part of his lucrative law practice. Moreover, he claimed to be unusually well qualified to undertake the duties he was proposing for himself. His self-commendation to the ambassador referred to his prewar residence in Reading and Carlisle, where he had had an extensive law practice, and to his subsequent legal career in Philadelphia, giving him a knowledge not only of where land was to be had, but also acquaintance with the men concerned in the business. Because he knew the country, no one would have a sounder judgment with regard to the lands most likely to be settled, and his law practice, which occasionally had extended to New York and New Jersey, would give him "the best means, without going ostentatiously to work, of making enquiries or of receiving information concerning purchases, titles, and persons."

It does not seem that the Dutch were impressed by Wilson's proposals. There is no evidence of any positive response in 1785, but Wilson, characteristically persistent, continued his efforts to obtain capital from what he considered a most promising source. In 1788 he appears to have planned "to embark for Europe,"[8] which almost certainly meant Holland, in order to undertake transactions in land. Though there is no evidence to indicate that he went—it is most unlikely that he did—he still continued his negotiations with Dutch financiers. In 1792 and 1793 he made agreements with a Dutch consortium over the sale of vast tracts of land in western Pennsylvania, and it appears that he tried to negotiate an arrangement very similar to the one he had proposed in 1785, by which he would become, on very favorable terms, manager on behalf of a group of Amsterdam investors of an area of one million acres for which he had acquired warrants.[9]

It was almost certainly in order to advance and extend this scheme that Wilson wrote the pamphlet now known under the title "On the Improvement and Settlement of Lands in the United States" but which in the original unedited version was entitled "Prospectus of an Association for the Promotion of Immigration from Europe."[10] It was the grandiose project here outlined which Wilson described to Theophilus Cazenove, the American agent of the Amsterdam group, as "the most extensive hitherto attempted in Pennsylvania, or indeed, in the United States, when the purchase and intended improvements are contemplated in one view."[11] Circumstantial evidence strongly indicates that the "Prospectus" was in fact prepared in order to induce Cazenove to persuade his Amsterdam employers to invest huge amounts of capital in the project outlined in it.

It is on the scheme he outlined in his "Prospectus" that Wilson's reputation depends as one who was motivated not merely by avarice and selfish ambition, but also by an altruistic desire to help to further the long-term interests of his country and its people. Wilson was not an ordinary speculator in land; he wanted profit, certainly, but equally certainly he wanted to play a recognized part in the extension of settlement and thereby to earn the fame he so much coveted. Wealth and fame may be personal aspirations, but it is to misunderstand Wilson to suppose that was all he sought.

The "Prospectus" is a mixture, characteristically Wilsonian, of imagination, idealism, over-optimism, naiveté, and irresponsibility. Its basic argument was that while America had an abundance of good land, its improvement was greatly retarded by lack of capital and labor; Europe, on the other hand, had an abundance of capital and labor, but there land was unobtainable except at a very high price. What, then, could be more sensible than "a proper union of the labor and capitals of Europe with the fertile and unimproved soil of America"? The amount of labor and capital in Europe would, he believed, increase rapidly in the immediate future.

On the eve of the revolutionary and Napoleonic wars in Europe he declared: "The numerous and expensive standing armies, which have checked population, will be diminished; the numerous and expensive establishments of nunneries and monasteries, which have prevented population, will be dissolved; and arbitrary government, which has had a more pernicious influence than either or both of these evils just mentioned, in lessening the numbers and the vigor of the human race, will be destroyed or relaxed." The prospect ahead of the United States was just as attractive: the new Constitution would ensure that the government would "expand in just and accurate proportion to the settlement of the country," since as new settlements developed new states of the Union would be created on terms of equality with the old. Under the liberal American system, major offices in new states would soon be filled by men of ability who had emigrated from Europe, while immigrants of lesser ambition would achieve for themselves and their posterity "the blessings of liberty, plenty, and independence . . . by settling under the free Constitution, and on the rich lands of the United States."

The practical problems confronting settlers on new lands, which clearly were a considerable deterrent to prospective immigrants, Wilson sought to minimize. It is true, he acknowledged, that forests presented certain difficulties to the settler, but he asserted they could be made capable of cultivation more easily than "the waste naked lands in Europe," which were poor and barren. Timber was a problem only to "an ignorant or a weak-handed settler." One with the proper knowledge and skill could make it "a source of ease, wealth, and pleasure" by using it for fencing, building materials, and tools, for converting by burning to pot and pearl ash, a source of profit, with a residue of excellent manure. Not unmindful of the quality of life, he suggested that an attractive environment could be created "by selecting the spots and fields proper for being cleared and cultivated, and blending them judiciously with those which should be left in their natural and unimproved state." "Even a *Farm* [sic] *ornée*," he went on, "may be planted and completed with less expense, with greater profit, and much more speedily in the wilderness of America, than it can be done in the smooth and unvariegated plains of Europe." Forests, then, need not deter. And even if they were something of a problem, it was a diminishing one as every settlement created made less difficult the creation of the next.

More important than this, however, was the fact that "every subsequent settlement, improvement, and farm bestows an additional value upon those which have preceded it." The process of settlement, in other words, was cumulative and reciprocal, with every other individual benefiting from each individual's activities. Surplus crops from older farms, for example, would help to provide the new ones. "A constant market," Wilson wrote, "will thus be regularly opened and regularly supplied; and the alternative vicissitudes of want and excessive plenty will be equally unknown. Everything produced will find a sufficient demand for its consumption; and every demand for consumption will find produce in sufficient quantities to supply it." The rate of progress as a result of this pattern was already remarkable, but was far less than could be achieved if European men and money were associated with it in sufficient quantities.

The rest of the "Prospectus" was concerned with the practical details of organizing an immense program of settlement in the West. Wilson attached very great importance to allaying misgivings by trying to ensure that the comfort and well-being of prospective settlers would as far as possible be provided for by thorough and humane planning. His imaginative proposals sometimes lacked feasibility but they nevertheless display a deep understanding of the practical problems, an awareness of the fears and hopes of immigrants, and a real desire to help them achieve "freedom, ease, independence, and happiness." Wilson establishes a claim to respect as a pioneer of planned immigration and settlement; had his plans been put into practice, the process of settlement might have taken a very different course, and a good deal of hardship and injustice avoided.

One great deterrent to emigration from Europe was, he asserted, fear of the hardships and dangers of a long voyage, a fear aggravated by the presence of wives and children. "The vessel," he suggested, "may be insufficient; the commander may be hard-hearted; the season may be unfavorable; the provisions may be of an ordinary kind; the water may be scarce; an improper number of passengers may be crowded together; sickness and infectious disorders may be the consequence."

Even if this prospect did not deter, the further prospect of arrival, friendless, in a strange country, with the necessity still of deciding where to settle and in the meantime of maintaining his family at great expense in the port of arrival, might dismay the prospective immigrant. Futhermore, even when the place of settlement had been decided upon, probably fortuitously, the hardship for his wife and children of the journey thither would daunt many a man, especially as few would be able to afford equipment that would lighten the journey. Once arrived at the destination the immigrant, encumbered with his family, would be faced with the task of building them a home and providing for their sustenance, "in a frontier or unsettled country and, perhaps, at an unfavorable season of the year." These depressing prospects might not be enough to deter those who were "forced by dire necessity, or impelled by resistless ambition," but they would deter the people Wilson was hoping to attract—those with some means, anxious to improve an already fairly comfortable situation in life. It was on people of this kind, he maintained, "that the settlement of a new country can be expected to be made on the best terms, with the greatest expedition, and with the largest share of private and public felicity." Many people in this position would welcome a plan which would enable them to migrate to America in comfort and safety, and "those who could devise and execute such a plan would perform a most precious service to individuals and to society, and would merit a rich compensation for their exertions and labors."

Wilson then presented his plan. As its prime purpose was to induce Dutch businessmen to invest large amounts of capital in western projects, it considered first the financial aspect. Public land about to be made available was to be bought in large amounts after having been first carefully surveyed, and should then be accurately subdivided into one-, two-, and three-hundred-acre units. Descriptions of these units "representing the lands to be neither better nor worse than in truth they are, should be carefully made," and the maps and titles clearly and properly drawn up. All this required ample supplies of money which must come from Europe. Wilson emphasized the difficulty that dogged him all his life: "The first axiom in this plan is—never to be in want of money." Those who invested in the project were to get "a reasonable proportion of the lands purchased, or of the net proceeds" as well as "a very handsome commission," payable in Europe, on lands sold. In addition they were to get a large share of the profits from the passage money paid by emigrants. The European directors of the project he urged "should be men of known and established character as well as property—such as will attract and deserve the confidence of those who propose to emigrate with their families and nearest connections."

Measures proposed for the transport and settlement of emigrants similarly were designed to inspire confidence. "The vessels employed in this service," he urged, "should be strong and good and seaworthy in every respect: they should sail well; they should be fitted out in the most complete manner; they should be abundantly supplied with every thing necessary and comfortable; they should be under the command of officers distinguished by their humanity as well as by their nautical abilities."

The next stage in the Wilson plan was less realistic, even with the injection of unprecedented amounts of capital, but it was in spirit akin to more practical proposals of a similar nature put forward earlier by James Oglethorpe[12] and subsequently by Edward Gibbon Wakefield.[13] Indeed, to use Wilson's own metaphor, it is possible to imagine a "chain of connection" among these three distinguished practitioners of colonization. Wilson recognized the enormous importance of proper preparation for the reception of immigrants. They were to be provided with proper accommodation on landing in America; their journey to their final destination should be organized in easy stages; and when they arrived at the land they had purchased "they should find, for their use, a house already built, a garden already made, an orchard already planted, a portion of land already cleared, and grain already growing or reaped." Moreover, facilities within a reasonable distance of the place of settlement should be established for the purchase of livestock, to obviate the need and cost of driving them long distances. How a labor force for these remarkable operations was to be provided he does not state, but he does observe that payment "at a reasonable rate" would have to be made by settlers in addition to the price they had already paid for their land. The utter impracticability of such a scheme puts in doubt Wilson's sincerity, but in matters of land and business the vision he displayed in matters of law and politics became not infrequently transposed to fantasy, to the detriment of the interests of himself as well as of others. If he deceived, he deceived himself also.

Knowledge of these arrangements made for their reception would, Wilson contended, dispel the fears which have deterred many families from emigrating. "The obstacles will appear to be smoothed; the dangers and difficulties will vanish; and the happy issue of the adventure will rise in pleasing prospect before the adventurer." He envisaged cooperative emigration under his scheme of groups of families from the same district, who, traveling together, would settle in the same place, "and may gain for themselves and secure for their posterity the possession and inheritance of liberty, property, plenty, and independence, without having been obliged to sacrifice, for a single moment, the comforts of life or society."

Wilson then proceeded to define the details of his plan more exactly. Careful selection of the ports of embarkation was necessary. His choice, not surprisingly, fell on Amsterdam as the most appropriate point for most of Europe. Hamburg was to be the embarkation point for northern Europe, Bristol or Liverpool for England, Greenock for Scotland, and Cork, Dublin, or Londonderry for Ireland.[14] Very careful selection of tracts of land, and the securing of indisputable titles he regarded as of vital importance to the success of the enterprise. These matters required expert and disinterested local knowledge and skill, and would therefore involve great but unavoidable expense if emigrants were to be given the guarantees of good land and a good title necessary to attract them to the enterprise.

The regions Wilson selected as the most suitable for the undertaking were "those to the westward and northward of Pennsylvania, on the southern and western shores of Lake Erie, and on the river Miami, which falls into that lake,"—an area including the Western Reserve and the Pennsylvania-New York border near the head waters of the Susquehanna and Delaware rivers, where Wilson already had extensive interests. This part of the United States he regarded as a particularly promising area in which to buy land, because of its good communications with other parts of the country both to the east and to the west. The lands were in what he termed a "great and eligible line of communication" extending from the Susquehanna and Delaware rivers to Lake Erie, and thence by way of the Miami, Wabash, Ohio and Illinois rivers to the Mississippi or by way of the St. Joseph River to Lake Michigan. The geographical factors may not have been quite what he believed, but his basic idea was sound. He also believed, again no doubt genuinely, that the climate of that region was a further attraction. "The climate," he asserted, ". . . is not less inviting than the situation and the soil. The country is in the same latitudes with the states of Massachusetts, Connecticut, New York, New Jersey, and Pennsylvania. By every information, we are led to believe that the severity of heat in summer and of cold in winter decreases in proportion as progress is made to the westward." Wilson, ever mindful of the interests of his country as well as his own, believed also that the United States would benefit equally from the development of settlement in this area. "Many reasons," he asserted, "public as well as private, satisfy me, after long and deliberate reflection on the subject, that it will be the interest of the United States as well as of individuals to pursue the settlement of farms and the establishment of states in the direction of the great line which I have described. In a great political view, it will be found to be the line of union and the line of strength."

A secondary area of settlement Wilson commended was along "the line from Lake Michigan to the Mississippi by the Fox and the Ouisconsing rivers," where he pointed out, accurately, that there was only one portage, and that of a mere three miles, giving, in fact, virtually unhampered communication by water between the Mississippi and Lake Erie. "It lies," he stated, again accurately, "through a country described by the latest and best accounts to be very rich and very level; and it is said to lead directly to the most valuable and extensive fur trade which can be found in America—that on the head waters of the Mississippi, and on the waters to the westward and northward of it." The lands on the Ohio and to the south of it Wilson thought less attractive to settlers than those he had discussed. Though the soil was as good, the climate was not, and communication with the Atlantic was less convenient. He was well aware that his plan was an extraordinarily extensive one, but he believed that it was practicable. "The very extent," he contended, "may sometimes aid the execution of a system," and this he believed to be the case with this plan. He believed, as he had reason to, that Cazenove, if Cazenove was in fact the recipient of the "Prospectus," was well able to "distinguish what is great from what is extravagant, and what is only extensive from what is impracticable." He believed also that Cazenove would be frank in his appraisal of the scheme. And, he informed him: "If I did not believe you animated with an ardent desire to promote systems formed on the scale of public felicity as well as on that of private interest . . . these proposals would never have been submitted to your view."

Wilson carried his detailed proposals to the extent of defining the return cargoes which the emigrant ships might profitably carry. He explained in more detail his plan for the transportation of emigrants across the continent: A "chain of houses and farms" at intervals of ten miles would enable them to find frequent refreshment and supplies, and toward the end of it there would be available to them, "at reasonable prices, a supply of horses, oxen, cows, sheep, hogs, and poultry, all of the best breeds; and farming utensils of the best kinds and construction." That the creation of the line of stages would initially be very expensive he fully acknowledged, but he maintained that "the rising value of the plantations, which ought to be larger and larger as we advance westward; the gradual increase of the stock and improvements on them; and the constant market for everything which they could produce would, in a short time, be sources of great profit to the proprietors, as well as of great convenience to the emigrants."

Two factors basic to any sound scheme for settlement, and yet which had been in the past, and were to be often in the future, callously or irresponsibly neglected, Wilson felt it important again to emphasize. "I cannot," he wrote, "insist too much upon the propriety and importance of small improvements being made on the different places of settlement, before the emigrants shall respectively arrive at them. These improvements, though small, are everything to a new settler. His family will derive great resource from even a patch of potatoes, carrots, turnips, cabbages, and other vegetables. Instead of losing his time, and wasting the scanty remains of his stock in cash (if of his stock in cash even any scanty remains are left) in searching and procuring the necessary sustenance of his family, he has the satisfaction to find the means of subsistence provided for him on the most easy terms, and placed within his reach." However impracticable this may have been in the circumstances of the West in the 1790s, it does reveal Wilson's awareness of the problems, and his concern for the welfare of the people he was seeking to attract. But was it in fact so impracticable? Wilson went on: "At first, those improvements will require very considerable advances in money, but the lands on which they shall be made will be an ample security for the reimbursement of the sums advanced; and, after the first series of settlements shall be made, those in every preceding series will find their account in making for others improvements similar to those which were made for themselves, and in receiving, after a short interval, the return of a sum equal to that which they have previously been obliged to expend."

Precision in the surveying of tracts—including subdivisions —was of the greatest importance. "No expense or pains," Wilson declared, "ought to be spared in examining, conveying, and laying off the lands with the utmost fairness and correctness; and in obtaining, in order to be able to give, a just account of their quality and situation, and of the timber growing upon them." In this way, a prospective purchaser without seeing the land would know with reasonable certainty what he was buying. "Correctness and fairness in the surveys," he contended, "will lay the foundation of the utmost certainty and regularity in conveying the titles from the proprietors of the large tracts to the purchasers of the several surveys. Hence will result that security which is an essential ingredient in the value of every real estate."

Under Wilson's scheme, every third survey was to be reserved, by lot, for the proprietors. This was not only because it would be profitable for them, as its value would increase, even if it were left uncultivated, by the cultivation of the land around it. There was also a broader purpose. The proprietors would be enabled to "exhibit, in particular places, the most instructive examples of every species of agricultural improvement"; they would be given a stimulus to activity "in promoting every plan which can accelerate the growth and value of the settlements, and the prosperity and happiness of the settlers; they would be able to make appropriate adjustments whenever a settler found that the quality of his land fell markedly short of what it had been represented to be, or that his title to it was defective. And, expounding a feature which he considered "to be of the last importance to the general utility and vigor of the system," he declared finally: "It will be in the power of the proprietors to lease, at easy and advantageous rates, farms to those who shall have come out on contracts of service, and shall have honestly performed the conditions of their contracts. An easy and advantageous lease will naturally pave the way to a purchase; and thus the most beneficial prospects will be opened even to those who possess nothing but their own labor and honest industry."

So comprehensive a scheme, with the prospect of great financial gain to all engaged in it, would require and command the services of men "well recommended by their integrity and their skill," whose reputation would be a guarantee of its proper execution. Grandiose in conception, it illustrates Wilson's characteristic fusion of the public interest with his own private interest, but to him the furtherance of the public interest was a necessary ingredient. Planned settlement on this scale possibly was no more feasible after the Revolution than before it, but in attempting it Wilson revealed the enlightened self-interest which marked so many of his activities. The project he outlined was perhaps viable so long as he got massive financial backing from the Amsterdam consortium. Though excessively optimistic in its assumptions it may have had a sufficient measure of realism to make it at least a partial success, which was all that was ever attainable in schemes of this kind.

How impressed the Amsterdam associates were by the "Prospectus" is impossible to determine, as the invasion of Holland by France in February 1793 put an end to the possibility of financial support from Dutch merchants for the foreseeable future. Wilson was left stranded, and though he struggled desperately thoughout 1793 to retain his interest in the lands in whose future he had such faith, he was in fact now deprived of what was his last reasonable chance of success in his western enterprises. From then on expedient followed expedient, and calamity calamity, until the final collapse of all his schemes in 1798. He continued to invest in new land, but more and more he was forced to disgorge others in a desperate attempt to save something of a fast-crumbling empire, and succeeded merely in aggravating his embarrassments. He even, in 1797, adopted the forlorn expedient of petitioning Congress to reverse the decision of the Continental Congress and validate the claims of the Illinois-Wabash

Company.[15] His final efforts to hold on to his empire display a distinct increase in the degree of irrationality which was never wholly absent from his speculative activities.

It was not only in his land enterprises that Wilson met with eventual disaster. Though his hopes of fortune, if not of fame, rested largely on land, there were other projects that he believed would enrich him and which, in most cases, would also benefit his country. In the event, however, they aggravated the extent of the final collapse. He was involved in the 1780s, often in association with his brother-in-law, Mark Bird, with various projects including iron works and saw mills in the neighborhood of Trenton, which he believed would become the capital of the United States.[16] After the collapse of these projects, in 1787, he devised an ambitious plan to construct a small manufacturing center on the Wallenpaupack River, at Wilsonville, where he hoped to build one of the largest cloth mills in America, with subsidiary dye and cloth printing works.[17]

Other ventures included part ownership of two vessels—one, the *Peggy and Nancy,* in the West Indian trade,[18] and the other, the *United States,* for the China trade. With the foresight so characteristic of him, he looked to China as a productive area for American commercial expansion, and the *United States* was dispatched there in 1784. Had it arrived, it would have been the first ship of American registry to reach Canton,[19] but it did not get farther than Pondicherry, in India, where it had to be sold to pay the wages of the crew, involving Wilson and his partners in heavy losses.

Another scheme that aroused high hopes but which does not seem to have been very successful was one in conjunction with, among others, Silas Deane, to supply the French navy with masts. This was during the War of Independence, after the French alliance seemed to open the way to a close trading relationship between France and the United States, an opportunity Wilson sought to exploit by securing appointment as advocate general for France in the United States "in order that he may be charged with all the causes and matters relative to navigation and commerce."[20] It appears that in association with Robert Morris and Silas Deane he planned to establish an agency in Nantes for the development of trade between the two countries.[21]

Reflecting the breadth of his interests, or his opportunism, Wilson became in 1793 a member—presumably a passive one as there is no evidence of active participation—of the "Society for promoting the Manufacture of Sugar from the Sugar Maple Tree, and furthering the interests of Agriculture in Pennsylvania."[22] Many of the major projects in which he was interested were being developed in the 1790s, financed from the large profits of his highly lucrative law practice (had he confined himself to this he would indeed have remained rich) and from massive borrowing. In his business, as in his land enterprises, it was the general financial collapse of 1796 which undermined his position beyond reasonable hope of early recovery. It was no consolation that many of his friends and associates—notably Robert Morris— suffered with him. Morris endured a debtor's prison; Wilson died, broken in spirit, in 1798. Benjamin Rush subsequently, in 1811, sadly observed to John Adams, "There was scarcely a single deceased person that was active in our Revolution that has not died poor in Pennsylvania."[23]

CHAPTER 11

*Some concluding observations
on the importance of the
contribution of James Wilson to
the historical development of the
United States.*

Whatever the reputation Wilson may have achieved among his contemporaries, as a jurist or even as a statesman, he did not achieve the
position he coveted, nor did his reputation long outlive those who
knew him. Friends and associates like John Dickinson, Robert Morris, Benjamin Franklin, James Iredell, Arthur St.Clair, Benjamin
Rush, and that most discerning of judges, George Washington, all
esteemed him highly as a man who possessed to an unusual degree
both knowledge and wisdom. Those who were acquainted with his
work in the Federal Convention acknowledged that his contribution
was of the first importance. "No man," wrote fellow delegate William
Pierce, "is more clear, copious, and comprehensive than Mr. Wilson"
whom he regarded as "among the foremost in legal and political
knowledge,"[1] and Washington thought him "as able, candid, and
honest a member as any in the convention."[2] Those who disliked the
principles of government with which Wilson was identified took a less
favorable view of him, and often charged him with intellectual dishonesty. He could, it was said, "bewilder truth in all the mazes of
sophistry, and render the plainest propositions problematical."[3] The
fears of his opponents as much as the praise of those who thought as he
did reflect the importance of the influence he had in the central issue of
the form of government to be adopted by the United States.

   That Wilson's fame soon underwent an eclipse is due in part to
the unfortunate circumstances in which he died; in part also to the fact
that before very long there emerged more dominating personalities
who proclaimed many, though never all, of the ideas which he had

advocated, and probably in part also to the paucity of his correspondence, the lifeblood of biographers, of which his friends sometimes complained.[4] Even the publication six years after his death of his law lectures and other public papers, under the editorship of his son Bird Wilson,[5] did not establish him as the peer of Madison, Hamilton, or Jefferson, none of whom can claim an unquestioned superiority over him as a Founding Father of the "Federal Republic," to use Wilson's own term, of America.

It was not until late in the nineteenth century that Wilson began to emerge from obscurity. A new edition of *The Works of James Wilson* appeared in 1896 under the editorship of James DeWitt Andrews; a biographical study was begun by L. H. Alexander but left unfinished at the author's death; Wilson's remains were removed in 1906 from the place where they had lain since 1798 and reinterred with honor in the precincts of Christ Church, Philadelphia; and he was publicly extolled at the dedication of Pennsylvania's new Capitol in the same year by President Theodore Roosevelt as an inspiration behind his "theory of governmental action."[6] The most appreciative of Wilson's latter-day admirers was, however, a fellow Scot, James Bryce,[7] the ablest and most influential of European expositors and interpreters of the American political system. Bryce had no doubt of Wilson's eminence—perhaps even preeminence—as a Founding Father, and it was he who wrote what remains the most perceptive of all tributes to him:

> The services which such a mind as Wilson's—broad, penetrating, exact, and luminous—can render to a nation can hardly be overestimated. In the long run, the world is ruled by ideas. Whoever gives to a nation, and most of all to a nation at the outset of its career, sound, just principles for the conduct of its government, principles which are in harmony with its character and are capable of progressive expansion as it expands, is a true benefactor to that nation, and deserves to be held in everlasting memory. Such a one was James Wilson.[8]

The measure of Wilson's achievements, Bryce accurately discerned, lies substantially in what in his mind constituted sound, just principles of government, in the degree to which they were in harmony with the character, or spirit, of the nation and in their inherent capacity for progressive expansion. So often did Wilson emphasize his fundamental tenet that all power had as its ultimate source the people, that no further exposition of it would seem necessary. There was, however, a unique element in Wilson's thinking, and this can be fully appreciated only by comparing his view of democratic government with those of contemporaries, and for this purpose, providing as they do a useful contrast, Hamilton and Jefferson offer the best illustrations.

Hamilton had much in common with Wilson. Both wanted strong government, though with Hamilton to the substantial exclusion of the states, whereas Wilson envisaged strong state governments complementary to a strong national government. Both recognized the vital importance of financial stability and economic viability. Both accepted the axiom that governments derived their just powers from the consent of the governed. But marked divergences took place over the nature and practice of democratic government. Hamilton, a republican by necessity if not perhaps from conviction, accepted democracy only in dilution. A believer in "mixed" government and an admirer of the British system, he recognized an admixture of democracy to be necessary to a well-ordered state. But in the United States he held it essential to dilute democracy with strong elements of monarchism and aristocracy. This sprang only partly from the conviction that the extent of the United States was too great to be governed under a purely republican system; it reflected also a lack of faith in the electoral discretion of the people and a fear of the harm which might be done by an ephemeral legislative majority which the government was too weak to withstand. Accordingly, though he accepted direct or indirect election of every branch of government except the judicial, his emphasis was heavily on indirect forms. The chief executive, wielding extensive powers, was to be in effect an elected monarch, but one elected by a complex system of indirect election which would place two bodies of electors between the people and the ultimate choice, thus reducing as far as was practicable the factor of popular "unreasonableness" he so much feared. Senators also were to be elected indirectly—though at only one remove from the people—and were, like the president, to hold office during good behavior. Only the House of Representatives resembled that favored by Wilson—directly elected, and consisting not of delegates but of men of independent mind who would act according to their convictions. An elite chosen in large measure by an elite, and exercising extensive power in the interests of the nation, was substantially Hamilton's notion of democratic government.

In many ways Jefferson's democratic concepts seem closer to

those of Wilson, though as he lacked Wilson's clarity of mind and was notably less consistent in his thinking, it is not always easy to compare them. They had in common, as with almost all other of their contemporaries, a belief in a "balanced" government of properly constituted monarchical, aristocratic, and democratic elements; both believed in the principle of "proportional representation" which to Jefferson meant in practice the abolition of the Virginia county unit system and its replacement by one based on equal individual representation; both believed in a broadly based suffrage, but both equally assumed that effective authority would fall to a natural elite of talent and virtue. In the adoption of democratic political methods, however, Wilson went much further than Jefferson thought it advisable to go. Jefferson advocated direct election only of the lower house of the Virginia legislature. He believed that the upper house should be based on different principles and interests, and at one point he favored appointment of senators for life, though subsequently he accepted a nine-year term as more appropriate. The Senate, according to Jefferson's view, should be chosen by the lower house, as "a choice by the people themselves," he observed in a phrase which Wilson would have anathematized, "is not generally distinguished for its wisdom." The Senate, as became its greater wisdom, should be independent of the people, and the maturity of its judgment safeguarded by a minimum age qualification five years greater than that advocated by Wilson for the national Senate. The executive similarly should be chosen by the lower house of the assembly—though much later in his life he began to appreciate the advantages of popular election of the chief executive of the state.[9] The executive thus chosen was to be deliberately weak. To help to ensure this it was to be elected annually, though Jefferson's own experience in the office led him subsequently to modify his view of the nature of the executive power. Weak government to Jefferson was at least in theory a virtue, and the strength of the national government created in 1787 was to him one of its defects.

Wilson believed in strong, effective government at the national and state levels, at the same time as he believed that the people should be the effective source of authority of the legislative and executive branches of government and, to a degree, given the importance he attached to the common law, even of the judicial branch.

If it can be argued that Jefferson was more solicitous than was Wilson for the general interests of the people, it can equally well be argued that Wilson had far more faith than Jefferson in the political judgment of the people. And if it can be argued that Hamilton was a more extreme advocate of a strong national government, it can equally well be argued that the schemes of Wilson were far more practicable and more likely to create an effective system that would survive. Wilson, the reputed aristocrat, had more confidence in the people than had Jefferson, the reputed democrat; Wilson, the defender of the political rights and interests of the people, was a more effective creator of strong public authorities than was Hamilton, who reputably put strong government above all other considerations.

Who then—Hamilton, Jefferson, or Wilson—most nearly accords with Bryce's criteria regarding sound, just principles of government in harmony with the character of the nation? If it is arguable that "the character of the nation" in the late eighteenth century harmonized as much with the ideas of Hamilton and Jefferson as with those of Wilson, it cannot so easily be argued that this remained so for long. Efficient government, drawing its authority always from the people, has become a distinguishing feature of the American system, and for this more is due to Wilson than to any other man of his time. The fears of many—notably Hamilton and including even Jefferson—that the people were not fully to be trusted, proved exaggerated; the essential requirement, which Wilson often drew attention to, of a responsible attitude on the part of a people as aware of their duties as of their rights, was adequately fulfilled.

Bryce's other criterion, the capacity for "progressive expansion," hardly needs elaboration. It was inherent in the Wilson system, and it is sufficient to point out that it was a quality which enabled the spirit of Wilson to succeed where Wilson the man had not, in extending the principle of democratic government closer to the limits he had aimed at in 1787—with regard, conspicuously, to the influence of the people on the choice of president, and to the election of senators directly by the people. It is enough in conclusion to quote with approbation the judgment of R. G. McCloskey:

> It is not too much to say that the ideas of James Wilson more nearly foreshadowed the national future than those of any of his well-remembered contemporaries. No one of them—not Hamilton, or Jefferson, or Madison, or Adams, or Marshall —came so close to representing in his views what the United States was to become.[10]

The story of Wilson, at the personal level, is a sad one. Admired but unloved in his day, his compelling ambition, powered by his enormous energy, failed, though only just, to obtain for him the position in the new nation he so desperately coveted. His life ending in disgrace, the memory of his vital contributions to the welfare of his country almost died with him, and even now resuscitation is impeded by prejudices and misconceptions which still persist. Perhaps it is now too late for Wilson to achieve with posterity the fame he so much desired, and others less deserving may continue to outshine him in the estimation of the people in whom he had put such great faith.

APPENDIX A

The Wyoming Controversy

The controversy between Connecticut and Pennsylvania over the Wyoming valley concerned the region which is now Luzerne County, Pennsylvania, with its main settlement Wilkes-Barre. The Susquehanna Land Company was formed in Connecticut in 1753 and in the following year it obtained from the Iroquois the rights to territory along the Susquehanna River, and after a delay caused by the Seven Years' War began a determined effort in 1769 to settle the area. In the meantime (in 1768) the Iroquois had sold the same lands to the Proprietor of Pennsylvania, and with the arrival of Pennsylvanian settlers serious violence amounting almost to civil war broke out between the two groups. Though this conflict ended in a victory for the Connecticut settlers, with the region in 1776 being designated as a county by the Connecticut assembly, Pennsylvania did not abandon her claim, and in 1782 tried by legal means to establish it. Congress in that year set up a Court of Commission (under Article IX of the Articles of Confederation) to adjudicate the controversy, and Wilson, supported by Joseph Reed, William Bradford, and Jonathan Dickinson Sergeant, was the leading member of the group appointed to present the case of Pennsylvania. The proceedings, held at Trenton, N.J., lasted forty-four days, in an atmosphere of acrimony which at times threatened bloodshed. (Dickinson Papers, Library Company of Philadephia, Item 38). That Wilson labored hard in his cause is attested by his colleague Joseph Reed, who wrote to George Bryan concerning him that "his argument is both laborious and judicious, he has taken much pains, having the success of Pennsylvania much at heart, both on public and private account"—a reference to Wilson's own financial interest in the lands at issue. (W. B. Reed, *Life and Correspondence of Joseph Reed* [Philadelphia, 1847], II, 390). Wilson's advocacy was successful, the commissioners unanimously recognizing the claim of Pennsylvania. The great constitutional importance of the Trenton arbitration was perceived by Wilson, who in presenting his case to the commissioners said: "You are now to decide a territorial controversy which with other nations would have been decided by the sword. This [is] a court of the first impression in any part of the globe." (Quoted in J. P. Boyd, *The Trenton Trial* [Philadelphia, 1937], p. 8). A valuable account of the Wyoming controversy appears in C. P. Smith, *James Wilson*, pp. 170–77).

APPENDIX B

The Treason Trials

The treason trials in Philadelphia in 1778 were the outcome of the British occupation of the city between September 1777 and June 1778. Several citizens who had reputedly cooperated with the British were accused of treason, and two—Abraham Carlisle and John Roberts—were found guilty and condemned to death. Carlisle was charged with having accepted a commission from the British and, though there was no evidence that he had ever carried arms, with having acted as guard at a city gate. Roberts was accused of having urged citizens to abandon the struggle and of conspiring to lead a British force to rescue a fellow Quaker, Israel Pemberton. Wilson was one of the defense counsel, in these and other similar cases, and his argument was based on the need to define treason very narrowly, in order to prevent abuse by the state of the law of treason to condemn political enemies.

A broadly defined law of treason, under which a great variety of offenses not directly concerned with waging war against the state, had often been used in many parts of the world to obtain convictions on a major charge on the basis of comparatively minor offenses. Wilson insisted that proof of an overt act—not merely vague accusations of treasonable intent—was necessary to an indictment for treason, pointing out that English law since the reign of Edward III had required in all cases of treason proof of an overt act, carefully defined. Despite the vigorous defense of the accused by Wilson and his colleagues, the court chose to define treason in the broad sense, and although acquittals were obtained in all other cases, Carlisle and Roberts were condemned to death.

An appeal to the Supreme Executive Council was unsuccessful, despite strong pressure from many prominent citizens of Philadephia, and the two men were duly executed. Pressure from those eager for vengeance in response to acts committed by others during the occupation triumphed over pressure from those anxious to ensure that justice was done. Wilson felt deeply on the issue, and subsequently strove to ensure that the chances of a similar miscarriage of justice should be reduced.

The treason clause in the Constitution of the United States (Art. III, Sec. 3), defining narrowly the crime of treason and providing essential safeguards for the accused against conviction on inadequate evidence, reflects the position taken by

Wilson in 1778 and its adoption was probably largely due to him. Subsequently Wilson stressed in his law lectures the importance of this narrow definition of treason. Quoting Montesquieu, he warned his students "that if the crime of treason be indeterminate, this alone is sufficient to make any government degenerate into arbitrary power." (R. G. McCloskey, *The Works of James Wilson*, II, 663). An excellent account of the treason trials may be found in C. P. Smith, *James Wilson*, Chapter VIII.

Wilson's defense of those accused of treason brought him unpopularity with the Philadelphia "mob," and appears to have stimulated the attack on his house—the so-called Fort Wilson episode—in 1779. Many contemporaries believed this to be so, though others thought that the fact Wilson's house was attacked resulted from merely accidental circumstances. For details of the Fort Wilson incident see especially C. P. Smith, *James Wilson*, Chapter IX; and also L. H. Butterfield, *The Letters of Benjamin Rush*, I, 240; W. B. Reed, *The Life and Correspondence of Joseph Reed*, II, 149–54, 423–28; W. H. Smith, *The St. Clair Papers*, I, 488n.

APPENDIX C

The Pennsylvania Constitution of 1776

The Pennsylvania constitution of 1776 was framed by a convention in which the more radical elements in the state were dominant, and which contained few members of much experience in law or government. The constitution that the convention adopted was designed to prevent an aristocratic elite from gaining control of affairs in Pennsylvania, and it reflected an extreme doctrinaire approach at marked variance with that displayed in most other states and which violated what had come to be widely accepted in America as sound principles of government. In particular it rejected the concept of "mixed" government, and on the grounds that "the people of this state have the sole, exclusive and inherent right of governing and regulating the internal police of the same," it put the real power in the hands of a unicameral legislature elected on a very broad franchise and in which, to reduce the danger of domination by long-serving members, membership was limited to four years in seven.

The check devised to prevent the General Assembly from acting contrary to the interests of the people was to publish bills for consideration by the people at large before final adoption in the next session, though there was provision for the enactment of laws "on occasions of sudden necessity" without such submission, which in any event was in practice an ineffective check on the conduct of the assembly.

The executive branch exercising minimal powers, consisted of a Supreme Executive Council comprising twelve members directly elected on a county unit basis under a system of rotation for a maximum of three years. "By this mode of election and continual rotation," the constitution stated, "more men will be trained to public business . . . and moreover the danger of establishing an inconvenient aristocracy will be effectively prevented." The chief executive, or president, was to be chosen annually by joint ballot of the General Assembly and council. The consitution also created a body called the Council of Censors, which was elected septennially on a county unit basis and which was required to investigate the conduct of officials of the state, and to ascertain whether the constitution had in any way been violated. The Council of Censors was empowered, if two-thirds agreed, to summon a convention to consider amendments to the constitution regarded by the council as absolutely necessary.

The constitution of 1776 is a long one, full of obeisances to the spirit of democracy. But in the minds of many of its critics, including Wilson, its effect would be to impose an irresponsible tyranny of the assembly, a belief apparently confirmed by the requirement that every member of the legislature take an oath to do nothing which would tend to lessen the rights and privileges of the people "as declared in the constitution of this state"—a provision which, in effect, if the constitution were strictly adhered to, made constitutional amendment by a new convention on the terms prescribed in the provision regarding the Council of Censors the only means of reforming the system.

The Pennsylvania constitution of 1776 was not only intellectually contemptible to men like Wilson or merely a threat to the influence of the upper class in Pennsylvania; it was, by violating the principles which were believed necessary to ensure free government, a threat to the democracy it was designed to safeguard. (For a detailed study of the constitution of 1776 see J. P. Selsam, *The Pennsylvania Constitution of 1776* [Philadelphia, 1936]).

NOTES

NOTES TO
CHAPTER 1

1. The comparative obscurity of Wilson's origin and, possibly, confusion with a contemporary namesake at St. Andrews, has given rise to the mistaken belief that his father was one of the founders of the Associate Presbytery which seceded from the Church of Scotland in 1733. William Wilson remained a member of the Church of Scotland of which he was a ruling elder.

2. Most of the knowledge we have of Wilson's early life is derived from a letter dated May 16, 1805, from Robert Annan to Bird Wilson, in the Rush MSS, Library Company of Philadelphia.

3. See below, p. 17.

4. John Dickinson was one of the most influential of Whig lawyers. He was the author of many pamphlets of the revolutionary period, notably *Letters from a Farmer in Pennsylvania* which had a profound effect on the development of the revolution in America. He was largely responsible for the drafting of the Articles of Confederation, and in the Federal Convention of 1787 he defended the principle of state equality, though he willingly accepted the compromise finally reached. Though at a number of points Dickinson's views differed in important respects from those of Wilson, master and pupil maintained a friendly relationship throughout Wilson's life.

5. Rachel Bird, who seems with her brother, Mark, to have inherited substantial property from her father, was the stepdaughter of Colonel Patton, an influential figure in the Reading district (see C. P. Smith, *James Wilson*, pp. 37–38).

6. The plan to create Vandalia, in the Ohio region, as a separate colony was supported by many influential Americans and immense importance was attached to its realization by those who were concerned with the development of the West. Its rejection by the British government, after great hopes had been raised in the course of

protracted discussions, therefore alienated many who now began to play a more active part in stimulating opposition to Britain.

7. The territorial provisions of the Quebec Act, which attached to the province of Quebec the most highly coveted of the western lands—those lying between the Ohio and Mississippi rivers and extending northward to the Great Lakes—were potentially severely damaging to those Americans who were interested in western development, and seemed to confirm the growing belief that they could no longer hope for a change of policy in a direction more in accordance with their interests.

8. Wilson stated that the pamphlet was written "above five years ago" when the nonimportation agreement following the imposition of the Townshend duties was in force, but that before it was ready for publication the crisis ended, and "it was, then, judged unseasonable" to publish it. (See Wilson Papers [MSS in the Library of the Historical Society of Pennsylvania, Philadephia], II, 13½). It is perhaps significant that it was at this time also that the prospects improved, for a time, of a much more rapid development of the West.

9. E. C. Burnett, *Letters of Members of the Continental Congress* (Washington, D.C., 1921), I, 175.

10. The Continental Congress was the commonly used but unofficial name for the revolutionary assembly which met first in September 1774 and continued in existence until March 1789, when it was superseded by a new Congress in accordance with the provisions of the Constitution of 1787. A distinction is often made between the Continental Congress of the period before March 1, 1781, when the Articles of Confederation came into effect, and the Congress of the Confederation of the subsequent period. However, as the Congress remained basically the same, and as contemporaries used the term Continental Congress throughout the entire period 1774 to 1789, that designation is used here with regard to the Congress before and after March 1781.

11. J. P. Boyd, *The Papers of Thomas Jefferson* (Princeton, 1950–   ), I, 464–65. (Copyright 1950 by Princeton University Press. Reprinted by permission of Princeton University Press.)

12. See Appendix A.

13. Arthur St. Clair was a close associate of Wilson. He was a fellow Scot, having been born in Thurso, and he had a similar interest in the development of the West, as well as in Pennsylvania politics. He was sent as a colonel in 1775 to take part in the retreat of the American army from Canada. From 1787 to 1802 he was governor of the Northwest Territory.

14. Burnett, *op. cit.,* I, 193, 197.

15. William Thompson, an Ulster Scot, was associated with Wilson at Carlisle, where he had been a surveyor and justice of the peace. An active Whig before the revolution, when war broke out he was appointed commander of the 2nd Pennsylvania Regiment, becoming brigadier general in March 1776. He was captured during the Canadian campaign, and returned to Pennsylvania on parole.

16. R. G. McCloskey, *The Works of James Wilson* (Cambridge, Mass., 1967), II, 747–48.

17. R. G. Adams, *Selected Political Essays of James Wilson* (New York, 1930), pp. 103–122.

18. *Pennsylvania Magazine of History and Biography,* LXV (1941), 459.

19 W. H. Smith, *The St. Clair Papers; The Life and Public Services of Arthur St. Clair* (Cincinnati, 1882), I, 324–25.

20. J. P. Selsam, *The Pennsylvania Constitution of 1776; A Study in Revolutionary Democracy* (Philadelphia, 1936), p. 110.

21. Burnett, *op. cit.,* I, 293, Diary of Richard Smith, January 1, 1776. The "Association" was a comprehensive scheme to bring about the abandonment of unacceptable British policies by means of economic pressures. Essentially, importation of goods from Britain or Ireland was to cease from December 1, 1774, and, unless the acts of Parliament complained of had been repealed by then, exportation of goods to Britain, Ireland, and the West Indies was to cease on September 10, 1775. In addition, steps were to be taken to render America as independent as possible of supplies from abroad by, for example, encouraging the breeding of sheep, promoting manufactures and agriculture, encouraging frugality, and discouraging any kind of extravagance or dissipation, such as horseracing, cockfighting or theatrical performances. Other provisions forbade merchants to raise prices as a result of any scarcity which might arise, and machinery for the enforcement of the Association, in the form of local committees, was established. It represented a determined effort by the Continental Congress to achieve a satisfactory settlement short of independence and, in its inception, without bloodshed. (See Merrill Jensen, *English Historical Documents,* IX [American Colonial Documents to 1776], Document No. 151.)

22. Burnett, *op. cit.,* I, 359, 404.

23. L. H. Butterfield, *The Adams Papers* (Cambridge, Mass., 1961), II, 240; see also Selsam, *op. cit.,* p. 116.

24. Butterfield, *op. cit.,* II, 239.

25. I. Brant, *James Madison* (Indianapolis, 1948–56), I, 228.

26. Dreer Collection, Letters of Members of the Old Congress (Historical Society of Pennsylvania), II, 29½, Wilson to Gates.

27. Brant, *op. cit.,* I, 227–28.

28. R. L. Brunhouse, *The Counter-Revolution in Pennsylvania, 1776–1790* (Harrisburg, 1942), p. 13.

29. Library of Congress, Pennsylvania Miscellaneous, IV, January 7, 1776–July 15, 1776.

30. Brant, *op. cit.,* I, 228.

31. Diary of James Allen (Historical Society of Pennsylvania), June 16, 1776–January 25, 1777.

NOTES TO
CHAPTER 2

1. R. G. McCloskey, *The Works of James Wilson*, I, 213.

2. Ibid., I, 133.

3. Ibid., I, 184.

4. Ibid., I, 121.

5. James Wilson, *An Introductory Lecture to a Course of Law Lectures; to which is added a Plan of the Lectures* (Philadelphia, 1791), p. 32.

6. Ibid., p. 64.

7. Oration delivered on July 4, 1788, in McCloskey, *op. cit.*, II, 773–80.

8. McCloskey, *op. cit.*, II, 577.

9. Wilson, *op. cit.*, pp. 18–19.

10. McCloskey, *op. cit.*, I, 238.

11. Ibid, II, 587–88.

12. Ibid., I, 242.

13. Ibid., I, 241.

14. Ibid., II, 592–93.

15. See below pp. 158–59.

16. Oration delivered on July 4, 1788, in McCloskey, *op. cit.*, II, 779.

17. McCloskey, *op. cit.*, I, 146.

18. Wilson, *op. cit.*, p. 59.

19. Ibid., p. 56.

20. Ibid., p. 46.

21. Speech in Pennsylvania Convention, 1789. Wilson Papers II, Historical Society of Pennsylvania.

22. J. B. McMaster and F. D. Stone, *Pennsylvania and the Federal Constitution, 1787–1788* (Philadelphia, 1888), p. 412.

23. McCloskey, *op. cit.*, I, 77.

24. McMaster and Stone, *op. cit.*, p. 230.

25. McCloskey, *op. cit.*, I, 1, note 1.

26. Speech in Pennsylvania Convention, 1789, Wilson Papers II.

27. McCloskey, *op. cit.*, II, 787–88.

28. Ibid., I, 406–7.

29. Ibid., I, 406.

30. Ibid., I, 296. See below p. 96. "Wanting to" is used in the archaic sense of "deficient in."

31. Ibid., II, 790.

32. Ibid., I, 242.

33. Ibid., I, 406.

34. Ibid., I, 406.

NOTES TO
CHAPTER 3

1. The Articles of Confederation, which formed the basis of the political structure of the United States from 1781 to 1789, continued the unicameral Congress already in existence. The principle of equality of the states was confirmed, with each state having one vote in Congress, and unanimity among the states being necessary for any amendment. Important legislation required the approval of nine of the thirteen states, thus making it possible for a minority of the states containing a small minority of the population to outvote a majority of the states containing a substantial majority of the population. The powers of Congress under the Articles were limited to those of making war and peace, of sending and receiving ambassadors, of entering into treaties and alliances, of coining money, of regulating Indian affairs, and of establishing a post office. No power was granted either to raise revenue independently of the states or to regulate commerce. There was no proper provision for the creation of an effective executive branch of government, executive powers being exercised by a number of separate committees. Similarly, there was no provision for the establishment of a judicial branch of the central government, though Congress could set up ad hoc courts for certain purposes. The Articles expressly stated that each state would retain "its sovereignty, freedom and independence" and described the arrangement entered into as "a firm league of friendship." It is possible that if given the power to raise revenue and to regulate commerce Congress could have developed eventually an effective government despite what to many contemporaries were fundamental deficiencies in the general political structure created by the Articles; it is clear that without those powers it could not.

2. W. C. Ford, *Journals of the Continental Congress* (Washington, D.C., 1904–37), VII, 122–23 (February 14, 1777).

3. L. H. Butterfield, *The Adams Papers,* II, 244.

4. E. C. Burnett, *Letters of Members of the Continental Congress,* II, 515n.

5. Ford, *op.cit.,* XXV, 868 (January 27, 1783).

6. Ibid., XXV, 879 (January 29, 1783).

7. Ibid., XXV, 876–77 (January 28, 1783).

8. J. P. Boyd, *The Papers of Thomas Jefferson,* I, 322; Butterfield, *op.cit.,* II, 245. Wilson's attitude toward slavery was ambiguous. He seems often to be a firm opponent of slavery, yet he owned a slave himself until 1794, and appears to have justified this, at least to himself, by drawing a distinction between ownership and absolute control of a person and the right to the labor of a person.

9. Ford, *op.cit.,* XXV, 854 (January 14, 1783).

10. Burnett, *op.cit.,* II, 215–17, Wilson to Robert Morris, January 14, 1777.

11. Courts of admiralty exercised jurisdiction over maritime cases in general, involving a great variety of issues arising from shipping. A very important part of admiralty jurisdiction, especially in the later eighteenth and early nineteenth centuries, concerned prize cases.

12. Robert Morris to James Wilson, January 31, 1777. Society Collection. Historical Society of Pennsylvania.

13. Burnett, *op.cit.*, II, 252, Diary of Benjamin Rush, February 14, 1777.

14. C. L. Ver Steeg, *Robert Morris, Revolutionary Financier* (Philadelphia, 1954), pp. 174–75.

15. Ford, *op.cit.*, IX, 947 (November 21, 1777).

16. For a list of Wilson's committee appointments see L. H. Alexander, "James Wilson; Nation-Builder," in *The Green Bag*, XIX (1907).

17. Butterfield, *op.cit.*, III, 411.

18. Ford, *op.cit.*, XXIV, 313 (April 30, 1783).

19. Ibid., XXV, 901 (February 18, 1783).

20. Butterfield, *op.cit.*, II, 241–42.

21. See, e.g., Butterfield, *op.cit.*, II, 243.

22. Ford, *op.cit.*, XXV, 962 (April 18, 1783).

23. Ibid., XXX, 296, 299–303 (May 22 and 24, 1786).

24. The Camden-Yorke opinion was a legal opinion issued in 1757 by the British attorney general and the solicitor general. It concerned only land titles in India where, it declared, grants of land made to British citizens by "the Grand Mogul or any of the Indian princes or governments" were valid without the need for confirmation by the British government. This opinion was seized on by land speculators in America to attempt to validate titles to lands purchased from Indians there, the form of the opinion circulated in America omitting the reference to "the Grand Mogul."

25. Ford, *op.cit.*, XXIV, 505–6 (August 12, 1783).

26. Ibid., VIII, 397–404 (May 29, 1777).

27. Robert Morris Papers, 1801–2, New York Public Library. Morris to Samuel Emery, January 11, 1802.

28. Wilson Papers, Historical Society of Pennsylvania.

NOTES TO
CHAPTER 4

1. M. Farrand, *The Records of the Federal Convention of 1787*, revised edition (New Haven, 1937), I, 49 (May 31). All references to the proceedings of the Federal Convention are to Farrand, and unless otherwise indicated refer to Madison's reports.

2. I, 359 (June 21).

3. I, 132–33 (June 6).

4. I, 361 (June 21).

5. I, 52 (May 31).

6. On June 30, Wilson modified his proposal regarding electoral districts which may transcend state boundaries by suggesting that each state should have one senator for every 100,000 inhabitants, with the smallest state (even though it would have fewer than that number) also to have one. This he portrayed as a concession by the large to the small states, and remarked, according to Paterson, that he would "not insist upon small matters if the great principles can be established."

7. I, 406 (June 25).

8. I, 151 (June 7).

9. I, 413 (June 25), Yates's report.

10. I, 417 (June 25), King's report.

11. I, 482 (June 30).

12. I, 482–84 (June 30).

13. I, 449–50 (June 28).

14. II, 4–5 (July 14).

15. I, 515 (July 2).

16. I, 550 (July 7).

17. I, 604–6 (July 13).

18. II, 10 (July 14).

19. II, 275 (August 13).

20. I, 545 (July 6).

21. II, 530 (September 6), McHenry's report.

22. See below, p. 75.

23. I, 375 (June 22).

24. II, 237 (August 9); 268–69 (August 13).

25. II, 217 (August 8).

26. II, 201 (August 7).

27. R. G. McCloskey, *The Works of James Wilson,* I, 411.

28. II, 548 (September 8).

29. I, 426 (June 26).

30. II, 260 (August 11).

31. II, 287–88 (August 14).

32. McCloskey, *op. cit.,* I, 322.

NOTES TO
CHAPTER 5

1. M. Farrand, *The Records of the Federal Convention of* 1787, I, 65–6, 70–1 (June 1). *See also* Chapter 4, Note 1.

2. I, 254 (June 16).

3. R. G. McCloskey, *The Works of James Wilson*, I, 293–94.

4. I, 97 (June 4).

5. II, 539 (September 7).

6. McCloskey, *op. cit.*, I, 440 *et passim*.

7. I, 66–7 (June 1).

8. McCloskey, *op. cit.*, II, 441.

9. I, 65–6 (June 1).

10. I, 94, 98, 100 (June 4).

11. I, 98–9, 102–3 (June 4).

12. I, 100 (June 4).

13. I, 106 (June 4).

14. See below, p. 74.

15. II, 301 (August 15).

16. II, 300–1 (August 15).

17. McCloskey, *op. cit.*, I, 323.

18. Ibid., II, 444.

19. II, 426 (August 27).

20. I, 68 (June 1).

21. I, 69 (June 1).

22. I, 80 (June 2).

23. II, 30 (July 17).

24. II, 56 (July 19).

25. II, 102–3 (July 24).

26. II, 103–6 (July 24).

27. II, 404 (August 24).

28. II, 493–94 (September 4). The Committee of Eleven put forward the following proposal for electing the president and vice-president:

Each state shall appoint, in such manner as its legislature may direct, a number of electors equal to the whole number of senators and members of the House of Representatives to which the state may be entitled in the legislature.

The electors shall meet in their respective states, and vote by ballot for two persons, of whom one at least shall not be an inhabitant of the same state with themselves and they shall make a list of all the persons voted for, and of the number of votes for each, which list they shall sign and certify, and transmit sealed to the seat of the general government, directed to the president of the Senate.

The president of the Senate shall in that house open all the certificates, and the votes shall be then and there counted—The person having the greatest number of votes shall be the president, if such number be a majority of the electors and if there be more than one who have such a majority, and have an equal number of votes, then the Senate shall choose by ballot one of them for president; but if no person have a majority, then from the five highest on the list, the Senate shall choose by ballot the president—and in every case after the choice of the president, the person having the greatest number of votes shall be vice-president; but if there should remain two or more who have equal votes, the Senate shall choose from them the vice-president.

29. II, 502 (September 4).

30. II, 522–23 (September 6).

31. Wilson concerned himself scarcely at all with the issue of the impeachment of the executive, an issue which could hardly have seemed at the time to be of immediately practical importance. Along with Madison he criticized a proposal that the executive "be made removable by the national legislature on the request of a majority of the legislatures of individual states" on the predictable grounds that this method would enable a minority of the people (in a majority of the states) to prevent the removal of a man "who had rendered himself justly criminal in the eyes of the majority" and would make possible intrigues against a just but unpopular executive. Conversely, fear of the leading politicians in a state might lead to improper concessions being made to that state. Wilson and Madison both thought it best to leave the states entirely out of the process of impeachment. On only one other point did Wilson contribute to the discussion of impeachment of the executive, when he opposed a proposal that the executive should not be impeachable while in office.

NOTES TO
CHAPTER 6

1. M. Farrand, *The Records of the Federal Convention of 1787*, I, 147 (June 6). *See also* Chapter 4, Note 1.

2. See, e.g., R. G. McCloskey, *The Works of James Wilson*, I, 4; J. B. McMaster and F. D. Stone, *Pennsylvania and the Federal Constitution, 1787–1788*, p. 354; Farrand, *op. cit.*, II, 73 (July 21).

3. McCloskey, *op. cit.*, I, 330.

4. I, 124–25 (June 5).

5. McCloskey, *op. cit.*, II, 497.

6. I, 98–105 (June 4).

7. II, 73 (July 21).

8. II, 298 (August 15).

9. II, 301 (August 15).

10. II, 429 (August 27).

11. I, 373 (June 22).

12. I, 164 (June 8).

13. I, 167 (June 8).

14. II, 391 (August 23).

15. II, 615 (September 14).

16. I, 356 (June 21).

17. I, 137 (June 6).

18. I, 154–55, 157 (June 7).

19. I, 322–23 (June 19).

20. McCloskey, *op. cit.*, I, 261–62.

21. I, 180, 183 (June 9).

22. II, 462 (August 30).

23. II, 456 (August 29).

24. II, 464 (August 30).

25. J. P. Boyd, *The Papers of Thomas Jefferson*, I, 327. (Copyright 1950 by Princeton University Press. Reprinted by permission of Princeton University Press.) The discussion in the Continental Congress took place on July 30, 31, and August 1.

26. I, 253 (June 16).

27. I, 483 (June 30).

28. McCloskey, *op. cit.*, I, 266–68.

29. I, 60 (May 31).

30. I. Brant, *James Madison,* III, 101, 112, 133–39.

31. II, 615, 616 (September 14).

32. II, 362 (August 21).

33. II, 376, 379 (August 22).

34. See above, p. 55.

35. II, 269, 272 (August 13).

36. II, 243–44 (August 9).

37. II, 268, 272 (August 13).

38. I, 587 (July 11); 595 (July 12).

39. C. P. Smith, *James Wilson; Founding Father, 1742–1798* (Chapel Hill, 1956), p. 123.

40. See Appendix B.

41. II, 310 (August 16).

42. II, 439 (August 28).

43. II, 439–40 (August 28); see Smith, *op.cit.,* pp. 247–48.

44. See above, pp. 39–40.

45. F. McDonald, *We the People; The Economic Origins of the Constitution* (Chicago, 1958), p. 170.

NOTES TO
CHAPTER 7

1. G. Hunt, *The Writings of James Madison* (New York, 1900–10), V, 57, Madison to Edmund Randolph, November 18, 1787.

2. J. B. McMaster and F. D. Stone, *Pennsylvania and the Federal Constitution, 1787–1788,* p. 143. [*See footnote on p. 207.]

3. McMaster and Stone, *op.cit.,* pp. 143–44. Wilson would have preferred the granting of general powers to Congress, and he was here explaining a feature whose introduction he had resisted (see above, p. 81).

4. McMaster and Stone, *op.cit.,* pp. 144–49. References to statements or quotations contained in a limited number of consecutive, or nearly consecutive, pages are given collectively after the last item in the series.

5. *Pennsylvania Gazette,* October 17, 1787.

6. McMaster and Stone, *op.cit.,* 183–84.

7. J. C. Ballagh, *The Letters of Richard Henry Lee* (New York, 1911–14), II, 457, Lee to Samuel Adams, October 21, 1787.

8. *Independent Gazette,* December 21, 1787.

9. William Findley, a very able politician much respected by his opponents, was the most effective of Wilson's critics. A citizen of Westmoreland County, he was a leading spokesman for western interests in Pennsylvania. He held various offices in Pennsylvania, including membership of the assembly and of the Council of Censors under the constitution of 1776. Findley's cooperation with Wilson in the Pennsylvania Constitutional Convention of 1790 nevertheless was a major factor in making possible its replacement by the very different constitution of 1790. Though a strong Antifederalist in 1787, Findley secured election to the national Congress in 1791, and there played a prominent part as a critic of much Federalist legislation.

John Smilie, another Westerner, also served in the Pennsylvania assembly and as a member of the Council of Censors. He was a strong opponent of the ratification by his state of the Federal Constitution of 1787, but accepted the Pennsylvania Constitution of 1790 and served in the first Senate of Pennsylvania. Subsequently he served at different times in the national Congress and the Pennsylvania House of Representatives.

Robert Whitehill, the most intransigent of Wilson's opponents, was an inhabitant of Cumberland County and a leading spokesman for the frontier. He played an important part in drafting the Pennsylvania Constitution of 1776 and was a member of the state assembly under that constitution. He resolutely opposed the ratification of the Federal Constitution of 1787, and as a member of the Pennsylvania Convention of 1790 he refused to give his assent to the new state constitution. He was a member of the national Congress from 1805 until 1813.

10. R. G. McCloskey, *The Works of James Wilson,* II, 759–60. Wilson's speech of November 24 appears in Bird Wilson, *The Works of James Wilson* (Philadelphia, 1804) and in McCloskey, both of whom give November 26 as the date on which it was delivered. The version in McMaster and Stone differs at several points from that given in Bird Wilson and in McCloskey. The McCloskey edition is the one usually cited here.

11. McCloskey, *op. cit.*, II, 760–63.

12. McMaster and Stone, *op. cit.*, p. 223. The McMaster and Stone version may reflect a revision by Wilson of his original draft.

13. McCloskey, *op. cit.*, II, 764.

14. McMaster and Stone, *op. cit.*, p. 230. The McCloskey version reads:
"Oft have I viewed with silent pleasure and admiration the force and prevalence, through the United States, of this principle—that the supreme power resides in the people; and that they never part with it. It may be called the *panacea* in politics. There can be no disorder in the community but may here receive a radical cure. If the error be in the legislature, it may be corrected by the constitution; if in the constitution, it may be corrected by the people." (II, 771.)

15. McCloskey, *op. cit.*, II, 771.

16. McMaster and Stone, *op. cit.*, pp. 230–1. The McCloskey version reads:
"In its principle, it is purely democratical: but that principle is applied in different forms, in order to obtain the advantages, and exclude the inconveniences of the simple modes of government.
"If we take an extended and accurate view of it, we shall find the streams of power running in different directions, in different dimensions, and at different heights, watering, adorning, and fertilizing the fields and meadows, through which their courses are led; but if we trace them, we shall discover that they all originally flow from one abundant fountain. In this constitution, all authority is derived from THE PEOPLE." (II, 772.)

17. McMaster and Stone, *op. cit.*, pp. 224–27.

18. Ibid., p. 316.

19. Ibid., pp. 383–84.

20. Ibid., p. 389.

21. Ibid., p. 320.

22. Ibid., pp. 227–29.

23. Ibid., pp. 234–35.

24. Ibid., pp. 242–43.

25. The porters of the Billingsgate fish market were notorious for their vituperative language.

26. McMaster and Stone, *op. cit.*, pp. 247–49.

27. Connecticut, Delaware, New Jersey, New York, Rhode Island, South Carolina, Virginia.

28. McMaster and Stone, *op. cit.*, pp. 250–54.

29. See above, pp. 88–89.

30. McMaster and Stone, *op. cit.*, p. 359.

31. Ibid., p. 404.

32. Ibid., pp. 352–53.

33. Ibid., p. 406.

34. Ibid., p. 403.

35. Ibid., p. 315.

36. Ibid., p. 308.

37. Ibid., pp. 385–86.

38. Ibid., p. 306.

39. Ibid., p. 327.

40. Ibid., pp. 319, 338–39.

41. Ibid., p. 391.

42. Ibid., p. 327.

43. Ibid., pp. 393–94.

44. Ibid., p. 400.

45. Ibid., pp. 337–38.

46. Ibid., pp. 396–97.

47. Ibid., pp. 306–7.

48. Ibid., pp. 399–400.

49. Ibid., p. 342.

50. Ibid., pp. 398, 401.

51. Ibid., p. 354.

52. Ibid., pp. 304–5.

53. Ibid., p. 402.

54. Ibid., p. 343.

55. Ibid., pp. 401–2.

56. Ibid., pp. 355–58.

57. Ibid., pp. 328–29.

58. Ibid., pp. 407–9.

59. Ibid., pp. 329–30.

60. See Appendix B.

61. McMaster and Stone, *op.cit.*, pp. 330–31.

62. Ibid., pp. 311–12.

63. Ibid., p. 347.

64. Ibid., p. 412.

65. Ibid., p. 344.

66. Ibid., pp. 394–95.

67. Ibid., p. 322.

68. Ibid., pp. 415–17.

69. See above, p. 81.

70. McMaster and Stone, *op. cit.,* pp. 323–24.

71. Ibid., pp. 415–18.

72. Ibid., pp. 490–91.

73. Historical Society of Pennsylvania. Broadsides.

74. McCloskey, *op. cit.,* II, 778–80.

* A more recent edition, published since this chapter was written, of the records of the Pennsylvania Ratifying Convention is Merrill Jensen; *Ratification of the Constitution in the States: Pennsylvania* [Vol. II of *The Documentary History of the Ratification of the Constitution*] (Madison, Wis., 1976). As the Jensen edition does not differ significantly for the purposes of this chapter from the earlier edition, the references to McMaster and Stone are retained.

NOTES TO
CHAPTER 8

1. H. M. Tinkcom, *The Republicans and Federalists in Pennsylvania, 1790–1801* (Harrisburg, 1950), p. 17.

2. See Appendix C.

3. *Pennsylvania Gazette,* September 19, 1787.

4. Historical Society of Pennsylvania. Broadsides.

5. Historical Society of Pennsylvania. Gratz Collection, Case 4, Box 15. William Thompson to James Wilson, April 14, 1777.

6. Historical Society of Pennsylvania. Gratz Collection, Case 1, Box 14, May 6, 1777.

7. W. H. Smith, *The St. Clair Papers,* I, 417–18.

8. Historical Society of Pennsylvania. Provincial Delegates, VI, 22. Wilson and others to Anthony Wayne.

9. C. P. Smith, *James Wilson; Founding Father, 1742–1798,* pp. 129–30.

10. R. L. Brunhouse, *The Counter Revolution in Pennsylvania, 1776–1790,* pp. 89–90.

11. B. A. Konkle, *George Bryan and the Constitution of Pennsylvania, 1731–1791* (Philadelphia, 1922), pp. 232–36; Brunhouse, *op.cit.,* p. 120.

12. W. H. Smith, *op.cit.,* I, 593 *et seq.*

13. L. H. Butterfield, *Letters of Benjamin Rush* (Princeton, 1951), I, 509. Rush to John Montgomery, March 27, 1789; G. W. Corner, *The Autobiography of Benjamin Rush* (Princeton, 1948), p. 178; Brunhouse, *op.cit.,* p. 222.

14. Tinkcom, *op.cit.,* pp. 11–12; Brunhouse, *op.cit.,* pp. 225–26.

15. R. G. McCloskey, *The Works of James Wilson,* II, 552.

16. A. Graydon, *Memoirs of a Life chiefly passed in Pennsylvania within the last Sixty Years* (Edinburgh, 1822), pp. 361, 363.

17. Quoted in Brunhouse, *op.cit.,* p. 298, footnote 113. William Lewis was a leading Quaker lawyer in Philadelphia, and was acknowledged by contemporaries to be one of the outstanding lawyers of his generation. As a dedicated Federalist he was normally a close political associate of Wilson's. In 1791 he was appointed judge of the federal district court for the eastern district of Pennsylvania.

18. Graydon, *op.cit.,* p. 363.

19. Ibid., p. 362.

20. McCloskey, *op.cit.,* I, 416.

21. Ibid., I, 414.

22. Ibid., II, 782–83.

23. Ibid., II, 785–86.

24. Ibid., II, 789–92.

25. Minutes of the Grand Committee of the Whole Convention of the Commonwealth of Pennsylvania which commenced at Philadelphia on Tuesday the twenty-fourth Day of November, in the Year of Our Lord One Thousand Seven Hundred and Eighty-Nine, for the Purpose of Reviewing, and if they see occasion, Altering and Amending the Constitution of this State [cited as Pennsylvania Convention (Committee) 1789–90], January 12, 1790, p. 37.

26. McCloskey, *op.cit.,* I, 440.

27. Wilson Papers, "Of the Unity of the Executive Department" (speech delivered in the Pennsylvania convention, January 13, 1790).

28. Pennsylvania Convention (Committee) 1789–90, January 16, 1790, p. 47.

29. McCloskey, *op.cit.,* I. 440.

30. Pennsylvania Convention (Committee) 1789–90, January 19, 1790, p. 51.

31. See McCloskey, *op.cit.,* II, 492–93.

32. Minutes of the Convention of the Commonwealth of Pennsylvania . . . for the Purpose of Reviewing . . . the Constitution of this State. February 19, 1790, pp. 114–15.

33. Ibid., February 23, 1790, p. 225.

34. Ibid., February 25, 1790, p. 140.

35. Minutes of the Second Session of the Convention of the Commonwealth of Pennsylvania which commenced at Philadelphia on Monday the Ninth Day of August in the Year of Our Lord One Thousand Seven Hundred and Ninety. August 27, 1790, p. 186.

36. Ibid., August 28, 1790, p. 193.

37. Ibid., August 19, 1790, pp. 165–66.

38. Ibid., September 2, 1790, pp. 211–12.

39. Ibid., August 31, 1790, p. 208.

NOTES TO
CHAPTER 9

1. Wilson Papers. Draft of Resolution to be adopted by the Committee to frame a Constitution for the United States. Marginal note against paragraph 13 concerning the judiciary.

2. Wilson's letter to Washington deserves to be recorded in full. He wrote, on April 21, 1789:

> A delicacy arising from your situation and character as well as my own has hitherto prevented me from mentioning to your Excellency a subject of much importance to me. Perhaps I should not even now have broke silence but for one consideration. A regard to the dignity of the government, over which you preside, will naturally lead you to take care that its honors be in no event exposed to affected indifference or contempt. For this reason you may well expect that before you nominate any gentleman to an employment (especially one of high trust) you should have it in your power to preclude him, in case of disappointment, from pretending that the nomination was made without his knowledge or consent. Under this view I commit myself to your Excellency without reserve, and inform you that my aim rises to the important office of chief justice of the United States.
>
> But how shall I now proceed? Shall I enumerate reasons in justification of my high pretensions? I have not yet employed my pen in my own praise. When I make these high pretensions, and offer them to so good a judge can I say that they are altogether without foundation? Your Excellency must relieve me from the dilemma. You will think and act properly on the occasion, without my saying anything on either side of the question. (Historical Society of Pennsylvania, Society Collection).

Whether or not Wilson would have been appointed had he not solicited the post is impossible to ascertain. But the tone of Washington's reply indicates that Wilson's letter might not have helped his cause. (See J. C. Fitzpatrick, *Writings of Washington*, XXX, 314.)

3. Extracts are from the original draft of the opinion in the Wilson Papers.

4. Eleventh amendment.

5. *McCulloch* v. *Maryland* (1819) and especially *Cohens* v. *Virginia* (1821).

6. See C. P. Smith, *James Wilson*, Chapter XXIII, and R. G. McCloskey, "James Wilson" in L. Friedman and F. L. Israel, *The Justices of the United States Supreme Court, 1789–1969* (New York, 1969), I, 79–96.

7. J. C. Miller, *Alexander Hamilton: Portrait in Paradox* (New York, 1959), pp. 406–7.

8. G. J. McRee, *The Life and Correspondence of James Iredell* (New York, 1857), II, 429.

9. Ibid., II, 327.

10. F. McDonald, *We the People*, pp. 58–59.

11. McRee, *op.cit.,* II, 516. Iredell to Mrs. Iredell, August 11, 1797.

12. Historical Society of Pennsylvania, Gratz Collection, Case 2, Box 14. William Bradford to S. Bayard, July 16, 1795.

13. McRee, *op. cit.,* II, 532.

14. *Pennsylvania Packet,* December 25, 1790, quoted in *Pennsylvania Magazine of History and Biography,* XX (1896), 75–76.

15. R. G. McCloskey, *The Works of James Wilson,* I, 86. Wilson's introductory lecture was published in Philadelphia in 1791 under the title "An Introductory Lecture to a Course of Law Lectures; to which is added a Plan of the Lectures." For convenience the McCloskey version, which differs only in the use of capitals and italics, is cited.

16. Ibid., I, 77.

17. Ibid., I, 184.

18. Ibid., I, 126 *et seq.*

19. Ibid., I, 348.

20. Ibid., I, 355–56.

21. Ibid., II, 502.

22. Ibid., I, 72.

23. C. P. Smith, *James Wilson,* p. 364.

24. McCloskey, *op. cit.,* I, 75.

25. W. F. Obering, *The Philosophy of Law of James Wilson; A Study in Comparative Jurisprudence* (Washington, D.C., 1938), p. 148.

26. McCloskey, *op. cit.,* I, 148, 149.

27. Ibid., I, 153–54.

28. Ibid., I, 166.

29. Ibid., I, 160–61.

30. Ibid., I, 164.

31. Ibid., I, 156.

32. Ibid., I, 160.

33. Ibid., I, 271–72.

34. Ibid., I, 274.

35. Ibid., I, 280–81.

36. Ibid., II, 822.

37. Ibid., II, 611, 627–28.

38. Ibid., II, 804.

39. Ibid., II, 628.

40. Ibid., II, 818.

41. Ibid., II, 805–6.

42. Ibid., II, 630, 806.

43. Ibid., II, 626.

44. Ibid., II, 634.

45. Ibid., II, 822.

46. Ibid., II, 618.

47. Ibid., I, 84.

48. See above, p. 50.

49. McCloskey, *op.cit.*, II, 711–20. Quotations are from pp. 718–20.

NOTES TO
CHAPTER 10

1. See, e.g., Historical Society of Pennsylvania, Yeates Papers, William Hamilton to Jasper Yeates, August 30, 1784, and October 8, 1786; Wilson Papers, V, Doc. 98B.

2. R. G. McCloskey, *The Works of James Wilson,* I, 19.

3. Ibid., I, 19.

4. Ibid., I, 159.

5. Ibid., I, 158.

6. Wilson Papers, "Heads of a Plan concerning the new States." Historical Society of Pennsylvania.

7. Wilson Papers, Draft Letter to the Dutch Ambassador, March 12, 1785.

8. L. H. Butterfield, *Letters of Benjamin Rush,* I, 449, Rush to Timothy Pickering, January 20, 1788.

9. Wilson Papers, V, Doc. 55½; New York Historical Society, Wilson to Charles Carroll of Carrollton, December 26, 1792; Elizabeth K. Henderson, "The Northwestern Lands of Pennsylvania, 1790–1812," in *Pennsylvania Magazine of History and Biography,* LX (1936), p. 139.

10. The "Prospectus" was written in 1792 or early 1793. Another copy, slightly revised, was later presented by Wilson to Benjamin Rush, under the title "On the Improvement and Settlement of Lands in the United States." The edition published in 1946 by the Free Library of Philadelphia reproduces the Rush copy, which excludes certain matters directly related to the negotiation with the Amsterdam group, and for no apparent reason slightly modifies the "Prospectus" at a few other points. Quotations from this work are here taken in every case from the "Prospectus."

11. Wilson Papers, V, Doc. 55, Wilson to Theophilus Cazenove, January 24, 1793.

12. James Oglethorpe was a pioneer of the concept of planned emigration and settlement. His scheme for the colonization of Georgia, in 1732, combined, though in a rudimentary form, selection of emigrants with preparations for their reception, and provided for advance planning of the economic and political organization of the colony.

13. Edward Gibbon Wakefield was an early nineteenth-century advocate of carefully planned emigration and settlement, carrying much further the concepts apparent in the ideas of Oglethorpe and Wilson. His theory of colonization provided for thorough surveys and careful preparation in advance of actual settlement, and he attached great importance to the quality of immigrants. The development of South Australia, and especially of New Zealand, was based substantially on the practical application of his ideas.

14. The version presented to Rush excluded the references to Hamburg, Bristol, Liverpool, and Greenock, and added Belfast and Limerick to the Irish ports of embarkation.

15. Wilson Papers, "Report of the Committee, to whom was referred, on the 13th ultimo, the Memorial of the Illinois and Wabash Land Company, by James Wilson, their President," February 3, 1797.

16. F. McDonald, *We the People,* p. 58.

17. C. P. Smith, *James Wilson,* pp. 369–70, 374.

18. McDonald, *op. cit.,* pp. 57–58.

19. W. B. Clark, "Postscripts to the Voyage of the Merchant Ship 'United States,'" in *Pennsylvania Magazine of History and Biography,* LXXVI (1952), 294–310.

20. W. C. Ford, *Journals of the Continental Congress,* XV, 1065, September 15, 1779.

21. R. A. East, *Business Enterprise in the American Revolution* (New York, 1938), p. 135.

22. Wilson Papers, Certificate dated March 8, 1793.

23. Butterfield, *op. cit.,* II, 1095, Rush to John Adams, August 19, 1811. (Reprinted by permission of the American Philosophical Society [publisher] and Mr. L. H. Butterfield.)

NOTES TO
CHAPTER 11

1. M. Farrand, *The Records of the Federal Convention of 1787*, III, 91–92. Pierce was a delegate from Georgia.

2. J. C. Fitzpatrick, *The Writings of George Washington from the Original Manuscript Sources, 1745–1799* (Washington, D.C., 1931–44) XXIX, 290, Washington to David Stuart, October 12, 1787.

3. "Centinel," quoted in K. M. Rowland, *Life of George Mason, 1725–1792* (New York, 1892), II, 281.

4. See New York Public Library, Emmet Collection. Arthur St. Clair to James Wilson, July 14, 1777; W. H. Smith, *The St. Clair Papers*, I, 378, 392.

5. Bird Wilson, *The Works of James Wilson*, 3 vols. (Philadelphia, 1804).

6. L. H. Alexander, "James Wilson, Patriot, and the Wilson Doctrine," in *North American Review*, CLXXXIII (1906), 971.

7. Though he was born in Belfast, Bryce was of Scottish parentage and he spent his youth in Scotland, being educated there at school and at the University of Glasgow.

8. James Bryce, "James Wilson: An Appreciation" in *Pennsylvania Magazine of History and Biography*, LX (1936), 361.

9. M. D. Peterson, *Thomas Jefferson and the New Nation* (New York 1970), p. 105.

10. R. G. McCloskey, *The Works of James Wilson*, I, 2.

BIBLIOGRAPHY

MANUSCRIPT SOURCES

Historical Society of Pennsylvania

The main manuscript source for a study of James Wilson is the Wilson Papers in the possession of the Historical Society of Pennsylvania.

Other collections held by the Society and containing relevant material are as follows:

James Allen, Diary
Broadsides Collection
Cadwallader Collection
Hampton L. Carson Collection
Conarroe Papers
Dreer Collection
Etting Papers
Gratz Collection
Lamberton Scotch-Irish MSS
Logan Papers
McKean Papers

James A. Montgomery Collection
Penn-Physick Papers
Provincial Delegates
William Smith Papers
Society Collection
Society Miscellaneous Collection
Sprague Collection
Stauffer Collection
Wayne Papers
Willing Papers
Yeates Papers

Library Company of Philadelphia

Rush MSS

Library of Congress

J. P. Morgan's Book of the Signers
The Confidential Correspondence of
    Robert Morris

Pennsylvania Miscellaneous
Arthur St. Clair Papers
United States Revolution (U.S.R.)

New York Historical Society

Papers of Charles Thomson   Miscellaneous Papers

New York Public Library

Emmet Collection   Robert Morris Papers 1751–1784

PRINTED SOURCES

Adams, Randolph G. *Selected Political Essays of James Wilson.* New York: Knopf, 1930.

Andrews, James De Witt. *The Works of James Wilson.* 2 vols. Chicago, 1896.

Balch, Thomas W. *Willing Letters and Papers.* Philadelphia: Allen, Lane and Scott, 1922.

Ballagh, James C. *The Letters of Richard Henry Lee.* 2 vols. New York: The Macmillan Company, 1911–14.

Boyd, Julian P. *The Papers of Thomas Jefferson.* Princeton: Princeton University Press, 1950–

Burnett, Edmund C. *Letters of Members of the Continental Congress.* Washington, D.C.: Carnegie Institution of Washington, 1921.

Butterfield, Lyman H. *Letters of Benjamin Rush.* Princeton, N.J.: Princeton University Press, 1951.

———. *The Adams Papers.* Cambridge, Mass.: Harvard University Press, 1961.

Corner, George W. *The Autobiography of Benjamin Rush.* Princeton, N.J.: Princeton University Press, 1948.

Farrand, Max. *The Records of the Federal Convention of 1787.* 4 vols. New Haven, Conn.: Yale University Press, 1937.

Fitzpatrick, John C. *The Writings of George Washington from the Original Manuscript Sources, 1745–99.* 39 vols. Washington, D.C.: Government Printing Office, 1931–44.

Ford, Paul L. *Pamphlets on the Constitution of the United States Published During its Discussion by the People, 1787–88.* New York, 1888.

Ford, Worthington C. *Journals of the Continental Congress.* 34 vols. Washington, D.C.: Government Printing Office, 1904–37.

Hunt, Gaillard. *The Writings of James Madison.* 9 vols. New York: Putnam, 1900–10.

Jensen, Merrill. *Ratification of the Constitution in the States: Pennsylvania* [Vol. II of *The Documentary History of the Ratification of the Constitution*]. Madison, Wis.: State Historical Society of Wisconsin, 1976.

McCloskey, Robert G. *The Works of James Wilson.* 2 vols. Cambridge, Mass.: Harvard University Press, 1967.

Maclay, Edgar S. *Journal of William Maclay.* New York: A. & C. Boni, 1927.

McMaster, John B. and Stone, Frederick D. *Pennsylvania and the Federal Constitution, 1787–88.* Philadelphia, 1888.

McRee, Griffith J. *Life and Correspondence of James Iredell.* 2 vols. New York, 1857.

Minutes of the Convention of the Commonwealth of Pennsylvania Which Commenced at Philadelphia on Tuesday the Twenty-Fourth Day of November in the Year of Our Lord One Thousand Seven Hundred and Eighty-Nine, for the Purpose of Reviewing, and If They See Occasion, Altering and Amending the Constitution of This State. Philadelphia, 1789.

Minutes of the Grand Committee of the Whole Convention of the Commonwealth of Pennsylvania. . . . Philadelphia, 1789.

Minutes of the Second Session of the Convention of the Commonwealth of Pennsylvania Which Commenced at Philadelphia on Monday the Ninth Day of August in the Year of Our Lord One Thousand Seven Hundred and Ninety. Philadelphia, 1790.

Reed, William B. *Life and Correspondence of Joseph Reed.* 2 vols. Philadelphia, 1847.

Smith, William H. *The St. Clair Papers.* 2 vols. Cincinnati, 1882.

Stowe, Walter H. *The Life and Letters of Bishop William White.* New York: Morehouse Publishing Co., 1937.

Syrett, Harold C. *The Papers of Alexander Hamilton.* New York: Columbia University Press, 1961—

Wilson, Bird. *The Works of the Honourable James Wilson, LL.D.* 3 vols. Philadelphia, 1804.

Wilson, James. *An Introductory Lecture to a Course of Law Lectures; to Which Is Added a Plan of the Lectures.* Philadelphia, 1791.

———. *On the Improvement and Settlement of Lands in the United States.* Philadelphia: Library Company of Philadelphia, 1946.

NEWSPAPERS

Pennsylvania Gazette   *Pennsylvania Packet*
Pennsylvania Journal

SECONDARY WORKS

The only biography of James Wilson is that by Charles Page Smith (*James Wilson: Founding Father*). R. G. McCloskey *The Works of James Wilson* contains an Introduction which examines Wilson's political and legal thought. Many biographies of contemporaries and monographs on subjects within the period contain information on Wilson or relevant material relating to him. *The Pennsylvania Magazine of History and Biography* has, over a period of ninety years, published a considerable number of articles relating directly or indirectly to James Wilson.

Abernethy, Thomas P. *Western Lands and the American Revolution.* New York: D. Appleton-Century Co., 1937.

Adams, Randolph C. "The Legal Theories of James Wilson." *University of Pennsylvania Law Review* LXVIII (1920): 337—55.

Alexander, Lucien H. "James Wilson, Patriot, and the Wilson Doctrine." *North American Review* CLXXXIII (1906): 971—89.

———. "James Wilson, Nation-Builder." *The Green Bag* XIX (1907): 1—9, 98—109, 137—46, 265—76.

Balch, Thomas W. "Thomas Willing of Philadelphia (1731—1821)." *Pennsylvania Magazine of History and Biography* XLVI (1922): 1—14.

Bining, Arthur C. "Early Ironmasters of Pennsylvania." *Pennsylvania History* XVIII (1951): 93—103.

Boyd, Julian P. *The Trenton Trial of 1782: A Significant Episode in Constitutional History.* Philadelphia: The Athaneum of Philadelphia, 1937.

Brant, Irving N. *James Madison.* 6 vols. Indianapolis, Ind.; New York: Bobbs-Merrill Co., 1948—56.

Brunhouse, Robert L. *The Counter-Revolution in Pennsylvania, 1776–1790.* Harrisburg, Pa.: Pennsylvania Historical Commission, 1942.

Bryce, James. "James Wilson: An Appreciation." *Pennsylvania Magazine of History and Biography* LX (1936): 358–61.

Carson, Hampton L. "James Wilson and James Iredell: A Parallel and a Contrast." *Pennsylvania Magazine of History and Biography* XLV (1921): 1–33.

Chapin, Bradley. *The American Law of Treason: Revolutionary and Early National Origins.* Seattle, Wash.: University of Washington Press, 1964.

Clark, W. B. "Postscripts to the Voyage of the Merchant Ship 'United States'." *Pennsylvania Magazine of History and Biography* LXXVI (1952): 294–310.

East, Robert A. *Business Enterprise in the American Revolutionary Era.* New York: Columbia University Press, 1938.

Ferguson, E. James. *The Power of the Purse: A History of American Public Finance, 1776–1790.* Chapel Hill, N.C.: University of North Carolina Press, 1961.

Graydon, Alexander. *Memoirs of a Life Chiefly Passed in Pennsylvania within the Last Sixty Years.* Edinburgh, 1822.

Harlan, John M. "James Wilson and the Formation of the Constitution." *American Law Review* XXXIV (1900): 481–504.

Hartz, Louis. *Economic Policy and Democratic Thought: Pennsylvania 1776–1860.* Cambridge, Mass.: Harvard University Press, 1948.

Henderson, Elizabeth K. "The Northwestern Lands of Pennsylvania, 1790–1812." *Pennsylvania Magazine of History and Biography* LX (1936): 131–60.

James, F. Cyril. "The Bank of North America and the Financial History of Philadelphia." *Pennsylvania Magazine of History and Biography* LXIV (1940): 56–87.

Klingelsmith, M. C. "James Wilson and the So-called Yazoo Frauds." *University of Pennsylvania Law Review* LVI (1908): 1–27.

Konkle, Burton A. *The Life and Times of Thomas Smith, 1745–1809.* Philadelphia: Campion and Co., 1949.

———. *James Wilson and the Constitution.* Philadelphia: Law Academy of Philadelphia, 1904.

———. *George Bryan and the Constitution of Pennsylvania, 1731–1791.* Philadelphia: W. J. Campbell, 1922.

———. *Thomas Willing and the First American Financial System.* Philadelphia: University of Pennsylvania Press, 1937.

Leavelle, Arnaud B. "James Wilson and the Relation of the Scottish Metaphysics to American Political Thought." *Political Science Quarterly* LVII (1942): 394–410.

Lincoln, Charles H. *The Revolutionary Movement in Pennsylvania, 1760–1776.* Philadelphia: University of Pennsylvania Press, 1901.

Livermore, Shaw. *Early American Land Companies: Their Influence on Corporate Development.* New York: The Commonwealth Fund, 1939.

McDonald, Forrest. *We the People: The Economic Origins of the Constitution.* Chicago: University of Chicago Press, 1958.

McLaughlin, Andrew C. "James Wilson in the Philadelphia Convention." *Political Science Quarterly* XII (1897): 1–20.

Miller, John C. *Alexander Hamilton: Portrait in Paradox.* New York, 1959.

Mitchell, Broadus. *Alexander Hamilton.* 2 vols. New York: Macmillan, 1957–62.

Obering, William F. *The Philosophy of Law of James Wilson: A Study in Comparative Jurisprudence.* Washington, D.C.: Catholic University of America, 1938.

O'Donnell, Mary G. *James Wilson and the Natural Law Basis of Positive Law.* New York: Fordham University Press, 1937.

Ohline, H. A. "Republicanism and Slavery: Origins of the Three-Fifths Clause in the United States Constitution." *William and Mary Quarterly* XXVIII (1971): 563–84.

Pole, J. R. *Political Representation in England and the Origins of the American Republic.* London: Macmillan, 1966.

Powell, J. H. "John Dickinson and the Constitution." *Pennsylvania Magazine of History and Biography* LX (1936): 1–14.

Rahskopf, Horace G. "The Oratory of James Wilson of Pennsylvania." *Speech Monographs* V (1938).

Rich, Bennett M. "Washington and the Whiskey Insurrection." *Pennsylvania Magazine of History and Biography* LXV (1941): 334–52.

Richards, Louis. "Hon. James Wilson at Reading, Penna." *Pennsylvania Magazine of History and Biography* XXI (1907): 48–52.

Rives, William C. *History of the Life and Times of James Madison.* 2 vols. Boston, 1866.

Rosenberger, Homer T. "James Wilson's Theories of Punishment." *Pennsylvania Magazine of History and Biography* LXXIII (1949): 45–63.

Rowland, Kate M. *The Life of George Mason, 1725–1792.* 2 vols. New York, 1892.

Selsam, John P. "The Political Revolution in Pennsylvania in 1776." *Pennsylvania History* I (1934): 147–57.

———. *The Pennsylvania Constitution of 1776: A Study in Revolutionary Democracy.* Philadelphia: University of Pennsylvania Press, 1936.

Smith, C. Page. "The Attack on Fort Wilson." *Pennsylvania Magazine of History and Biography* LXXVIII (1954): 177–88.

———. *James Wilson: Founding Father, 1742–1798.* Chapel Hill, N.C.: University of North Carolina Press, 1956.

Stillé, Charles J. "Pennsylvania and the Declaration of Independence." *Pennsylvania Magazine of History and Biography* XIII (1889): 385–429.

Thomas, E. Bruce. *Political Tendencies in Pennsylvania, 1783–1794.* Philadelphia: Temple University Press, 1938.

Tinkcom, Harry M. *The Republicans and Federalists in Pennsylvania, 1790–1801.* Harrisburg, Pa.: Pennsylvania Historical and Museum Commission, 1950.

Ver Steeg, Clarence L. *Robert Morris: Revolutionary Financier.* Philadelphia: University of Pennsylvania Press, 1954.

Williamson, Chilton. *American Suffrage from Property to Democracy, 1760–1860.* Princeton, N.J.: Princeton University Press, 1960.

Wilson, Bird. *Memoir of the Life of the Right Reverend William White, D.D., Bishop of the Protestant Episcopal Church in the State of Pennsylvania.* Philadelphia, 1839.

Wilson, Janet. "The Bank of North America and Pennsylvania Politics, 1781–1787." *Pennsylvania Magazine of History and Biography* LXVI (1942): 3–28.

INDEX

Congress (of U.S.), 48–49, 51, 53, 55, 61, 74–75, 81–83, 91, 104–07, 110–11, 114–18, 148, 163–64

Connecticut, 35, 50, 78, 185

Considerations on the Nature and Extent of the Legislative Authority of the British Parliament (Wilson), 6–7, 9–12

Constitutionalists (in Pa.), 125–27

Constitution of the U.S., 40, 55, 57, 61, 68, 70–73, 82, 84, 86–95, 98–106, 110–11, 113–21, 128–29, 135, 137, 142–48, 156, 168

Continental Congress, 7, 10–12, 26–38, 30–36, 38, 40–41, 79, 175

Cork, 171

Courts of Admiralty. *See* Admiralty, Courts of.

Criminal Law, 156–58

Crown, Prerogative of, 7, 9–10

Deane, Silas, 176

Declaration of Independence, 11, 13–15

Delaware, 50, 79–80

Delaware River, 165, 172

Detroit, 11

Dickinson, John, 5–6, 10, 12–14, 30–31, 77, 125, 178, 191

Direct Taxation, 91, 114

Dublin, 171

Edinburgh, University of, 4

Electoral College, 64, 68–69

England, Anglo-Saxon. *See* Anglo-Saxon England.

An Enquiry into the Principles of Political Economy, 37

Equity, Courts of, 88

Erie, Lake, 35, 172

Executive (of U.S.)
  appointment of, 63–69, 109, 200–01
  form of, 58–60, 105, 109–10

powers of, 59–63, 73–74, 109–10

relations with legislature, 61–62, 68–69

term of office, 63, 66–67

See also Federal Convention; President (of U.S.).

Federal Convention, 9, 34, 40, 42–43, 86, 93–94, 97–100, 102, 107, 110, 117, 126–27, 141, 178
  balanced government and, 45–46, 52
  committee of detail, 53, 67, 81
  executive branch and, 58–60, 63–69, 79–83, 200–01
  judicial branch and, 62, 60–75
  legislative branch and, 43–54, 56–57, 81–83
  state-federal relationship and, 46, 51–52, 56, 63–64, 71, 75–82
  See also Congress (of U.S.); Executive (of U.S.); Judiciary (of U.S.); Legislature (of U.S.); *and* President (of U.S.).

Federal-State relations. *See* State-Federal relations.

Findley, William, 93, 98, 103, 111–12, 127–30, 135, 204

Foreign Affairs, 107, 112, 114

Fort Pitt, 10

Fort Wilson, 187

Fox River, 172

Franklin, Benjamin, 48, 61, 81, 122, 178

Freedom of the Press, 89, 104

Freedom of Thought, 104

French Revolution, 154

Gates, Horatio, 13

Genêt, Edmond Charles, 148

George III, 61

Georgia, 49–50, 161

Gerry, Elbridge, 64, 66

Glasgow, University of, 4